Love Finds a Way

<u>Other books in the series:</u>
Love has a Name (#1)
To Love Again (#2)

<u>Also by Christina Hill:</u>
Love at First Flight

Love
Finds
a Way

A Novel

Christina Hill

Copyright © 2023 Christina Hill

The characters and events portrayed in this book are fictitious. Any similarity to real persons, living or dead, is coincidental and not intended by the author.

ISBN-13: 979-8-9857199-4-9

Edited by: imPRESS Millennial Books
Cover design by: Christina Hill
Cover Photo: Canva

To those who fight the battle in their mind every day.
You are seen. You are loved. You are brave.

PROLOGUE
October 2015—Age 19

Jacob

Dear Kit,

It's weird writing you a letter you'll never read.

My roommate is gone and it's just me, sitting in our dorm room at the Journey Center. It's quiet. So quiet that I can hear my own thoughts, and they're screaming at me. I'm so damn sick of it.

Even though it's only been one year, two months, and ~~three~~ four days since I got arrested, I still remember everything. The things I admitted to and those I didn't. I've got a past, like you, and one that includes the gang leader, Bobby, also like you. I never expected to find *us* again. To love a sister I said goodbye to a long time ago, but I did. You may not understand why I've kept everything from you, but in a lot of ways, I think you do. Deep down, I think you know you'd do anything for the ones you love.

You did everything you could for me, and that's what I'm doing for you.

I've been working through all my shit in therapy, and my therapist says writing is a good way to get stuff out—especially for someone like me who has kept too much locked inside for only me to know and nobody else to find out. So, that's what I'm trying to do…get it out. Except I'm not planning to show you this letter, because I love you. Remember that, okay?

It's been eating me alive these past couple of years, and now that I have family in the picture, now that you and Beau are in my life, it keeps me up at night. The information I have, the past I've been witness to, it all makes me feel ~~guilty~~ evil. But, I'm not. I just know what will happen if I open my mouth and tell somebody. It'll hurt people. It'll hurt us and now that there is an us—a family—I'd rather let it die with the old me. The one who went to prison, did drugs, and sold them. But I have to get the words out before they kill me.

So, I'm writing you a letter. I'm going to tell you everything I know, not just because I have to get it out, but because I feel I owe it to you and the past you survived. The women you've told me about and the prostitutes you worked with, I owe it to you and I owe it to them.

It's easier to think of people as a *them*. You don't know *them*, so it's easy not to care. Yet, when you give *them* a name, it changes everything. When they become a sister, a friend, or a neighbor, *them* isn't a collection of random people anymore. They're an individual, and it's personal. So, even if I could keep it all inside, I couldn't. Not when *them* is named Kit.

We've lived a ~~good~~ great life this last year. Aside from the part where I was in prison, you visited me in jail often, and I know if you could, you'd visit me here in rehab, too. Your letters keep me going while I'm in this blackout period where contact with the outside world is limited and all I have are my thoughts.

But maybe not seeing you face to face is why everything's coming up now. You're not here to ruffle my curls and for me to complain about it, even though I really don't care. I like that you do that. It reminds me of the times we had when things weren't so heavy. But they are now, and you're not here. It's just me, my memories, and this pen. A dangerous combination for someone like me who knows too much.

I hope one day I'll have the courage to admit to you what I'm going to write. That I can tell you to your face, preferably years later, and confess what I know. Maybe things will change by then. People will be caught, jailed, and killed by the time I tell you. Maybe Bobby will pay for what he's ~~done~~ doing. I hope so.

Remember, I'm doing this because I love you.

Don't forget that in the facts I'm about to tell you, okay?

Don't forget me.

CHAPTER ONE
September 2016—Age 23

Ruby

Reaching into the purse draped across my shoulder, I dig out a box of cigarettes and a lighter. The box is almost empty, but the last two will get me through the rest of the night. I've been working the blade since I was seventeen but smoking cigarettes even longer. My mother got me into them kind of like she got me into prostitution, too. Not directly. But every family has a history, and this is mine.

I pull a slim tobacco stick from the box and hold it between my lips, light it, and take the first drag, sinking deeper into the rough wall behind me. The sky is dark with no stars to speak of, not like they'd be seen here in the city, anyway. The glare from the tall, lighted buildings in downtown L.A. would distract from any old star God could create. But the taste of the tobacco as it passes my lips? Magic.

I rub underneath the edge of the black-haired wig and feel the sweat beneath it. It covers the bright, thick red hair I've always hated since it's the same color as my mother's. I hate the wig, too, and most of the time I don't even know why I still wear it. It's been a part of me for a long time, including the stilettos, high-cut skirt, and low-cut top. All of it is like a second skin to me now; a second skin that keeps me employed.

Adjusting the wig so it sits properly again, I see a car roll by the sidewalk slowly. Standing up straight and wiggling my fingers in a suggestive *hello*, I wait to see if they'll stop. They don't, so I slump back against the wall once more and take another drag. The smoke fills my lungs, giving me life, even if the warning label says they'll be the death of me. I study the cigarette; it's the only thing keeping me sane on nights like this. It's slow. Too slow. I rarely walk the blade anymore. I've got clients, regulars, friends of friends that I usually meet in my motel room, but not tonight. I need money and don't care how or where I get it.

I'm glad I don't have a pimp on nights like this where I might have to turn tricks for them, too, to make up the difference. Pimps can be more trouble than they're worth, and I don't like sharing my money. They're greedy. Other than drugs, prostitution is the most lucrative street business there is in Los Angeles. I'm not about to rely on anyone else to fill my pockets; I'll do it myself. It's what my mother did, and it's what I've been doing the last few years, too.

I can't afford a slow night, though. It's putting a damper on my plans and an even bigger dent in my savings. I've got some money stashed away. It isn't much, but I'm hoping it'll buy me a bus ticket to somewhere other than L.A. I don't want to stay a street girl forever. I never meant to be here this long, anyway. But here I am.

Another car passes quickly with no intention of stopping. I tamp down the end of my cigarette butt on the wall and slip it back into the box, moving casually up the sidewalk with enough sway in my hips to stop the next car in its tracks. My mother taught me how to walk like this. It's not like she wasn't good for anything. She conceived me in a rundown motel room—where I grew up—and showed me how to do a lot of things, until she couldn't.

Ten years old. That's how old I was when I woke up beside her, stretched my arm out, and yawned like it was a normal morning, but it wasn't. When I looked over at her, my mother's lips were purple, her face blue, and her skin cold to the touch. She died right next to me. An overdose, they told me. An overdose that killed my mother and put me in foster care. An overdose that took everything good in my life away. Not that there was a whole lot of good to start with.

My mom, Jillian, wasn't a horrible person, just a bad mom most days. The memories I have of her are alright. She had the decency to lock me in the bathroom when she had visitors and always gave me her food if we didn't have enough for both of us. She'd been good to me. It was the woman my mother transformed into, when she was on drugs, that I didn't know and still resented. She was practically a stranger despite seeing her more often than her sober version. My mother did what she could for me, which is exactly why I'm going to do whatever I can to get my daughter back.

The sidewalk below my feet is uneven. Jagged pieces jut up with poorly filled cracks that force me to look down and watch my steps so I don't trip. They are likely the same cracks my mother walked on when she was hustlin'. Not much has changed, other than the fact she's gone and I'm still here, making a name for myself the only way I know how.

My girl is three now, with blonde hair that reaches the middle of her back and eyes as green as mine. She's staying with a foster family while I clean up my act. They're the worst. Not because they aren't nice, but because they have my daughter and I don't. I shouldn't have been drinking. Willow was asleep in the car, safely in her carseat. Falling asleep in the motel while she was still outside had never been my plan, but I was so tired, I couldn't keep my eyes open. I should've been better, though. She needed me to be better. The owner heard her crying and called 911. Things would be different if CPS hadn't been called, and I hadn't purchased the vodka.

I'll do it, though. I'll save enough money to get my daughter back and move away from here. Los Angeles is the black hole of prostitution. Once you start, it's hard to climb out of it in one piece. There are too many pieces and sometimes, they don't fit back together again. But if we leave, we can both start fresh. Maybe I'd even be able to work a normal job.

I side-step another pothole and hear the soft hum of a vehicle slow down behind me. It creeps up, giving me enough warning, but I don't turn around, yet. I let the driver sample my body with their eyes before I have to stare into them. When I finally pivot, I see the man leaning his left arm on the edge of the window, his face darkened by the shadows that the night sky and street light create together.

The man tips his chin toward me. "Hey."

I shift to my other foot, hoping to get a better look at his face. "Hi."

"You working tonight?" he asks with a curious tone.

I size him up. Tall. Full midsection. No beard. Clean. "Yeah, I am. You interested?"

"How much?" His words are quiet, like he doesn't want anyone to hear.

Maybe he feels guilty for being here. Does he have a wife and kid at home waiting for him? Probably. But money doesn't discriminate, so neither do I.

"Sixty for messin' around, eighty for everything else."

He studies me, doing a drawn out, exaggerated perusal up and down my body. I try not to flinch or push out my chest any further than I already am. I know he's going to pay. He stopped, and when that happens it's as good as done.

"Alright. Get in," he tells me in a strong voice.

I reach my hand out, giving him a nonverbal clue as to what comes first.

He reaches for his wallet sitting in the cupholder and pulls out four twenties to cover our time together.

I close my fingers around the money. "Meet me around the corner in the alleyway." I point in the direction I'm referring, and he lifts off the brake pedal and rolls forward.

I start walking, folding the cash and tucking it into a pocket inside my purse with the rest of my cash. It's not safe to carry cash around. It only takes one customer to steal from you to teach you that. I learned to hide it in a slit I made between the inner and outer lining of my purse. It'll do for now until I can drop it off at my place.

His car pulls into the one-way alley, and I dread the next few steps before I'm offering a nonrefundable service to this unfamiliar man. I heave a sigh and smooth my hands over my skirt. I'm not nervous. I moved past that a long time ago, but I still have to mentally prepare myself. Some men aren't so bad. I'd even say there are some experiences I enjoy, but those are rare. So rare that when it does happen, it reminds me I'm not a robot. I have feelings, desires, wants, *needs*. But I can already tell this guy won't be one of those. There's little to no attraction there. No, this guy will just be another job. Someone else to please.

I bend around the corner of the wall and see him leaning against the door of his car. I let out another breath and keep walking toward him, using the tempo of my hips, the seductive smile on my lips, and the money in my purse to fuel me. When I reach him, I don't see the look in his eyes I'm used to seeing from men who are about to get everything they paid for. His eyes aren't hooded and his breathing isn't frantic. He stands straighter and faces me. I hesitate. He doesn't move.

Something feels wrong here.

His steely eyes bore into me, and I regret taking this man's money. He's the wrong kind to take money from.

"Hands behind your back. You're under arrest for prostitution and solicitation."

CHAPTER TWO
September 2016—Age 20

Jacob

"Jacob?"

"Yeah?" My voice is hoarse so I clear it and try again. "Yeah? Kit, what's going on?"

Kit sighs. "Thank God. I've been trying to call you all morning."

I pull the phone away from my ear to check the time. "It's only nine."

"Exactly. So why aren't you answering your phone? Aren't you working today?" Her voice has an edge of accusation. Always the big sister.

"Not today. I'm off. I was playing guitar." There's an edge to my voice now as I mess with the guitar pick, passing it between my fingers. I tap the speakerphone button and push a hand through my long, curly hair. "Aren't you supposed to be on vacation?"

She lets out a heavy sigh. "I was. I mean, I am."

I haven't heard this kind of worry in her words since she found me on the streets a couple years ago. She's making me worry. Did something happen?

I lean the guitar against the wall. "Is Beau okay?"

"What? Beau? Yeah, why would something be wrong with my husband?" she replies in a confused tone.

"You just…you sounded…never mind. What's going on?" I stretch my arms up and rub the soreness in my bare shoulder.

My muscles ache from working out with my roommate, James, yesterday, but I don't let a day go by that I don't do some kind of physical activity. It keeps me sane.

She breaks into my thoughts like the annoying song that plays every time she calls. She insisted on it, though, saying I needed a ringtone just for her.

"Look, I need your help," she says.

I don't even try to hide my short laugh. "Alright, something must really be up."

"It is. I wouldn't ask if I had another option," she pauses. "Sorry, that came out weird. I just meant I shouldn't even be asking you, of all people, to do this."

That makes me feel better. "Kit, just tell me. What has you all wound up calling me at nine in the morning when you're supposed to be enjoying your vacation with Beau?"

"Andrea and Jordan are visiting Aunt Cindy today, Janet and Olive are working, and Dina is visiting her boyfriend's family out of town. Everyone else is busy."

She called every single one of her friends already?

I stand up and start pacing my small apartment bedroom in only the boxers I slept in. "I don't work today. I'm free and can help you. Just tell me what you need."

"You're right. Okay, it's my friend, Ruby."

I push the curtains aside and stare at another building that's so close, the window barely adds any light to the room. Working at a restaurant downtown is one thing but living there would be impossible. I found an apartment near Kit and Beau in Burbank, California. It requires that I live with a roommate just to afford it, and I have to commute twenty minutes into the city for work, but at least I found a place. L.A. is cluttered with people looking for places to live.

My mind is searching for any familiarity with the name Ruby. I know most everyone Kit does and the name Ruby doesn't come to mind. "Who's Ruby?"

She doesn't speak and the quiet on the other end of the line makes me think we got disconnected. It would make sense. Doesn't Mexico count as an international call? "Kit, you there?"

"I'm here." She continues. "Ruby and I worked together on the streets, you know, turning tricks…that kind of work."

She really doesn't need to explain it. I was familiar enough with the work she had done a long time ago. But she doesn't know just how well-acquainted I was.

I push my hair out of my face again and sigh. "Yeah, okay, and…"

"And she's in jail," she finishes, and I'm glad she's on the other end of the line and can't see my face.

I'm not surprised. Prostitutes get picked up all the time, but I already know what's coming next before she says anything else.

"You want me to pick her up?" I ask in a low voice.

"Yes?"

"Why do you say it like a question?" I ask.

"Because it is a question. If you don't want to or…can't, I'd understand. I can try calling someone else." Her voice trails off as I clutch the phone tighter.

I'm not thrilled about going back to the jail that I got out of a year ago. Turns out spending a year someplace doesn't make it feel like home. It was ten times better than life on the streets, but it wasn't always easy. Would I be recognized? Months have passed so likely not. But do I want to go? Hell no. If Kit weren't the one asking, I wouldn't even consider it.

"I'll go," I say before I can change my mind.

"You will?"

I nod, like she can see me. I can't believe I'm agreeing to this. "Yeah. I got it. She's downtown?"

She clears her throat, and I can almost picture her playing with the ends of her short hair. "Mhm. Same place."

I switch the phone to my other hand and lean against the window frame. I don't know where these feelings come from. Why does it feel hard to breathe?

She rattles off more details. "I've already paid her bail. She's ready to go whenever you can get there."

I stand straighter and rub the back of my neck. "Cool. I'll get ready and leave soon."

"Jacob?"

"Yeah?"

She pauses. "Thank you for doing this. I know I'm asking a lot for you to go back there. But know how grateful I am that you're doing this for me…and Ruby."

Ruby. The name means little to me or my memories, but I'm about to find out who this *friend* is. Why hasn't Kit ever talked about her before? Are they close? Or, is Ruby just calling out of the blue to scam my sister out of her money? Something about this situation makes me feel angry all of a sudden knowing Kit might be the vulnerable one.

"Sure. I'll text you later. And Kit?"

"What?"

"Try to have some fun, alright?"

She laughs and it seems to do the trick in breaking some of the tension. "I will. Swear."

I hang up the phone and go to my closet to pull out my standard t-shirt and jeans. They're my last clean pair since I'm due for a laundry day. That was supposed to be today but not anymore. Now I've got to drive back to the jail I left this time last year. I have to walk in there and pretend like I don't feel guilty for something I haven't done. To ignore the looks of a warden who might know me. I don't know, maybe they'll take one look at me and sense that I'm trouble, or that I was.

I'm not anymore. Trouble, that is. I'm free of that label, but that doesn't mean I don't look back over my shoulder and wonder when all the shit I did will come back to bite me. It haunts me. Kit's worried tone today was enough to make me think she discovered every last part I've tried to keep hidden. I hate looking back over my shoulder, but for a guy like me, I don't think I'll ever get that privilege to not.

I let out a long exhale as I shove my feet in my Vans sneakers and tie them quickly before reaching for my car keys. After working my ass off as part of the maintenance crew—a required job during my rehab program—and saving for a full year, I had enough money to put down on a car. It isn't new by any stretch, but it runs. I can get to work, the gym, the grocery store, and Kit's house with it, which is really all I need.

Walking down the two flights of stairs, I trudge toward my Toyota with slow movements. I should stop off and get a coffee, maybe a breakfast sandwich, or the groceries I need to buy. *Ruby can wait.* Maybe she isn't after Kit's money, but I don't know that, yet. I won't until I look her in the eye.

Before I reach the car, I run my hands through my shoulder-length hair and grip firmly while I contain it in a low bun. I started growing it out when I got booked into jail and haven't cut it since. It's curly as hell and always gets in my eyes if I leave it down, so I rarely do, but it marks the time that's passed. It's like a visual reminder of the distance from then until now.

When I approach my car, I notice the passenger door is ajar.

"Shit," I say out loud.

I could have sworn I locked my doors last night. Moving closer to the passenger side, I look around the rest of the lot just to make sure whoever broke in isn't still lingering. It's quiet. No movement anywhere from neighbors, residents, or thieves so I open the passenger door slowly and peer around, looking into the backseat, driver's side, and eventually the trunk when I pop it open. I never leave valuables in my car, so I know there wasn't anything to steal, other than the car itself. But they did take something else I needed—laundry soap.

Dammit. Really?

I slam the doors and stomp to the driver's side door.

All I can say is that this friend better be grateful.

CHAPTER THREE

Ruby

He's standing across from me. Staring.

His gaze is so intense at times, it's like he's counting the freckles that climb across my nose and fill both of my cheeks. So, I look at the cat clock hanging on the wall. Every second the large hand moves, the cat's tail moves side to side. It doesn't fit here, but it gives me something to watch as we wait. His eyes aren't roaming the exposed parts of my body or revealing a glimmer of desire, which makes me all the more uncomfortable, so I cross my arms over my chest. I'm doing my best to hide but it's hard.

The room isn't all that small. It has a door, a few chairs, and a reception desk that leads to storage lockers that have my things in them. The place only feels small because Kit's brother is sucking all the air out with his presence. I stand in front of the desk waiting to get my purse and wig back after enjoying a one-night stay in the slammer.

I'm not sure what I'd been expecting when Kit told me her brother would be picking me up. The few glances I've risked tell me he's about my height with heels on, has a square jaw, strong biceps, and a man bun, which I don't hate. But I don't let my eyes linger. Not when I'm off the clock and definitely not when he's Kit's family.

He doesn't seem to care if I'm interested or not. His eyes bore into me with a fire I don't want to examine.

I lean my hip into the waist-high countertop while I tap my heeled foot on the ground, waiting for the woman whose name tag reads Barbara to bring me my things. It's only one purse and a wig. It shouldn't take this long. Every second feels like an hour, and I'm not sure how much more staring I can handle. Sweat builds on my upper lip and my hands start to shake. I need to get out of here. I need a drink to take this edge off. It was bad enough getting eyed up and down by every warden *and* inmate in this place. My red hair is like a flashing neon sign that screams, "Look at me, I'm fucked up and paying for it." It's anything but subtle.

My back hurts, my feet ache, and I'm exhausted since I've barely slept in the last day.

"I'm Jacob," he says from what feels like the other side of the room. He's only a few feet away, staring—of course—at the side of my face.

He doesn't look like a *Jacob*. The Hulk would be more fitting.

I tighten my arms around myself and stare straight into the wall without offering a response. He's picking me up. That's it. It's not like we need to be friends.

He clears his throat, like he's going to say more, but Barbara walks back in with my things before any more awkward introductions can happen. "Thank God," I say with a relieved sigh.

She pulls the items off the counter when I reach for them. "Hold your horses there, dearie. I need to confirm these are all we have for ya."

Facing the counter, and another cat tail tick later, I want to lunge for my purse and tell her this is all I have. There's barely anything more to my name. Just my purse, which holds my escape money, wig, and lipstick.

I clench my jaw tightly as she clicks around on her computer until she finally reads off my full name. "Ruby Red?"

"That's me." I'm no longer hiding the irritation in my voice, but then again, I don't think I've been trying all that hard.

"Ruby Red?" Jacob asks from behind me.

I glance over my shoulder at him. "Yeah?" My tone is biting, and the kink he's forcing me to stretch out in my neck doesn't give a damn. "Is there a problem?"

I pivot halfway around, and he shoves his hands into his front jeans pockets. "No. No problem. It just doesn't sound like a *real* name."

I scoff. "A *real* name? As opposed to…what?"

I know exactly what he's thinking. Ruby Red sounds more like a working girl's name than the fake one I use—Jasmine—but I want to make him say that out loud.

I thought I could make him sweat, but he doesn't look rattled. He's about to say something when Barbara clears her throat loudly. "If you two are done here, then I can finish the checkout process."

I swivel back toward the counter. "What else do you need?"

Barbara sets my few items on the counter. "Just one purse and a black-haired wig?"

"Yes, that's it." My reply is clipped, but Barbara doesn't care. She deals with people like me all day.

All she does is push up her glasses and makes a few final clicks on her keyboard. "Alright, that does it." She slides my items across the counter.

I clamor for them, not even trying to hide my desperation. Leaving the wig on the counter, I grip my purse with one hand while I use the other to search frantically for the small slit to confirm my money is still there. I let out a sigh when I feel it.

"Ready?" Jacob's voice reverberates off the walls and reminds me I'm not alone.

I turn all the way around and snap my gaze to his, finally taking note of his caramel eyes. They are light in color, contrasting with his other dark features. He's clear across the room, but there's something familiar about his eyes. Swallowing, I drop my head and snatch my wig from the counter. I don't need to be studying the color of his eyes. I need to get back to my motel and count every single dollar in my purse—twice. It feels like it's all there and I should know, I hold it often enough, but I need to confirm.

He hooks a thumb toward the exit. "My car is in the visitor's lot."

Moving toward the door, I follow but stay silent. The less talking the better. I don't want to have to explain why I'm here—though I'm sure he already knows—and I don't do small talk.

I pinch the bridge of my nose as the bright sun causes my eyes to water. I'm supposed to see my daughter this weekend. I'd hoped to have more money by then so I could buy her something, but I don't. I have to pay my weekly rent with this money. This hiccup in my schedule wasn't supposed to happen. But at least I'm getting out sooner this time. If I miss a visitation, it goes in the file and the file is what separates me from Willow. It tells the case worker, foster family, and judge that I'm not a fit parent and shouldn't get my child back. Fuck them for thinking that'll actually happen. I'm going to get her back. I'll get the money and buy us both an apartment. We'll have enough food, and Willow will have her own room filled with so many stuffed animals and toys. Maybe even a princess bedspread like I always wanted.

We reach Jacob's car, and he walks to the passenger door to open it. He waits for me to climb in, but I stop and stare at his hand gripping the door. "What are you doing?"

His brows pinch together. "Opening the door."

I shake my head. "I can open my own door." Taking the remaining steps with a forceful stomp of my heels, I yank the door out of his hands.

He's bothering me now. Who does he think I am? Some highly bred woman that expects men to open my door? No. I can open doors for myself, make my own money, and take care of my daughter.

He puts both of his hands up in surrender. "Fine."

I'm staring directly into his eyes. Not up. Not down. Straight into those light hazel pools of honey. Now I know why his eyes are familiar. I've seen these eyes before.

I shake my head to break me from my trance. "Fine," I say with a snap, never letting go of the door.

Those eyes might be familiar, but they don't hold memories I want to remember. I want to bury those memories. Again. *How is this happening?* It was bad enough getting arrested and now this? Now *Jacob?* He told me his name was Dylan when we first met.

Jacob walks around the front of his car and slides into the driver's seat. I push the door open a little more and climb in, too. The cab is quiet until he turns the key in the ignition, and the song he had been listening to blasts through the speakers at a volume that causes me to jump.

He turns it down without so much as an apology mumbled in my direction. I should be nicer to him considering he is Kit's brother, and he picked me up from jail. But now that I know who I'm dealing with, I don't care about being nice. Nice doesn't erase the past. Does he remember? Do I look familiar to him? Probably not. It's been a while. I don't flatter myself with the idea that he'd remember we slept together.

The car ride continues in silence with only the faded sound of music in the background and my sporadic directions to turn or continue. He doesn't say anything or offer any pointless conversation that would be a strain for both of us. Instead, we just cruise down the freeway in the middle of the afternoon like any car that isn't stuck in traffic would do, which is rare for this city. His left hand is resting lazily on top of the steering wheel, and he doesn't appear as discontent as I feel. I could use a cigarette or a stiff drink. I'll make sure to get both when I get home.

"Do you get picked up often?" he asks casually as if this isn't a prying question.

I'm not answering him. I won't do it. But I struggle to hold my tongue when the tattoo on the inside of his bicep outs him right away. I recognized it immediately. It's a gang tattoo. These are common in my world. I've got one on my side from the one and only time I had a pimp. They're a way to keep track of who's in the gang or part of the "family." In other words, who's owned and who isn't.

One breath leads to two, and I can't take it. "No, but it looks like you might." The words are out, hanging between us.

He twists his arm and stares down at the intricate emblem no more than two inches tall and wide. Who knows if that tat ever put him in jail like my profession did, but chances are, he knows someone in the slammer.

"I got out a year ago," he says.

I might feel bad for pushing and prying like he was. But I tell myself I shouldn't. This is Dylan or Jacob, I don't know for sure, yet. Does he really not recognize me? I tamp down the emotions rising up and the voice that tells me I'm forgettable. The same voice that's made a full-time job of reminding me of such things. I don't know why I want him to know who I am, but I do. If I was worth the brain cells it takes to keep memories like the ones we shared, maybe I'd be worth more than how I feel. I swallow every feeling and thought, like it doesn't matter. It can't.

"Good for you," I say sarcastically, biting my nails and acting as if nothing could bother me. I won't let it.

He's silent, pretending like he's just dropping his sister's friend off and not a prostitute he paid to have sex with years ago.

I'm almost home. A few more miles and then I'll get out, shove a "thank you" in his direction, and never see him again. This is what Jasmine would do. She's the one who wears the black wig, fakes it for a living, and acts like her heart isn't beating. She wouldn't say anything about the one night with the one man who made her feel like she wasn't just a prostitute. Jasmine wouldn't remember that night in her loneliest moments and wish for one more conversation, one more kiss, one more tender word spoken about her.

Jasmine wouldn't do anything Ruby does.

Some days it's easier to be Jasmine.

CHAPTER FOUR

Jacob

I couldn't forget that red hair if I tried. It's so bright, like a lamp in the dark, and it's not even nighttime. I bet it would feel the same if I ran my fingers through it like the last time.

She still doesn't know who I am. I've stared at her long enough to know she is for sure who I think she is. Ruby has looked at me—even if only for a handful of seconds—but she still doesn't recognize me. Did she forget? Could I blame her? I'm not sure if I should say something or just let it be. It's not like we're going to see each other again after this, but that's what I said the last time I saw her and now look at us. Driving in a car together, not saying anything, which isn't too far off from the first time we met. Except...yeah, maybe it is pretty different.

Last time, she had me pinned in the backseat of a car and kissed me like she was hungry, hair tickling my face as I gripped handfuls of it.

I shake my head clear of the memory and try to focus on driving instead of the way my whole body responds to those snapshots. I'll drop her off wherever she's been directing me to go, and then I can just go home and forget her. I don't have to say anything. She doesn't remember and probably for the best, because I guarantee she wouldn't be in my car if she did. She would've slapped me—hard—like I deserved. But she didn't. She's been cold and distant, but I can't say I wouldn't be, either, if I were in her position.

I glance over at her and see her looking out the passenger window. Clearing my throat, I ask, "Where to now?"

"Take the next left turn where the burger place is, and then about a mile down that road," she says to the window.

I clutch the steering wheel tighter taking note of the fact that her place is only a handful of miles from my apartment. I'm close by. So close that we could've run into each other at the grocery store. The one on Fifth that always has at least one window busted out. Has she been there? Probably not, because if I saw her, I would've known who she was immediately, just like I did today. Her wavy red hair isn't the only thing I recall about her. The freckles that bridge her nose and the tops of her shoulders are still there. I've traced her heart-shaped face and slender body with my hands, too. She has a small tattoo on her ribcage that means the same thing mine does. And I know for a fact what she sounds like when the doors are closed. It's hard to ignore our history when she's sitting right next to me.

"That was my turn. Didn't you hear me?" she snaps.

Dammit. I need to get her out of my head. "Sorry. I'll flip around."

I pull into a fast food parking lot and put my car in reverse, trying to focus on my turn and not Ruby's body again. My hand cradles the edge of her seat as I look in the rear window to back up. It's inches away from her shoulder. The same one with freckles. It doesn't matter that she's wearing a jacket over a black skin-tight dress, because I know they're there. I've kissed them.

I move my hand quickly and grip the gear shift, pushing it firmly into drive and pulling forward toward the parking lot exit. Pressing the automatic window button down farther, I let more air into the cab. There's less in here than I need right now.

"Take a left," Ruby says, pointing to a motel.

I look up at the sign that reads, *Mote*. It's missing an *L* and by the looks of this place, I don't think it'll be getting it back anytime soon.

"You live here?" I didn't mean for it to come out like that. I guess it just feels wrong to drop her off at a place like this. I don't even have to guess what goes on behind these doors. I already know.

"Yeah. I do," she bites back.

I swing into the sparse parking lot and park in front of the row of doors, keeping my mouth locked shut and not saying anything else. I've already insulted her enough by asking if she lives here. I know she must think I'm judging her for living here. But I'm not. I just don't think this place looks safe…at all.

The engine is still running, and I watch as she pulls her dress down a little more. Clutching her wig close to her chest, Ruby reaches for the door handle and the next thing I know, my mouth is unlocked and opening.

"Hang on."

Her green eyes stab me in the chest. It's the first time she's *really* looked at me since I opened her door. For every second she holds my gaze, the knife twists deeper. I'm such a jackass for how I left. For feeling and whispering so many things in her ear, and then up and leaving like I had a right to. In my mind, I did. I was young, reckless, and money-hungry, making more than I'd ever seen in my life and feeling like a king because of it. I thought leaving was the smart thing to do, and maybe it was, but I didn't do it the right way. She may not recognize me, but I can see the cut of pain I gave her among the others that are there now, too.

She turns her head first, peering out the windshield. "Of course. Where are my manners? Come inside." She gets out of the car and shuts the door, a little harder than I'm expecting.

It takes my mind a minute to catch up, and I realize what's happening here, or at least what it looks like. "Shit," I mutter to myself as I stay glued in the driver's seat.

She waits for me at the front of my car, and I know why. She thinks I'm expecting payment for picking her up, and she's willing to give it.

I scrub a hand down my face. *Dammit.* Now what? I know what I should do. What the stable, been-through-therapy-and-rehab version of myself should do. But this is Jasmine. I mean, Ruby.

I reach for my door handle and step out, rounding the hood to face her.

"My room is down this way. Follow me." She starts walking, and I almost want to follow her. I do want to follow her, but I don't. I'm not doing that again. I shouldn't.

"Ruby."

She whips around to face me and juts out an impatient hip. I can see the pinched smile she's giving me and for some men that might read as an invitation but to me it looks forced. She doesn't want to invite me in but feels obligated to, and I hate that I'm not the only man who's made her feel like that. Like she *has* to and not that she *wants* to. There was a time she wanted to, but that isn't the case anymore. I ruined that—*us*.

I study the freckles that leap across her cheeks and are painted in a rose color. It looks natural like she's been in the sun for longer than she should. *Angel kisses,* she'd called them as I attempted to kiss every one of them.

I push my hands deep into my front pockets and stay exactly where I'm standing. I drop my gaze to the ground and start kicking at a small rock. "I'm not coming to your room."

I look up and search her face, but she isn't looking at me, only past me somewhere over my shoulder. "Fine." She stands straighter. "Thanks for the ride."

Turning slowly, she walks toward the farthest door closest to the street. I don't want to follow her, but I don't want to leave her, either. I don't want to tell her who I am, but I want to apologize. I'm not ready for this goodbye just like I wasn't ready to say hello.

I rub the back of my neck. "Ruby, I'm not coming to your room, but are you sure you should stay here? Kit isn't home, and I know she'd be cool if you wanted to stay at her place for a while."

Her feet stop moving and she speaks over her shoulder. "I'm a big girl. I can take care of myself. Bye, *Jacob*."

My name catches flame on her tongue.

She keeps walking until she reaches her door. Digging out a key from her purse, she sinks it into the lock, turns the knob, then pushes inside. The door closes, and I let her go like I did the first time. I have no right to ask her for anything unless it's an apology, and that would mean fessing up.

CHAPTER FIVE

Ruby

I close the door and lean against it, releasing a shaky exhale. I can't believe I made it through without cracking. The car ride, heavy silence, and then my offer.

Placing a hand over my racing heart, I try to calm down. I don't know why taunting him sounded like a good idea. I was curious if I invited him in, as payment for a ride, if he'd accept. I wouldn't have followed through on it. At least, I tell myself I wouldn't. But what does it say about him? Does it make him a stand-up guy for not coming inside when he paid me for sex the first time we met? Or, am I just not appealing to him anymore? Either way, I'm glad that's over, and now I'm safe behind a closed door that I can choose to open or not. It's a long-term stay motel that acts like an apartment but doesn't require all the money like one. It might be rundown and sketchy-looking, but my door has a lock and that's what I pay for.

The room is dark, so I flip on the light and a soft glow highlights the space in a yellow-orange tinge. I lift the stained curtain that hides the window to see if Jacob is still out there. He is. Staring at the ground and kicking the ground with his foot, hands shoved deep in his pockets. It doesn't help that I can still remember the feel of his lips on mine, or the way his hands cradled my cheek. *He still left*. And the worst part is that he had a right to. I was a prostitute, and he was tangled in some kind of street business I didn't ask questions about. It's not like one night could change any of that.

I drop the curtain. Knowing that he's Kit's brother only makes things worse. Jacob needs to stay a memory and nothing else. Kit can't find out about us, or our friendship will be over. I'll keep my mouth shut. Let's just hope he doesn't figure things out.

I peer around the room. There's one queen bed with ratted, thinning sheets that is still unmade from when I slept in it last. A set of dresser drawers, broken TV, chair, desk, and standing lamp complete the furnishings in the small room. For seven-hundred dollars a month, it's home.

I kick off my heels and walk to the bathroom opposite the front door to turn the shower knob to warm. I need to wash away the grime from the last couple of days and get rid of the memories of Jacob. His name still feels weird rolling off of my tongue. He was always Dylan in my mind. Those eyes belonged to Dylan. Those lips? Dylan's. It's a cruel joke from the universe to have seen him today. I can never have what I really want. Something I thought wasn't just a one-night stand was really nothing more and nothing less. I should've known not to hope for the *more*.

Staring at my reflection in the mirror, the condensation in the bathroom builds, covering my shoulders, neck, and head until I can no longer see myself. It's a relief, really. I don't like looking at my reflection for long. It tells me things I'd rather not know. Like the dark circles beneath my eyes letting me know how tired I am. My reflection doesn't explain *why* I'm tired, it only accuses me that I am. Or, the snarls in my frizzy hair that look like I just rolled out of bed, which isn't far from the truth. Maybe I don't like mirrors, because my face is blurred. Not that there's anything wrong with the mirror, just me.

While the water heats, I exit the bathroom, mindlessly move toward the dresser, and reach behind the TV. The glass bottle I hid here is half-full, less than what I want but enough for now. I hide everything. My money, liquor, gum. Anything that belongs to me, I hide. There are too many people walking in and out of here to trust they won't steal something. My mother did the same. She hid her things just like she hid me in the bathroom when she was screwing someone. I guess I got good at hiding.

The top sticks, but I finally unscrew it and take a swig, ignoring the stinging burn in my throat. I enjoy it too much to care. I slink out of my jacket and shuffle back into the bathroom, pulling one strap of my dress off my shoulder, and then another. Removing my bra and panties, I drop everything in a heap at my feet before grabbing the neck of the bottle again and stepping into the shower. It's warm and welcoming and feels like a giant exhale comes to life.

Tipping my head back, I take another drink. I'm rushing, and I know it. But I want to forget before I can remember anything. I spent not even twenty-four hours in a holding cell, and I'm wiped. It's nothing like the forty-eight hours last time. I didn't have a Kit in my life to bail me out then. I face the inconsistent trickle of water, doing my best to keep the bottle out of its way. At least the temperature of the water is warm this week. Oftentimes, I can't even count on that.

I close my eyes and dip my face in the stream, letting it erase my makeup. The shower head only has two settings: hit you so hard that it stings, or off. I wish I had a tub to soak in. The motel I grew up in did, and that's where I learned to hold my breath. I'd sink under the water and slowly blow out bubbles of air. It was quiet under the water. The sounds were all muffled and faint, making it feel like I was truly alone. The times I couldn't hide, I'd think about being under the water and holding my breath, silently counting up in my head.

It doesn't work the same in a shower. The sputtering waterfall pelts my forehead, and I let the droplets roll over my open lips while I inhale and exhale. I think that holding my breath would be nothing compared to breathing underwater. If I could breathe underwater, I'd never have to surface. I could sink down and be fully surrounded by the quiet. No one would bother me, and I'd never have to swim up for air.

Testing my own ability, I tilt my face up and try to take small breaths. It doesn't work, and I start violently coughing to spit the water out of my mouth and lungs. Bracing myself on the wall with my hand, I fill my body with the air it craves. The only thing I've proved is that I can't do the impossible. But one day, I will. I feel it in my bones. I'll sink beneath the water and find my peace. I think about it often enough.

Taking another drink from the bottle, I lean my shoulder against the wall. If it weren't for Willow, I'd be practicing more. But I'm not, because she needs me like I needed my mother. I'm the only family she has left, and I have to get her back.

I flatten my back against the cold tiles and slide down, letting the water coat one-half of my body as I bend my knees. Staring at the bottle, a punch of guilt hits me. I'm the one holding it, and I hate myself for it. I'd still have Willow with me if it weren't for this damn bottle.

The tears start to build behind my eyelids and I let them, because tears make me feel human. I have emotions, even if they come up at weird times. I drop my head and look down as the water mixes with the tears sliding down my cheeks. I've told myself I'll fix things; I can get better. I'll do better. But then life reminds me that I'm just like my mom, letting my addiction become more important than my daughter.

I lost my mother to hers, and now I'm losing my daughter to mine.

CHAPTER SIX

Jacob

I should leave. I don't know why I'm still here other than the look in Ruby's eyes right before she turned and walked into her room. It was relief mixed with…sadness. Was she sad I didn't go inside with her? I can't stand leaving her like this again as if I were dismissing her so easily. So I'm here, leaning on the hood of my car, arms and ankles crossed, trying to decide what comes next. Leaving would mean I may never see her again. Staying might give her the wrong idea.

I rub my forehead with one hand. Kit could check in with her when she gets back. Does she have Ruby's number? I know where she lives now, but it wouldn't be a good idea to have Kit drop by when Ruby might be working.

I push off my car and reach into my front pocket for my phone. Why do I care so much? Is it guilt? I exhale and look back at Ruby's door. I need to call Kit and see if she has Ruby's number. Maybe I can encourage her to call and check in. That would make me feel better about leaving, knowing that Ruby had someone to talk to.

I tap Kit's contact number and hold the phone up to my ear as I start pacing again. It rings for an ungodly amount of time before someone finally picks up, but it isn't Kit.

"Hello?" A deep voice asks.

"Beau. It's Jacob. Is Kit there?"

Beau's response is calm like he doesn't have a million questions needing answers like I do. "Hey, man. Yeah, she's here but in the shower. Want me to have her call you back?"

I pause and raise my hand to rest on my hip. *Do I?* I don't answer.

"Did you already pick up Ruby?" he asks.

"Yeah, she's back at her motel," I confirm while staring at said motel.

"Cool."

The silence spans the distance between Beau's phone and mine.

"Jacob? You alright, bro?"

"Yeah…yeah, man, I'm good." I clear my throat. "Do you know if Kit has Ruby's number?" I try not to sound interested, only concerned. I am concerned, so that's not a lie, but I'm more interested than I want my words to let on.

"Uh, I think so? Let me check."

I wait impatiently, kicking the curb with my shoe.

"Looks like Kit has it," he says.

Air pushes from my mouth. "Sweet. Thanks."

"Is that all you needed?"

I look at Ruby's door again. I want to knock on it so badly, but I don't have a reason to. She doesn't want to come stay at Kit's house, and it's clear she doesn't want help. But maybe I could invite her to something, and I could see her again. Maybe I'd tell her that I remember her. Or not. I don't know, yet, but we could at least talk more.

"Jacob?"

I shake my head. "I'm here. Hey, your birthday party is next Saturday, right?"

He laughs. "Yup. Kit was adamant about throwin' this party. She said we need somethin' to celebrate."

I lick my lips. "Why don't I invite Ruby to come, too? She seems like she could use some friends right now. You cool with that?"

He doesn't hesitate. "For sure. Kit hasn't seen her in a while, so I'm sure she'd love that."

I want to ask him what *a while* means, but I clamp my mouth shut. Instead, I grip the phone tighter and stare at the missing *L* in the sign. I'll just tell Ruby it was Kit's idea. "Alright, I'll invite her."

"Cool bro, I'll catch you later," he says before the line disconnects.

I slip the phone back into my pocket and run a shaky hand over my jaw. With that over with now, I actually have to knock and talk to her again. I start moving toward her room. I'll invite her, and then leave. Emphasis on the *leave*.

I'm in front of her door, looking straight at the peephole I can't see through. My hands start to sweat as I knock once. I shift from one leg to the other, stuffing and unstuffing my hands in my front pockets. I toy with the hem of my shirt and wait for her to answer.

Nothing.

Is she looking at me? I smile in case she can. I'm not back here to cash in on her offer, but she doesn't know that. Did she fall asleep? If so, I feel bad for knocking. Maybe there was a man or client inside waiting for her? My mind starts shooting off all kinds of possibilities, which has me knocking harder this time.

I knew this place wasn't safe. I ball my fist and start pounding. "Ruby! Hey, Ruby!" I'm making a scene but I only care about the intruder that could be holding her at gunpoint.

The lock turns and clicks as someone pulls the door open. Ruby is standing just beyond the frame, eyes wide, hair dripping wet, and clutching a towel around her body.

My lungs deflate, and now I'm not sure what's worse: believing Ruby is in trouble or seeing her in nothing but a towel. I gulp and jerk my eyes up to her face.

Keep your eyes up.

Her attitude is practically spewing at me like fire in shades of green, and the skin around her eyes is tinted dark from her makeup. "What the hell?"

I realize what a dope I must look like, knocking like a crazed man, and then looking like one as I stare so hard just so my eyes won't drop lower. "Sorry. I-I…" I open my mouth, then close it. "Kit wanted me to invite you to her house this Saturday. It's, uh…it's actually a birthday party for her husband."

I watch as her anger dissipates but only a touch. Ruby's thick hair is dripping so much water down her face and neck, but I refuse to look down, even though I'm sure there's a puddle beneath her bare feet.

"You were pounding on my door to invite me to a party?"

I nod confidently. "Yup."

She lets out a weak laugh. "I don't do parties."

Accepting her answer is what I should do. It's not like I do parties, either, but this is different. This party is for Beau. He towers over me in more ways than one, and if I'm half the man he is, I'll be alright. He was showing up to my jail cell almost every other day and was there for me when I needed people. I think Ruby could use some friendship. I imagine her life gets pretty lonely.

I shouldn't stoop this low, but I know her type and what will get her there, because I've been in a similar place. I've been desperate enough for food and drink that I would find it wherever I could. "There'll be free food, beer, and wine. You know, typical party stuff."

She bites the inside of her cheek and shifts her weight to her other foot. "Fine."

"Fine," I parrot with a wry grin I'm trying hard to keep contained. "I'll let Kit know."

"*I'll* let Kit know," she says to my half-turned body.

"Fine by me." I shove my hands back in my pockets and walk back to my car.

But Ruby can't let me have the last word. "Fine."

I smirk and let myself look back over my shoulder once. The hard line of her mouth, rigid shoulders, and rosy cheeks say that things are not fine.

CHAPTER SEVEN

Ruby

These visits are never easy. I wonder every time, without fail, whether she'll forget who I really am. I don't expect her to know me, and there are times I think it might be easier if she didn't. Easier for her, not me. The goodbyes are the worst. After a year of these visits and the nagging guilt of losing custody of my daughter, I still can't get through one without crying.

It's only been a week since I got out of jail, and I worked every night from then until now to add a few more dollars to my stock after rent and food. Willow doesn't know that I'm saving up money for us. I have a plan to get her out of the system and back with me, preferably far away from here. She's only three and wouldn't understand, anyway. But with every visit, I leave feeling guilty that I'm not making money fast enough, and by the time I do save up, it'll be too late. She won't want to live with me or consider me her *real* mom.

Tess, her social worker, was agreeable to keeping our scheduled visit today, even though I spent a night behind bars. It's not like my profession is a secret. There's no way I could keep anything from Tess and still see my daughter. She doesn't judge me for it, knowing that I need to survive, but these visits are closely monitored. The foster parents are there, Tess comes, and it's always in a public place like the park we're meeting at today.

The bench is hard as I lean back and stare up at the sun. My flowing skirt slides up my thigh as I cross and uncross my legs. Despite the spaghetti tank I'm wearing, it's hot. So hot that I regret not bringing an elastic to pull my waist-length hair back. I usually have one on my wrist along with the many other bracelets I wear. But I must have forgotten it in my rush to leave and make it here on time. Twirling the braided leather bracelet around my arm, I scan the park again. Being here early is important to me. It proves to Tess, the foster parents, and Willow that I'm reliable. So what if I'm a prostitute that's barely making it? I'm here early, and I'll keep showing up for my daughter. It's my favorite part of every week, because Willow and I get to live in a world that's just us again, even if it only lasts an hour. It's the best hour out of the one-hundred and sixty-seven other hours in a week.

The nerves reach my crossed leg, and I bounce my foot up and down, up and down, hoping the rhythm will calm me. Willow doesn't fully understand who I am in her life, and it hurts as much as a stab in the side would. She calls me "Mama" but lives with another woman and her husband. We sometimes have a picnic together, but I don't make or share meals with her multiple times a day. I'm a distant relative to her at best. But we share the same DNA, she has my smile, and when I look at her small face, I'm selfish enough to keep showing up. Maybe one day she'll call me mama, and I'll feel the love behind it.

Willow doesn't know her biological father, and he's a spotty memory for me at best. That's the thing about my line of work, pregnancy is a hazard of the job. I didn't mind it, though. Finding out I was pregnant and knowing the father could have been one of four people, didn't bother me. It was easier. They weren't involved and likely wouldn't have wanted to be, even if they did know. But I wanted Willow from the moment I took a test to confirm she was growing inside of me. I can understand now how my mother must have felt. She could have aborted me like I could have aborted Willow. But when you're never alone yet always lonely, a child that is just yours becomes a comfort—a peace in the middle of chaos and a friend where none exist.

The reality of having a child, though, is a lot different.

My mother, Jillian, was an addict. She wanted me, but that's only step one. Want doesn't put food in a child's belly. Want doesn't forget to unlock the bathroom door when a client had left hours before. And want doesn't overdose and kill themselves with your kid in bed next to you. Sometimes I wonder if I would've been better off aborted. But I don't wonder that for long, because then I'd have to consider if I'm doing the same thing to Willow.

It wasn't all bad. On her good days, my mother would buy a giant bag of jelly beans, and we'd spend hours on the floor of our motel guessing the flavors. She'd rent a movie from Blockbuster, and I'd snuggle up so close to her that I could smell the flowery scented perfume she wore and feel the silky texture of her nightgown on my cheek. These were the moments I lived for. The times that were her and me against the odds.

But the odds won anyway.

Laughter rings out behind me, and I peer over my shoulder and see a head full of blonde hair bouncing wildly as she approaches. *Willow. My girl.* Unfolding my legs, I stand quickly, rubbing my hands together in anticipation.

Her skin is like porcelain, smooth to look at and softer to touch. Her light hair is a stark contrast to my red, but it's the only feature that makes us different. Her eyes are green, like mine. Her skin is fair with freckles, like mine. Her slim, pointed nose is also like mine. There is no question that she is *mine*.

Liquid jealousy runs down my back with my sweat seeing Molly, the foster mom, trail behind Willow. The anger turns red hot and builds inside of me as she catches up to hold Willow's hand.

That should be me holding Willow's hand.

I've always worn my feelings on every square inch of my face. Molly knows I'm not her number one fan—she stole my daughter and is trying to be her mom for fucks sake. And I hate that she's all the nicer to me because of it. I want her to despise me like I despise her. The only way I can handle being around her is to remind myself that Willow won't be with Molly and Stan forever. I'll get her back, and then I'll be the one she wants to hold hands with.

Willow drops Molly's hand and runs in my direction but not to me. She runs to the bench for the cherry-flavored slushie I bring every time we see each other. I used to drink half of it and save the rest for her, but Molly didn't like Willow having all that sugar, so I started buying Willow her own.

She cradles the large cup between her two small hands as I sit down. "Hi, Willow."

Taking another sip, she squints up at me. "Hi."

Molly and Tess approach us and offer a simple greeting. No Stan today, I notice, and sigh with relief. He makes me uncomfortable. Not because he's a man with wandering eyes, but because he's not. He only ever looks at my face, smiles, waves, and keeps his distance. It's unnerving and weird, because in my world, that's not normal.

"Hot day we're having, huh?" Tess asks, wiping a hand across her glistening forehead.

What is it with people always wanting to talk about the weather?

"Yup. It's hot." I don't come here every week to talk to them. I'm here for Willow and every word they speak to me are words I don't get to share with Willow.

Tess nods and points behind her. "We'll be over at the picnic table if you need us."

"Let us know if you need anything, though," Molly adds.

"Sounds good." I won't need them. I never do.

The two women leave, and now it's only Willow and me. She's balancing the slushie on her small leg and drawing the red-colored ice up through the straw. "Ow!" she says, touching her hand to her head.

I smile and sit beside her. "Brain freeze?"

"What's dat?" she asks.

"It's when you drink something super cold really fast and it makes your whole head feel frozen," I explain.

"Frozen?"

"Not actually frozen, but just extremely cold."

She shrugs and takes another drink, forgetting about the burning cold sensation.

"How've you been?" I ask.

She doesn't look up at me or answer my question.

"Look at my new shoes!" She angles her foot toward me, so I can see the picture of some character she seems to like enough to have on her shoes.

"Wow! I love them." And it's true, I do love them but not for the reason she thinks. I love them because she does. I should be grateful that Molly and Stan can buy these things for her, but at the same time I'm not, because it just reminds me that I can't.

I make a mental note of the character on her blue sneakers. "You kind of look like her."

Willow tilts her other foot to the side so she can look at the blonde girl with a long braid. "She looks like me."

I laugh. "That's right. But she doesn't have your pretty green eyes."

She stares up at me, the sun bouncing off of her golden hair.

"Like your eyes." She points a small finger at my face.

She noticed. Tears prick at the corners of my eyes. "Yeah, just like mine."

She reaches out and touches my hair. "You have orange hair."

I look down at where she grabs my hair. "I guess it is kind of orange. But you know what?"

"What?" She lifts her cup for another sip.

"You don't have to have the same hair color to be family," I say.

She swings her legs back and forth since they can't touch the ground. "Really?"

My eyes roam the playground. "Really. It's true."

"Molly isn't my mom."

I can't disagree and as much as I don't like Molly and Stan, they are the ones caring for her right now. But I also suck at lying, especially to my own daughter.

"You're right. Molly isn't your mom…but she's taking care of you."

She plays with the straw. "You're my mom."

The tears won't leave, and I have to blink them away before responding. "I'm your mama. Forever and always."

"Forever?" she asks.

I sniffle. "Not just forever. *Infinity*."

Her eyes grow big. "Who's infinity?"

Wiping under my eyes, I shift to face her. "Infinity goes on forever. It doesn't end. I'll never stop being your mama." I swallow the growing lump in my throat. "And I'll never stop loving you."

Willow nods, then jumps off the bench, sets her slushie down, and grabs my hand. "C'mon. Let's go swing!" She grips my hand tightly and I squeeze back, loving the feel of her small fingers in mine.

Infinity doesn't seem long enough when it comes to Willow.

CHAPTER EIGHT

Jacob

"Hey, man. You good?" Beau asks, bumping my shoulder. His skin is dark, his smile light.

I nod once, sitting forward on the edge of the couch cushion. "Yeah. I'm alright. Just tired."

It isn't exactly a lie. I am tired. But I'm also on edge knowing that Ruby is supposed to be at the party tonight. Maybe she won't come. I can only hope that's the case. The more time we spend around each other, the more opportunity she has to figure out our previous connection.

Beau slides his hands in his pockets. "Can I get you something to drink?"

"Sure." I force a smile. "Water is good."

I stopped drinking and smoking when I got to jail, because I had to. Then, I was in rehab. Now, I'm two years sober and don't want to start that clock over.

"You got it." Beau walks back into the kitchen as I slump farther into the couch.

Beau and Kit live in a small house in the suburbs of L.A. It's a two bedroom, one bath place with a yard the size of the guest room. Kit has found a lot of the furniture and decor secondhand like this dark green velvet couch I'm sitting on. It's soft and doing an okay job of easing my nerves as I run my hand back and forth along the armrest.

"Bored already?"

I startle at the sudden voice speaking to me.

"Sorry. I couldn't help it." Monica, Kit's former social worker, shuffles closer.

I stand and lean down to embrace her. "Monica, hey. It's great to see you."

She pulls back with a giant smile. "How have you been?"

Instead of admitting Ruby has invaded my thoughts this past week, causing little sleep and even less focus, I tell her what everyone does when asked this question. "Good."

She squeezes my arm. "Are you sure about that?"

My smile widens. She can always tell. "I'm sure. Life is good."

What I really mean to say is life is confusing. One minute I'm minding my own business, the next I'm facing a woman I had sex and a strong connection with, left without a word, and then couldn't stop thinking about her for years. Life is flat-out harsh.

"How have you been?" I ask.

"I can't complain. The kids I get to work with are still the best part of my day," she says with a wink. "I love when I get to see their lives change."

I smile again. She's practically beaming at me. Guilt nags at my thoughts. Everything resurfacing with Ruby makes it feel like not much has changed. Sure, I've been through the blender of growth, but my past mistakes are haunting me in the form of a beautiful redhead.

"It's so wonderful to see you, Jacob. I'm going to go catch up with Kit," she says.

I point straight ahead. "She's on the back porch with Olive and Dina."

She pats my arm a few times before heading in that direction, passing Beau on her way. They exchange a hug, and Beau brings me a water bottle.

"Cheers," he says, clinking his amber bottle with my clear one and taking a drink.

"Thanks." I let the cold water slide down my throat before clearing it. "So, what's it like being an old man now?"

"Watch it," he teases before taking another sip. "Twenty-eight is hardly old man territory but for a twenty-year-old baby, I guess it is."

I tip my head to the side. "Touché."

The doorbell dings as I take another drink.

Beau heads for the door, his long strides getting him there in half the time. "And so it begins," he says over his wide shoulder while opening the door.

My stomach drops as he opens the door. I expect to see Ruby behind it, because that's the only face my mind is capable of producing. But it's not Ruby.

Kit's best friend, Andrea, steps inside and hugs Beau while her husband, Jordan, trails her, infant car seat in hand. I haven't seen their baby, yet, since she was born two months ago. Moving closer, I greet them and bend to get a look at the baby.

"Amelia Grace," Andrea says with a smile when I stand again. "Do you want to hold her?"

I freeze. I've never held a baby and this one is so small. Her plump cheeks are the biggest thing about her.

"I don't think you want me to hold her." I laugh nervously as I follow them both into the living room.

"I'll hold your water," Jordan says with a smirk, like I don't really have a choice.

I hand it to him and glare. "Don't take a drink. I don't want your lipstick on it."

Jordan laughs as Andrea straightens, cradling Amelia in her arms and thrusting her toward me. I bend my arms awkwardly to conform around her small body. "Is this right?"

Andrea lowers my elbow so Amelia's neck fits snuggly in the crook of my elbow. "Now it is." She takes us both in. "Relax, Jacob. You're going to pull a muscle with how stiff you are. Look," Andrea says, pointing at Amelia, "she likes you."

I drop my gaze to the yawning baby in my arms. She's even smaller than she looked in the car seat. Her fingers stretch, and I can't help but smile at the sheer size difference of mine. Every one of her features are miniature versions of Andrea's. The shape of her face, curve of her nose, and the dark wisps of hair are just like her mom's.

"She's perfect," I whisper.

"She is," Andrea replies.

Amelia turns her head into my bicep and starts nuzzling me. It tickles as her nose brushes my skin, and her mouth begins to open and close. "Is she okay?"

Amelia lets out a cry that makes me wonder what I did wrong.

"She's just fine. Hungry, but fine," Andrea says, lifting the infant from my arms.

Jordan slaps my shoulder, then hands me my water bottle. "Don't worry too much. We're all as good as chopped liver when Amelia's hungry."

"Is Kit outside?" Andrea asks over the cries.

I nod, doubting that Amelia really is alright like they seem to think she is when she's crying like that.

"I'll go feed her out there," she says as Jordan gathers all of their things, and there's a lot of them.

"You're a natural, dude." Beau shoots me a look as he passes. It almost sounded sincere, but the tilted smile on his face tells me he's teasing.

I shove him, and the beer in his hand sloshes. "You're on door duty for that." He points at me while exiting the room.

Fine by me.

It's quiet for now since a lot of the guests have already arrived. Except one. But I'd rather be alone, anyway. Sliding my palms back and forth, I ease back down onto the couch. If Ruby shows up tonight, I have to play it cool. Kit will notice that I'm acting weird around Ruby and will call me out on it. She's good at that.

A familiar feeling creeps back into my thoughts.

I should have told Kit.

Keeping things from her isn't like me anymore. My life was built on secrets before she came back into the picture, and I swore I wouldn't keep anything else from her. But Ruby is my past. I'm keeping the past where it belongs. No need to bring something up that would only cause more rifts. It isn't worth it.

The doorbell rings, blaring for my attention. Standing, I wipe my hands on my black jeans and take even strides to the door. This door is nothing like Ruby's. It's painted one solid color—black—and isn't chipping with dents and scratches scattered over it. But I'm not knocking on her door this time. She's basically knocking on mine. Putting my hand on the knob, I twist and open. Red hair the color of fire fills my vision.

I gulp. If I'm not careful, I'll get burned.

CHAPTER NINE

Jacob

My gaze lingers on Ruby's face before scanning her body from head to toe. I do it before I'm even thinking clearly, following the lines of her tight, white dress as it hugs her waist, hips, and stops mid-thigh. Scolding myself, I look up. She's rubbing a hand up and down her arm, dodging my eyes like we're playing a game of table tennis. If I thought I could put her at ease, I would. But I don't think I'm the one to do it.

I swallow, then smile to soften the mood. "You came."

She glowers at me. "You invited me."

"Kit invited you," I say and regret opening my mouth. Could I sound like more of a dick?

She rolls her eyes. "That's right, so where is she? I'd rather talk to her."

I deserved that sharp comment. But I don't apologize. It's better this way. If she hates me then she won't like me, and I don't think I could handle her liking me. I've already proven that by walking away from her.

I hook a thumb over my shoulder. "She's in the backyard with everyone else."

Stepping through the front door, she starts walking toward the back of the house. She smells so good. Nothing like she did after picking her up at the jail. I mean, she didn't smell bad. But tonight, a sweet floral scent follows her around.

I didn't want the words we shared tonight to start and end like this. I need to say something that isn't dickish for once.

I shut the door and turn on my heel, speaking to her back. "You want something to drink?"

She stops and faces me, the full weight of her irritation boring into me. Shrugging and staring at the bottle in my hand she asks, "Anything besides that."

I nod, passing in front of her and gesturing for her to follow me to the backyard. The thoughts of how well her dress fits her, the effortless waves of her long hair, or the intoxicating smell of roses that fill my senses as I pass have lived in my head until now. "You look great."

I'm thankful her back is to me as I trail her through the living room and kitchen. I don't want to see the confused look on her face. One minute I'm acting like a complete tool about inviting her, and the next I'm complimenting how she looks. What the hell is wrong with me tonight?

"Thanks," she grinds out under her breath.

I leave it at that and let the silence be the foot in my mouth I need to shut up.

Stretching around her, I open the sliding glass door to the backyard, gesturing for her to exit first. Kit's laugh echoes above the rest, but she sobers as we walk out together but not *together*.

"Ruby, you're here!" Kit rushes over, throwing her arms around Ruby in an embrace I think is only half-welcomed. Ruby tenses like she isn't used to being hugged, then she folds her arms around Kit in some kind of awkward hug that includes a few pats to the back.

Seeing her here, with my family and close friends, is harder than I thought. She's smiling, for one. And her smile is worth the wait it takes to see it. There's a sliver of a gap between her front teeth and the corner of her eyes crinkle. I need to stop noticing. So, I head to the cooler beside the house and pop the lid, reach for a beer, and use a bottle opener before offering it to Ruby.

She takes it with a small nod and a brief glance at me. I guess I hoped for more, because as I turn away and walk back toward the house, disappointment sours in my gut. I tell myself it's old feelings mixed with a healthy dose of regret. I walked out on Ruby after sharing more than a bed with her. Looking back, I know that was a jerk move. I liked her and based on our conversation that night, she liked me, too. But we couldn't change who we were. Hell, we can't change it now, either. She's still a prostitute, and I'm Kit's brother. No sense in feeling regret when I can't change things, and if I can't change them, why revisit old feelings?

I shake my head and lean against the house silently watching people swirl around me, taking sips of my water every so often and wishing I had something strong, at least for tonight. Life is good now. I have my family back, my roommate and friend, James, plus a few mentors. Everything else is behind me. And after tonight, Ruby will go back to being my past. I'll never see her again just like before.

Try telling that to my eyes that keep drifting in her direction for the rest of the night.

I'M SITTING ON the swinging bench seat after the party moved inside, nursing another water when she joins me. I haven't talked to Ruby since we walked outside earlier tonight and almost can't believe she's standing in front of me now, hair draped over one shoulder, leaning on one leg, and cradling a fresh beer in her hand.

"Can I sit here?" she asks, pointing at the empty seat beside me.

"Huh? Oh, yeah. Go ahead." I push my fingers through the mess of curls tangling around my shoulders. I took my low bun out of the elastic earlier and don't have the energy to wrangle it back into submission now.

I stop my back and forth rocking long enough for her to sit down.

"Do you always hide outside during parties?" she asks while sitting.

I swallow but keep my eyes trained on the chain link fence across the yard. "No. Just not in the mood for a party tonight, I guess."

She nods and drinks her beer, a different kind than earlier. "I hate beer."

The swing starts rocking once again thanks to the nerves coursing through me. I can't stay still when she's around.

"Why are you drinking it then? There are other drinks," I say.

"Those aren't any fun." She crosses her legs, and it draws my attention.

I skim the length of skin from her knee to the hem of her dress, then quickly look away. Are her legs angled toward me? Or, is this swinging bench just that small?

"So, who is *Jacob*?" Her words are slurred, mocking even.

I don't respond right away but grip the neck of my water tighter, noticing how she emphasized my name. Does she know who I am? Where is this coming from? Her voice drips with honey from the alcohol but the sting is close by. It's a question I don't know how to answer, or that I should. The more she knows about me, the more likely she'll remember me. I need to keep things impersonal.

I look over at her, a lazy smile drapes across her naked lips and her eyelids are half-lowered, studying me. The red in the whites of her eyes tells me she's drunk, or at least well on her way. Maybe this is where her sudden interest in me comes from: alcohol.

"What do you want to know?"

She kicks off her flip flops and curls her legs beneath her on the swing, facing me completely. "What do you do for work?"

I peer down at the bottle resting on my thigh as if it's the most interesting thing here. It's not, but I pretend anyway. "I work at a restaurant in the city."

She flips her hair over her shoulder, and I follow every movement, like she's doing it in slow motion and just for me. "Do you have your own place?"

Her question shouldn't catch me off guard. It's a simple question with a simple answer, but I still pause before replying. "No, I have a roommate."

She crosses her arms and chews on her bottom lip. "Where do you live?"

"Not far." *Shit.* I shouldn't have said that.

Ruby drains the rest of her beer and leans closer to me, her breath tickling the side of my face. Raising a hand, she runs a finger along my jaw as I keep my eyes trained forward. "I like to have fun. Do you?"

Heat crawls up my neck and my mouth runs dry. What the hell is happening? This isn't playing it cool and keeping my distance. I'm doing the exact opposite by letting her touch me and not moving away. I need to move away. I'm convinced she doesn't know who I am, because if she did, she'd be getting closer to punching me, not asking if I like to have "fun."

My pulse thrums beneath my skin, and I can hear my own heartbeat in my ears. Closing my eyes, I swallow the extra saliva in my mouth. I open them and turn my head to look at her as she sits back slowly. Her eyes are still bloodshot but hooded in the waning light. I trace her parted lips with my eyes, then shake my head and look at my lap.

Snap out of it, Jacob.

"I don't like to have fun," I say.

The silence ticks on.

She drops her hand. "Did you ever like to have fun?"

Her question makes my blood run cold. We aren't talking about any kind of fun; we're dancing around the fun that we've already had together. The kind of fun that I need to stay far away from for the sake of my own mental health. I'm not the same guy hustling on the streets anymore and enjoying every piece that life—and women—had to offer.

I scratch my jaw. "Yeah, I *did* like to have fun but not anymore."

It sounds like a rejection, and I hate that. I'm not rejecting her, but I am rejecting the *fun* she's talking about. She doesn't move but rather sits in silence, staying still as I use my feet to push the swing. Considering how much time has passed since either of us has spoken, I figure we've moved on. That is until she stops our swinging, grabs my water, chugs it, hands the bottle back to me, and stands. "Suit yourself," she says, walking back to the house.

I let my mouth hang open. Somehow her agreement still sounds like an invitation. One that I want to accept with every cell in my body. I'm practically humming with pent up desire. But I stay seated. I won't go down that road again, especially with Ruby.

Because of Ruby.

CHAPTER TEN

Ruby

Instead of joining the rest of the party, I weave through bodies and head straight down the hall to the bathroom. Stumbling through the door, I close it and lean my head back, breathing heavily.

He said no. Again.

I'm not asking him so I can get rejected over and over. I keep asking him, because one of these times he'll cave and say yes. And when he does, I'll take him to the edge, and then leave him hanging. He deserves to know how it feels.

Leaning forward, I brace myself on the counter and drop my head. I knew I shouldn't have come tonight, but my curiosity won out. He told me he had a sister the first time we met—that they had gotten separated—but now that I know who that sister is, I wanted to see them together. I wanted to see how they acted, talked, and laughed with one another. Now I wish I hadn't. Kit is my friend and former coworker from the streets. She's the one I've called for help. I don't have any family or friends, but I do have Kit. I remember when we reconnected on the streets. She was there looking for Jacob. God, if she'd known I'd slept with him a few months before that she would have kicked me out of her life a long time ago.

After I slept with Jacob, we talked. I never do that with clients. Ever. They pay, they have sex, they leave. But this time I let Jacob stay, because when he opened his mouth, I heard a pain that sounded like mine, and I wanted to know where it came from. Was it built the same way? How'd he get to working the streets, too? I knew he sold drugs. No one carries that much cash, and his wallet was full of it. But he wasn't on anything from what I could tell, and he didn't fit the typical dealer stereotype I was used to.

He ordered us food, and I let him talk and ask questions, then I let him fall asleep in my bed. It was no surprise that by morning, he was gone. Giving too much too soon is never a smart move. *Men don't want that*, my mother used to tell me. They want what they want without strings or attachments. I gave too much to Jacob, but I won't make that mistake again.

Kit is the only person in my life I can trust. I can't let her find out that I slept with her long-lost brother. Or, if I sleep with him again. If she does, I can kiss our friendship goodbye. There's no way she wants a prostitute tainting her family after it took her so long to get out of the game. Revenge sex isn't a good idea, because of Kit but also based on how I feel. All of those memories and old feelings are surfacing, and I'm not thinking clearly. I need to remember who I'm dealing with. Just another man who used me and left me. He took what he wanted and paid me for my services. There are no attachments or expectations. It's business. That's it.

I turn the faucet on and cup my hands, filling them with cool water before splashing it on my face. Bare of makeup, my skin prickles from the cold water but I do it again, hoping to sober up before leaving. This is my first time at Kit's house, and I know for sure I'm not coming back. With Jacob and Kit back in each other's lives, he'll always be at things like this. Parties, birthdays, celebrations. I usually don't even come to these in case I run into someone I've slept with. But this is Kit. I thought her place would be safe, but as long as Jacob is here, it's not. He makes me want too many things. I forget who I'm supposed to be and instead start hoping for things that can't happen. It's dangerous.

Patting my face dry and taking another steady breath, I turn the door handle to exit into the dark hallway. The noise from the party is faint from back here, but my ears are ringing. I don't get very far and have to stop abruptly. A figure hovers on the other side of the door jam, and my breath all but stops. The ringing in my ears quiets and the pitch black hallway is aglow with the soft light from the bathroom.

Dylan. I shake my head. *Jacob.*

"Are you okay?" he asks.

I try to focus on his face, but it's hazy, so I settle for the floor. "Fine."

There's no other response other than this when I'm in his presence. Everything has to be fine. No other emotion will do if it doesn't start and end with *fine.*

He reaches to grab my elbow as I sway. "You don't seem fine. Let me take you home."

He braces my shoulders with his firm grip before I can respond. His hands are warm against my bare skin, and it's the only thing I feel. It's all I need to feel. But the rest of me is numb. I look up at him, choosing to focus on his stubbled jawline and neck. Big mistake. I'd consider running my hand along the rough surface if my arms weren't pinned to my side. Is his face closer? Did I lean in? Did he?

I shake off the trance and push past him. He starts walking behind me, propping me with his hands any time I tip too much to the side, and moving us down the dimly lit hall, back through the living room, and to the front door. "You don't have a jacket, right?"

I pat the purse slung across my body and shake my head. "Just this."

People I don't know or can't remember their names wave goodbye and open the door for us to pass through. The important part is that we didn't run into Kit. Leaving with Jacob wouldn't look right, and even with my buzz I'm aware enough to know that.

My legs are wobbly as he leads me to his car parked at the curb like everyone else's. The cool air is like a slap to the face, but I welcome it. I could use it right now when my mind is living in the past and my body is fully wanting in the present.

He settles me into the front seat, shuts my door, and jogs to the driver's side. The car roars to life and another blast of music greets us, startling me.

He laughs. "Sorry."

I don't respond. I'm too busy watching his curly hair dance around his shoulders. He must have run his hand through it a few times already, combing through curls haphazardly since they stand in different directions. His hair is a lot longer than the last time I saw him—the piercing in his ear and tattoo on his forearm are new, too—and I have the sudden urge to run my hand through the mess of it to see if it feels the same. Is it thick like I remember? Will the curls loop around my fingers if I comb through it?

He's too busy securing his seatbelt to see my hand reach over, but his whole body tenses when I push my fingers through his hair, trailing the curve of his head. He closes his eyes, and I do it again and once more after that, telling myself *this* will be the last time. I follow the length of a curl with my pointer finger and thumb, pulling lightly then letting go and watching it bounce. My hand is back on my side of the car, but I wish it wasn't.

He clears his throat and rushes to put the car in gear, pulling out of the parking space. He doesn't acknowledge my wandering hand, but I know he felt it. There's a power in knowing my touch has an effect on him and yet, a low simmering irritation that he's trying to ignore it. He's trying to ignore me.

He was the one who left *me*.

He won't do it again, though. He won't leave without seeing how it feels to be the one left behind. I'm the one who was embarrassed, not him.

I close my eyes to stop the throbbing in my head. He had a right to leave. Payment had been taken and services had been provided. It was everything that came afterward that still makes me angry. He took some of my memories. The ones I opened up about and shared with him and no one else. He held me cradled against him; my hips, legs, and back formed perfectly against his. We laid there for so long, I couldn't tell where he started and I ended. We just were.

And then, he was gone.

I woke up cold, without a note or a text. He vanished, and I never saw him again until he picked me up at the jail and those same lips he sang me to sleep with were talking to me. He doesn't know how that feels. I'm always the one being left. Men come and go, in and out of my motel room like a revolving door. They leave, all of them, including Jacob. But I'm the one who stays.

We ride through side streets and the five freeway, and I stare blankly out the window. The buildings get taller and brighter the closer we drive. The bus drive to Kit's house took twice as long with all the stops and detours, but in the car, we're flying. We pass cars faster than they pass us and the rhythmic movement of the vehicle tires me even more. But I don't have a chance to close my eyes before Jacob parks the car in front of the motel. We aren't in Kit's neighborhood anymore.

I lift my head away from the window and swing my gaze to him. His hand tightens around the steering wheel. "You're home."

My motel door is directly in front of us, framed by the windshield. If I weren't the kind of person who wanted revenge so badly, I'd get out of the car and go inside. I guess I'm not. "Aren't you going to walk me in?"

I want him to hurt like he hurt me. It doesn't make any sense; I'm blind with rage. I should just chalk it up to another night with a different man who paid and left. But I can't do that. I'm not the bigger person.

Jacob looks straight ahead, his jaw clenching beneath his cheek. He shakes his head but doesn't say anything. He gathers his hair into a low bun like earlier. All business. No fun.

I clear my throat and soften my tone. "*Please* walk me to my door. Come on, my legs feel all wobbly and weird right now."

His shoulders relax, and he reaches to open his door. I bite my lower lip to keep from smiling. He won't leave here without something to show for how he treated me.

He helps me stand and slips a solid arm around my waist, as we make slow work toward my door. He's trying to keep his distance, but I don't let him. I bump my hip against his, lingering for as long as he'll let me. My arm is slung around his shoulders, and I start playing with the short hairs at the nape of his neck, making him shudder.

He sucks in a breath and adjusts to add more space where there isn't any. "Do you have your key?"

Before he pulls his hand from my waist, I grip his arm to hold it in place. I turn into him, pressing my chest against him and hearing his intake of breath. I look up through my lashes like an innocent woman without hidden motives. "Will you help me find it?" Our mouths are close as I whisper against his lips.

His back is to the door as his nostrils flare with every breath he takes and his hooded eyes stare down at me, trying not to see me but failing when I fill his line of sight. Ignoring the key tucked in my purse, I run my hand up his core and over his chest. It's firm and strong, different than before but better. I ignore the pulsing energy it sends shooting through my body. Instead, I bend a finger around the neckline of his t-shirt and gently tease the sensitive skin beneath it. Dropping his head back, he stares up at the night sky. My gaze is drawn to his Adam's apple bobbing as he swallows back the building fire I know I'm kindling.

I want him to feel every bit of desire that we both remember and when he does, I'll blast him with the same rejection he offered me. I won't need to admit who I am or for him to recognize me for this to work.

But when his hands settle on my hips, I'm the one who's inhaling sharply, my body beginning to tremble.

No, no. This isn't how it's supposed to go.

I press my body closer to his, unable to stop myself. I'll need to be closer if I'm going to push him away. He'll have to reach a point of no return before I can rip the rug out from beneath him. I need to stay strong. Keep focused on why we're touching. It isn't for pleasure; it's for payback.

Our breathing is labored and perfectly in sync when he spins me around until my back is pressed against the door. I part my lips, feeling every delicious angle of him snug against my curves. I close my eyes. I don't want to see my desire reflected in them.

Stay focused.

His breath is warm on my face, and I squeeze my eyes tighter. This is too hard. We're too close, and I'm not prepared for the sensations he's pulling out of me. I wait for his lips to find mine. Maybe it'll be better once we're kissing. My body will kick into autopilot like it usually does.

He doesn't kiss me, though. Lifting his hand, he trails light fingers along the length of my jaw. "Ruby Red," he whispers close to my cheek.

The way he says my name in a low growl drips down my body like oil being poured out. Slow, silky, and warm. I feel it everywhere—in my core and limbs, fingertips and spine. It pools low between my legs.

I finally open my eyes, needing to prepare myself for whatever comes next. I need to take control, because this…this can't happen. Not with him in the lead.

I'm met with his light eyes searching my face. I should look away if I know what's good for me. We need to speed this up. This slow motion video is making it harder to convince my body this isn't really what I want.

The night air is cool on my bare arms and legs, but my body is too warm to spend time being cold. I reach up and tug at his hair tie, letting the curls fall around his face while I run my hands back down his chest and grip the hem of his shirt. Men don't need a lot. They just need enough to feel desired and when they do, it's over.

I touch my lips to his, testing the taste of them. Sweet mint fills my senses, and I want more. Our kiss is so light, but I feel every connection point. His bottom lip between my lips, his tongue brushing against my mouth, and the corner of his top lip that's lined with stubble. Every part tastes just like I remember him. I continue to press short pecks around his mouth and trade the cotton bunched tightly in my hand for his skin. He rocks his hips closer to mine and his whole body quakes as my hands explore the hard lines of his stomach.

His forehead rests on mine and his long hair tickles my face, creating a secluded tent around us. "Ruby."

Taking my name as a sign of his pleasure, I continue, letting my hands climb higher and then lower.

"Ruby," he says again, but this time, his voice sounds more serious.

I don't let it dissuade me, though. It's only more fuel. He wants this, and we both know it. I hook a finger into his jeans near his hip and begin sliding it around toward his belt buckle.

"Fuck," he says, while grabbing my hand. He isn't angry. His voice is strained like this is taking every ounce of his willpower. *Good*.

Pulling my finger out of his jeans, he drops my hand to my side and steps back. He runs both of his hands through his hair, tugging at the ends all while staring at me.

"Ruby, we have to talk," he says.

I pull my dress down farther and raise a hand with my key. "I found my key. Let's talk inside."

"No." His voice isn't harsh but it is firm as he stares at the ground. "Shit."

His eyes are angry when he looks at me again, and I know he won't be coming inside. That willpower is back, creating a forcefield that, by the look and feel of it, is stronger than ever. His hands rest on his hips, and though he's breathing deeply, the thin line of his lips and steely glare in his eyes are setting the course. He doesn't want me.

I can't explain why this feels like another stab of rejection from him, but it does. Heat fills my cheeks. I should have just hated him and called it a day. Touching him only invited him to reject me—again. I was supposed to be in control, but it didn't work. Why didn't it work?

"I need to tell you something." His voice is on the low and weighty setting.

I shake my head. "Don't." I want nothing more than to open my door and escape inside. This is so embarrassing.

"Jasmine," he says, and I pause. *He knows who I am.*

I turn slowly, but our attention is stolen by the black SUV that creeps by. The windows are closed and dark, making it impossible to see anyone on the inside until the window begins to roll down slowly. A man with dark hair and a snarl plastered on his lips flicks a cigarette onto the pavement. I normally wouldn't think twice about this sort of thing. People lurk, especially men. But I know that snarl. I've seen it before.

The way Jacob's hands ball into fists makes me think he has, too. He stiffens, grits his teeth, and mutters, "Fuck."

The drive-by is brief. The man rolls his window up and peels out of the parking lot in seconds. Without taking his eyes off the vehicle, Jacob says, "Open the door and get inside. Now."

The night air might as well be freezing considering how much my teeth are chattering. "Excuse me?"

Stomping toward me, he fishes the key from my hand, eyes wide and scanning the small motel parking lot. With fumbling hands, he inserts the key into the lock and pushes the door open, leading me inside with a firm grip on my arm.

"What the hell is going on?" I ask, yanking my arm away.

My voice rises and sounds shrill in the small space. He knows who I am. He's known this whole time.

I peer over to the top drawer of the nightstand where I have a knife. I didn't think I'd need to use it with him, but if he's like some of the others, then I might have to. "You need to leave." I inch closer to the bed, my destination set on the contents of that drawer.

He slams the door, securing every lock, and drawing the curtains before he peeks out. His breathing is the only sound I hear besides the loud thump of my heartbeat. He slaps the back of the closed door so hard, I feel the ground shake beneath my feet. Pacing the room, he ignores me. I have so many questions, but none of them matter. I scoot backward slowly, careful to avoid jerky movements that'll give me away. I'm almost there. A few more steps and I'll have protection against this caged animal.

The thundering racket of my pulse becomes too loud in my own ears. My hand on the drawer, I pull it open and grab the knife, holding it out in front of me. "You need to leave."

He stops, releases his hair from his own grip, and locks eyes with me. His expression morphs from lunatic to the most concerned man in the room. "I'm not gonna hurt you."

I hold my breath, as the knife stands between the two of us. "You already did."

Jacob raises his hands in surrender and takes a few steps back.

"Get out."

He puts his hands in front of him. "Can we just—"

"Get out!" I yell louder this time.

He drops his head and nods. Studying the wall, as if it will give him the words he needs, he nods again and reverses the locks on the door, then opens it to leave. He hesitates. "That was—"

"I know who that was."

And I know who *Dylan* is, too.

He exhales, looks at me with pleading eyes, then walks out.

I drop the knife, rush to the door and lock it.

I grit my teeth and cradle my head in my hands. If I had any doubts about who Jacob really is, it all comes into focus. That selfish prick. I get it now. It's all summed up in one name that no one on the streets likes to hear: Bobby.

CHAPTER ELEVEN

Jacob

"Come on, it has to be here. Where is it?"

My breathing is labored as I flip through papers, open boxes, and tear through my closet. But I still can't find it. I know I didn't throw it out. Not with all the information written in that letter. There's no way I'd be so careless.

"I knew I should have burned it," I mumble to myself.

Peering around the room, I've created a mess that's produced nothing. I can't find the letter I wrote to Kit, and now it looks like I've been robbed. Dammit. I rub my forehead, sweat beading there already. Bobby's damn grin keeps replaying in my mind. He's back, picking up where we left off. Where he's the gang leader, and I'm the lowly lieutenant that he's got by the neck. He doesn't need a reason to show up, but he never does anything without one. He's another person from my past making sure I don't forget that I have one. But I'm not completely powerless. I've got dirt on him that if he knew, he wouldn't have smiled like he did. That's why I have to find the letter.

I drag my hands down my face, scratching the scruff lining my cheeks and neck. I know I freaked Ruby out last night. She had a knife pointed at me for fuck's sake. I called her *Jasmine*. I was going to explain everything. That I know who she is and who I am—who Bobby is—but by the look on her face, I didn't need to explain. She needed me out.

And I need this letter in a safe place. The truth lives in my memories and that single piece of paper, nowhere else. Thinking about someone else finding it sends a sinking feeling throughout my entire body. If someone read it…

Standing, I step over the contents of my room and scan everything in case I missed it. Clothes, shoes, books, paper, trash. No letter. It's either lost or hidden, and both options don't help. It's the most valuable thing I own at this point, and it's what's kept my family intact these last couple of years. No one knows about it—especially Kit—and I need to keep it that way. Secrets are okay if they're used to protect, and that's what I'm doing. I'm protecting.

A knock on my door steals my attention, as my roommate pushes it open. "Wow," he says. "Are you spring cleaning, or what?"

I stare at the disaster, then back at him. "Or what."

"I would offer to help, but I don't want to," James says, rubbing a hand over his smooth head.

"Thanks." I glare at him and rub the back of my neck, hoping the stress eating away at me isn't noticeable. "I was looking for something, and I didn't really pay attention to the piles I was making."

His eyes widen. "Clearly."

I put my hands on my hips. "What are you doing today? You workin'?"

"It's my day off, and I was going to work out. I came to see if you wanted to join but it looks like you're a little busy." He waves a hand toward the chaos at my feet.

"Thanks, but I can't. Not because of the mess. I have to get to work soon." I look at the floor. "I'll deal with this later."

"Imma head out soon." He moves to exit then turns back around. "You sure you're cool, man?"

I fight the urge to wipe at my brow again. "Yeah. I'm good." It's all lies.

James is my best friend outside of Kit and Beau. We went through the recovery program together and got along, which wasn't the case with everyone. I'm not exactly the easiest friend to have. Maybe it's the lying, or the fact that I've never had real friends, only the kind that like to stab you in the back.

"That's bullshit, but I'll hound you later," he says, then walks out with a flippant wave.

Shaking my head, I high-step over the piles I created when I tore them out of my dresser and start searching for my work clothes. I'm in the kitchen but still required to wear the standard white button up and black pants. Add an apron and that's the full extent of my uniform. Washing dishes for a living is putting food in my fridge and gas in my car, but it isn't what I want to do forever. I don't know what job I'd want to do for that long.

Yanking out each dresser drawer open to look for a pair of socks, I pause. This motion feels familiar and not just because I do this every day. I smooth my hand along the inside of the drawer. It's not here. I grab my socks and go to turn around, but I feel the need to check again. Turning back, I pull the drawer out completely, thinking I'll get a better look at all the corners and angles, but something falls out with it.

The letter.

I don't bother putting the drawer back. I set it on the ground and quickly snag the envelope at my feet. I found it. It's in my hands, and I can see it with my own eyes. I sigh with relief, clutching the envelope tighter and dropping my head back.

"See ya later." James' voice cuts through my thoughts, and I jerk my head up, then back to the letter.

"Bye," I say quietly. Too quiet for him to even hear.

I need to go, but I have to put this envelope somewhere that I won't forget. Where the hell is that? I look around my room. The nightstand, gym bag, closet? No. I'm not tryna lose it again.

This letter shouldn't even be here. I planned on destroying it before, so maybe I should do that and be done with all this worrying. It would be safer that way. Less risk. It's been a while since I've read it. Is it really as bad as I remember? Probably. Okay, yes.

There's a reason I didn't burn it or get rid of it all this time. Not because I ever planned to hand it over to the person I wrote it for—Kit—but to have a written testimony in case something went down. If Bobby ever came back, ready to pick a fight, I'd have this. And with Bobby showing up last night, I know getting rid of this isn't an option, yet.

Spying my journal on the bedside table, I pick it up and flip through the pages, stashing the letter inside. I'll read it again later when I have more time. It's not like the memories don't live in my head already. I know what kind of shit Bobby was into, or is, which is why he likely wants to cover his bases. The evidence is damning. But I'm not looking for a fight. No. I just want to keep my family safe. Ruby, too.

I strip down and pull my black pants on, then button up my shirt. It's not like I'm a stakeholder in her life. The first time we met, I came and went easily. I should do that again. I should avoid her based on how things went last night when I chose not to leave right away. Her hands in my hair, on my skin. I'm only a man. It's simple, really. When a beautiful woman touches me, my body is going to react. So, there needs to be no touching, and that means no Ruby. Being around her is like playing with fire. It won't end well if I stick around.

She knows now; it's all out in the open. She knows I'm Dylan, or rather, Jacob.

I pull on my Vans sneakers and tie the laces. I need to keep her out of this thing with Bobby, but maybe I should apologize. She deserves that. We don't have to touch. We can just talk.

The thought of her waking up alone this morning makes my gut churn with unease. I was such a jerk—kissing her, and then leaving like I did. I freaked out over seeing Bobby, and then said her street name, wishing she hadn't heard me say it before walking out her door, like a dog with its tail between its legs.

I'm stuffing spare clothes into my gym bag for after work with such force that I break the zipper when closing it. I run anxious fingers through my hair. *Damn it*. This wasn't how I wanted things to happen. I never planned on telling her, but I just couldn't help myself. I couldn't stay away from her. Why don't I ever listen to myself?

I smooth out my hair and redo my bun, grabbing for my now broken gym bag and leaving the mess in my room for later. I can't think about this right now. About Ruby or Kit. Their future, or mine. If I take my eyes off of the present, off of Bobby, he'll take that as an invitation. I have no plans to tell Kit that I saw him last night. She'd only freak out. But in my rush to leave last night, I didn't get to tell Ruby to keep this between us. I'll need to tell her not to say anything. Great, an apology with a request.

I exhale, hand on the door frame, and look over my shoulder to where the letter is. It holds every one of my last remaining secrets.

The secrets I need to keep hidden.

I SKIP EVERY other step as I bolt up the stairs to my apartment. Kit's car is in the visitor space, but I'm not expecting her. Since when does she just show up like this? Usually she'd text, but this time she didn't. Why is she here? My heart beats faster than it did during my run at the gym.

Did Bobby show up at her work?

Does she know about the letter?

Cresting the last step, I twist the knob and barrel through my unlocked front door. "Kit?" My high-pitched voice echoes in the space.

"In here," she says from my bedroom.

My stomach drops, as I trudge through quicksand to get to my room. She's here. In my room. The letter is in my room. I can't let Kit find the letter. She wouldn't read it though, right? There's no name on the envelope. It's blank but not sealed. Standing beneath the door frame, I'm expecting the worst—Kit finding and reading that damn letter, or crying because she saw Bobby. Instead, she's spinning in a full circle in the middle of my room, scrunching her nose.

She doesn't look at me. "Your room is disgusting."

The journal is still by my bed, the letter poking out the top. It's not in her hands. I let out a sigh, too big for the moment, and look at Kit. "I'm…organizing."

She crosses her arms, shrugs both shoulders and stares at me. "Why?"

No tears. There are no tears in her eyes, I confirm. "Spring cleaning…I guess." I drop my gym bag inside the door and attempt to take a step inside the room.

It's a lost cause with all the stuff littered everywhere. Some of the clothes are clean, too, and I don't want to step on them. If I'm too close to Kit, anyway, I'm sure she'll hear how hard I'm breathing. Between the running and fear, I'm tapped of breath and energy.

"Why are you in here?"

She points behind me. "Your door was open."

I nod and narrow my eyes. "Are you planning to help me clean it up then?"

Kit scoffs. "No way. Unless you want to pay me, I'll let you deal with this." Her hand waves over the floor that isn't visible.

"Not happening."

"If you say so." She shrugs and walks past me, bumping my shoulder before heading out of the room. "I brought you a sandwich. You weren't at church this morning, and you didn't answer your phone, so I had to make sure you weren't dead. It's the sisterly thing to do."

Following her into the kitchen, my stomach growls on cue as I grab for the sub sandwich and unwrap it. "Thanks." I plop down on the barstool chair at my kitchen counter and shove the first bite into my mouth, because I'm starving and I'd be smart to avoid Kit's comment. I didn't go to church, because I didn't remember. There were a few other things on my mind.

"I worked," I say between bites.

"Mhm." She squints and cocks her head. "I thought you don't work on Sundays?"

Big sister is always in my business. "I don't but had to switch shifts with someone so I could go to Beau's party. And then I went to the gym." I rush to change the subject. "Where's Beau?"

"With Jordan. Something about a football game." Kit leans against the counter, unwrapping her sandwich and tucking any stray veggies back into the bun. It's a weird habit of hers. "I'm glad you're not dead," she adds.

I give a pinched laugh before taking another bite. I know she's joking. We've been through a lot together these last couple of years. She worries about me, even though she tries to play it off like it's no big deal. You don't stop worrying after getting separated in the foster system only to find your brother works for your old pimp and ends up doing time because of him. At least not easily. There's truth to her words, and I don't take it lightly. Mostly.

I chase my food with another bite and wave a hand in front of my body. "I'm very much alive. I've got aching biceps and sore pecs to prove it."

"Okay, we get it. You work out," Kit teases and rolls her eyes. "So…how's Ruby?"

I cough, choking on a jalapeño. It went down the wrong way. Or, maybe Kit's question did. Pounding a fist to my chest, I take a minute to answer. "What do you mean?"

"You okay there, buddy?" She walks over and slaps my back, like I'm a choking child. "I was just asking since you took her home last night but didn't come back to the party. Was everything alright?"

I clear my throat once more, buying time. These are exactly the kind of questions I don't want to be answering and why I was avoiding Kit in the first place. What am I supposed to tell her? That I kissed Ruby—the woman I paid to have sex with years ago—and then had a drive-by visit from Bobby? Fuck no. I can't say any of that.

"Right. Yeah, she, uh…" I rub the back of my neck. I'm screwed. "She just needed a ride, so I took her home." That's it, or at least all I'm going to say. I shift in my seat and bite down on my sandwich again to fill my mouth with something other than words I'll regret.

She shakes her head and walks to the fridge. "I thought so."

She sighs and opens the door, pulling out a couple of waters. "Thanks for doing that. I would have driven her, though. You don't have to help her every time. After picking her up from jail, I wasn't expecting you to keep doing stuff like that."

I wasn't expecting to, either, but I wasn't going to let Ruby leave on her own to ride the city bus in her state. She was halfway to wasted and well on her way to a bad decision—other than the one she made with me outside her motel. I still don't get what came over her, or me for that matter. She seemed annoyed when I picked her up from jail. It didn't make sense since I was the one doing her a favor. I chalked it up to a rough night in the cell. But last night was a complete shift. Fire and ice—warm one minute and freezing me out the next. She was perfectly fine sticking her tongue down my throat, and I was fine with it, too.

She unscrews the cap and hands me a plastic water bottle that I take an extra long drink from. My mouth is dry from all this side-steppin' I'm doing around the truth.

"It was Beau's party. It made more sense for me to take her home so you wouldn't miss anything. Really, it's fine. She's… nice."

A jolt of electricity shoots south of my waist at the memory of how *nice* Ruby is. How nice she feels. How nice she looks. How nice our bodies moved together. I tilt the bottle back and don't stop drinking until it's empty and I wipe my mouth.

"So, uh. Have you and Ruby been friends for a while?" I'm fishing and I know it. I need to leave it alone and drop all these questions about Ruby. The more I know isn't going to help.

She stares at her bottle. "Yeah. I guess there's something about our shared experience that's bonded us. I know she's still turning tricks on the streets, going on dates to earn money and all that, but I want to be here if or when she decides to leave."

I squeeze the empty bottle and try not to scoff. Ruby didn't seem ready to leave the streets. She seemed perfectly content to continue doing dates and pleasing the horny men of Los Angeles. She told me she wanted to leave L.A. and prostitution when we first met, but she never did. I was the one who got out. "Has she ever said she wanted to leave?"

She nods and my mouth slowly falls open. "She has plans. I think she wants to get out of the area, but her daughter is in foster care here, so she's trying to get her back first." Kit takes another bite of her sandwich.

Daughter?

Did I know this? I take back what I said. Maybe she does have a reason to stop the sex work. I think back on the night we spent together. I wasn't drunk or high at the time and would've remembered if she said she had a daughter. Did she mention anything about her recently? Maybe in the car?

"I don't know all the details," Kit starts, setting her sandwich on the counter and wiping her hands. "She doesn't share too much about her or the situation. It's gotta be hard, though." She shakes her head and raises her brows.

I close my mouth and tame my voice. "So, Ruby has a daughter. How old?"

She picks up her sandwich. "Yup. I think she's three now."

I widen my eyes. Three years old? I do a quick mental calculation. The first time I met Ruby was three years ago. The first and only time we slept together was three years ago. *Holy shit.* My leg starts bouncing beneath the countertop. "Why doesn't Ruby's daughter stay with her dad?"

Stop asking questions.

You don't want to know.

You don't need to.

She flips her dark hair over her shoulder and shuffled on her feet. "I don't think she knows who the father is. It's not like it's that hard for slip-ups to happen." She continues to eat her sandwich and drink her water like the world isn't tearing in half.

Thoughts enter my mind without an exit, and soon, I'm making up stories I'm not prepared to consider. What if…she could be…no. There's no way.

"You look pale," she says. "Are your biceps hurting?" She smirks.

Shaking my head, I reach for my water bottle and remember it's empty. "I think I'm just tired after work and my workout. I'm gonna go shower and take a nap."

"Alright, I have to go anyway. I'm supposed to be grocery shopping." She takes another sip, then throws away our trash. "Any chance we can meet up to work out this week?"

I raise an eyebrow as I stand. "You want to work out with me?"

Pushing out a hip, she crosses her arms. "Don't look at me like it's a crazy idea. We've talked about it before."

"You've never come with me, though."

She waves a dismissive hand. "I will this time."

I tip my chin toward her, glad for the change of subject. "How about tomorrow morning?"

"I'll meet you there. Promise."

"Fifty pushups if you don't."

"Ugh. Are you going to be like this at the gym, too?" she complains.

"Maybe." I wrap her in a quick hug and walk backward. "Don't forget to lock the door behind you."

She's already strutting down the hall with her back to me, flipping her hand in the air. "Yeah, yeah. I will."

I stride to the sink and fill up my water before heading to my room. The door clicks shut, and I'm alone with my thoughts. They're crazy. I need to stop thinking like this. The kid isn't mine. It can't be. I scrub a hand down my face. Life is a mess. I'm lying to Kit about too many things when it was only ever supposed to be one thing—the letter. Now, it's my connection to Ruby, the kid, and seeing Bobby pop up out of nowhere. It's too much. I haven't had to deal with any of it for years, and now everything's hitting at once.

I sit on the edge of my bed, unscrew the water bottle, and drink. I don't stop until half of it is drained. I could probably deal with everything else if Bobby weren't in the picture. He's been quiet for two years, and there's been no trace of him. Not like I'd kept any of my old connections in place after going to jail, but there have been no threatening notes, no calls, hit men, nothing. He all but disappeared from our lives, or so I hoped.

Snatching a few clothes to change into, I turn my attention to the journal beside my bed and the letter tucked between the pages. I know it's ridiculous, but I can't let this letter out of my sight. It's too risky. What's written inside would change things—everything, actually. It would change everything. Kit and I have been good. Our relationship is strong since the past has stayed in the past. But all of that would die a slow, painful death if she read it. I need to keep it with me. No close calls.

Grabbing the journal, I pluck the envelope out of its grip and hide it between the clothes in my hand and head to the shower. I shut the bathroom door and stare into the mirror. Does Ruby's daughter have brown skin like mine? Does she have red hair like Ruby? Would I be able to tell if I saw her?

I brace my hands on the edges of the counter. "Don't go there," I grind out under my breath.

It doesn't matter if the timeline seems to match up. Kissing Ruby then and now was a mistake, and I wasn't thinking about anything outside of that moment. Consequences didn't exist when her mouth was on mine. But in the real world, they do.

Shaking my head, I feel sick. So much for changing.

I pick up the envelope hiding beneath my clothes and hold it. The past is knocking on my door while the future possibilities all but drop in my lap. I don't know how to make sense of everything. But there is one thing I know I need to do.

I have a redhead to see.

CHAPTER TWELVE

Ruby

My head hurts.

Moaning into my pillow, I try to roll over. Nope. It hurts too much. The searing pain pounds inside my skull. I don't have time for this. I need to work today.

The dryness in my throat causes me to gag. It's so raw. I need water. I roll over and feel around on the nightstand, unable to open my eyes yet. Items fall and crash into one another as I fumble around, so I peel my lids open and scan the bedside table. I can't lift my head to get a better angle, it feels too heavy and tired, but it doesn't look like there's any there.

Great.

I rotate until I'm on my stomach, but now it feels like I'm going to puke. The room is spinning as I push up to a seated position and stumble forward on shaking legs to the bathroom. What happened to me? I fall through the door and grab hold of the sink then the toilet. I need to throw up. It's coming.

Oh, right. It's what happens most nights. I drink too much, pass out, then vomit. All before noon.

Bowing over the toilet, I get rid of the many ounces of alcohol I consumed last night. Plus the ramen noodles and questions plaguing me. So many questions. All of them race through my brain, and I press my hands to either side of my head. Not now. I don't want to deal with these now. Bobby. Jacob. Kit. Willow. Everyone demands my thoughts.

"Stop!" I yell, and then start a coughing fit.

Drool hangs from my mouth, and I gasp for air. I use the wall to balance and clutch my head as it spins in circles. Why are there so many questions? Why am I asking about questions with a question? I brace my stomach with a hand and sink to my knees, hoping I won't be sick again. The peeling black and white tile floors keep me from falling farther, which my body somehow feels is possible.

I wipe my mouth with the back of my hand and fall back against the wall. Water. I need water. I open my eyes and crawl toward the sink then use the edge to pull myself up. I need water. Flipping the faucet handle up, the splutter of water exits the pipes and only lets a few drops of liquid fall into the sink basin.

"No, no, no. I need water," I beg. I rush to pull the handle up and down, but it doesn't work. There's no water still. The owner said a pipe burst, but that was two days ago. I thought it would be fixed by now. "Dammit!"

I slink down, back to the cold tiles. Sweat beads on my forehead. I just need to lay down. Just for a little bit. Lying on my side, I curl my legs up. The cool floor feels good, and I close my eyes again. I could stay here all day. Maybe I will. When was the last time I took a day off? Money doesn't come if I don't work so never.

I focus on the in-and-out pattern of my breath until the ache in my stomach leaves, my body cools off, and I have enough saliva to coat my tender throat. What am I supposed to do? If I could just get water somewhere, maybe I'll be fine for another week. I've done it before. Living without water isn't all that bad. I'll survive.

Buying a few water bottles at the gas station down the street will be cheaper. I just have to get there. Chills roll through my body like a wave, and I shiver. I'm cold now, but I don't have the energy to give a damn.

I close my eyes tighter.

Jacob.

He left. Vanishing into the night like the rest of them.

He said my street name, and then hopped in his car to leave. It didn't matter that I couldn't sleep, or that when I did, every noise woke me up. I wish it was because of Bobby, but it wasn't. I couldn't sleep, because Jacob outed himself. He knew exactly who I was and still…God, I'm such a fool. Now, I know who he is.

Apart from Jacob, word on the street is that Bobby isn't who you want to do business with. Between the drug cartels and prostitution, he has enough power, and too much of it is never a good thing. It would be better to avoid him, and I've managed to do that until last night. Does Jacob have beef with Bobby? He told me he's been to jail. Was he there because of Bobby?

I rub my forehead and roll to my back. The small movement is enough to make my stomach groan. *Please don't puke again.* I'm too tired to get up.

My head is still throbbing. I could do without all of the questions. The drinks were supposed to get rid of them. They did last night but not today. They're back, and I can't keep up with them.

Why did Bobby show up?

Why did Jacob freak out over seeing him?

How long did Jacob know it was me?

What would Kit say if she knew about Jacob and me?

Why do I keep thinking about our kiss?

What about Willow?

Willow.

She's the place where all of my thoughts lead. Everything I do or don't do affects my ability to be her parent. I want to be good at it, but right now, that's hard to believe.

I grip the edge of the toilet seat and slowly pull myself up to sit. I'm still wearing the dress from the party last night, and now it smells. I need to take it off. I need to shower. I need water. I need food. I need my head to stop hurting. But I can only solve one of those issues. I push the straps down off my shoulders and slide my dress down past my bra, stomach, and legs until I slither out of it and toss it across the bathroom. I reach over and flush the toilet, then lean back against the wall again.

Willow deserves better. Better than my mother and better than me. She deserves Molly. She was made to be a mom. For reasons I don't know and don't care about, she couldn't have kids and decided to take someone else's. She took mine.

My stomach gurgles again and more saliva fills my mouth. I swallow and swallow until I can't. I hold the sides of the toilet and vomit again. There's nothing left in my stomach, but my body doesn't get that. It keeps gagging and constricting until I'm sucking in a lungful of air. What if this is all I'm good for? Getting drunk and screwing.

I wipe my mouth before I attempt to crawl back to my room. I'm so thirsty. I need something to soothe my throat and my thoughts.

I pause multiple times before I make it back to my bed. There's a clear bottle with a few swigs of vodka calling my name. I knit my brows together and squeeze my eyes shut as I position my heavy body on the edge of the bed and drink deeply. Sputtering coughs fall from my mouth, spraying alcohol across the room and on my bare legs. I use the sheet to wipe my mouth as my throat burns, and I feel like I could be sick again. But I don't go back to the bathroom. Instead, I fall back on the bed and curl up in the sheets.

Willow doesn't belong in a place like this where pipe bursts and don't get fixed quickly, or with a mother like me. I never deserved to be Kit's friend, or Jacob's anything. I'm no good at relationships. I've never had one that's lasted.

I close my eyes and my body relaxes some. My breathing is steady once more, and the pounding in my head quits as long as I'm completely still. But my face contorts and scrunches as a surge of emotion rises up.

I don't deserve to be here.

To live.

To have a daughter.

Who fucking cares? I don't. Jacob doesn't.

The tears are painful as they leave my eyes. Every one of them weighs five pounds. Every. Fucking. One. I press my pillow into my face to stop them. I need them to stop. I bite the soft fleshy pillow and scream. I scream until I don't have any air left and I'm gasping. More coughing. More gagging. More tears.

I pull the pillow away at the last second, gulping air and wincing. Coward. I'm a fucking coward. If Willow didn't have me in her life, she'd be free. She'd be able to live her life with Molly and Stan. Why can't I do it? Why can't I kill myself? It would be so much easier for Willow if I could.

The tears don't stop. Not when I pressed the pillow to my mouth. Not when I hide under the flimsy sheet. And not when I fall asleep with tears streaking down my face and pooling on the bed. They continue to slip down my cheeks, like they'll never stop.

Can you die by tears?

I wish.

CHAPTER THIRTEEN

Jacob

I'm late to work. Two times this week. The last couple of days have been a blur of late nights thinking about way too much. I haven't had time to go visit Ruby, and it feels like a big, hairy unsettled issue. Add the fact my pulse races whenever I think of Bobby's drive-by appearance. He came out of nowhere and disappeared just as fast, causing me to question if I'd even seen him. But the way my stomach knots tells me I did.

Jumping out of my car, I slam the door and hurry to the back entrance of the restaurant. It won't matter to my boss that I've worked here for more than a year since leaving the Journey Center. There won't be second, third, or fourth chances out here in the real world. I could've lived and worked on campus to earn more money, but I chose to leave. We all needed to adjust back to real life eventually, and it was time to stand on my own two feet. This job affords me that.

I shove my things in one of the employee lockers in the break room and drape an apron over my head while I redo my bun. Working in the kitchen means I don't have to deal with customers or other employees, since I'm the only one in the back most nights. I prefer it that way. I can throw in my headphones and run dishes through the washer, making hours pass quickly.

I tie the apron straps around my waist just as I round the corner and almost ram into my boss.

"Jacob," he says, stopping abruptly. "You're late."

The clock hanging on the wall just past his shoulder tells me I'm twenty minutes late. "Sorry. It won't happen again."

He studies me, trying to determine if I'm full of shit. I'm not, but I do need this job. "Make sure of it," he says, then passes me.

I exhale and head to the industrial dishwasher. There are stacks of dirty dishes piled on the end of the stainless steel counter waiting for me. It doesn't take much time to fall behind, considering how busy this place is, which is a wonder based on the prices listed on the menu. I'd have to give up my whole paycheck just to afford one meal here.

I put my headphones in and tuck the cord beneath my apron as I scrape plates and rack them. A loud beat fills my ears and drowns out the sound of rushing water washing off the grime on the plates I send through the washer. I repeat the actions over and over and over again. More dishes come. I clean them. They dry. I put them away. The repetition is familiar and is what got me through my time in jail. We had jobs, yard time, therapy, and meal times. I could count on the schedule playing out the exact same way every day. No setbacks. No changes, and I like that about this job, too.

The clapping beat and voices harmonize to create a mix I never get tired of. I push another load of dirty dishes through the scalding hot water and point my feet side to side, balancing on my heels and lightly bending my knees to the music while I wait. I shuffle and slide, pivot and dip. The room gets warm fast, and I have to push stray hairs off my forehead.

Like music, dancing is my outlet. I keep pace with the pulse of the song and let the motions flow through me. There's enough freedom in dance to play around with and attempt new things while still feeling in control of my body.

A light tapping on my shoulder has me whipping around and raising my fists. Adrenaline races through my body, but I coach myself to chill out. I breathe and lower my balled hands. *It's just Reggie.*

I take my headphones out. "What the hell, man?"

Reggie's new around here and doesn't know not to sneak up on me like that. I guess he does now.

He holds his hands up. "You didn't hear me. How else was I supposed to get your attention?"

Shaking my head, I check my phone for the time. It's almost eleven, and the restaurant just closed an hour ago. "Sorry. I was focused."

Reggie nods but keeps his distance. "Someone's here to see you."

I flip the switch on the washer, so it quits running after it spits out the last rack of steaming hot dishes. "Who is it?"

He shrugs and starts to walk backward. "They didn't give a name, but they're at a table by the hostess stand."

Using my apron, I dry my hands. "Alright. Be right there."

The adrenaline spike of thinking I was being attacked doesn't lessen as I run through the short list of names of people that could be here, especially at this hour. I check my phone, but there are no new texts or missed calls.

Ruby doesn't have my number, so she wouldn't be able to call. But does she know where I work? Maybe I mentioned the name? Did Kit? I don't know. We left things in a weird spot, which is saying something based on how things ended the first time. I've been busy, but it's also because I don't know how to ask about her daughter. I don't know if I should leave it alone. Did I miss my shot? I'm not about to answer that honestly. The kiss weighs heavy on my mind, too, every time I think about it. But I need to suck it up and talk to her. Maybe that's why she's here, because she wants to talk, too.

I struggle out of my apron and hang it on a nearby hook. The kitchen area is one swinging door away from the main dining room. There's constant activity pushing in and out of this door during business hours, but now it's quiet. This is why I like working the closing shift when I can: quiet.

The picture of her red hair falling down her back is already in my mind as I exit the kitchen. Sinking my fingers in it was just like I remembered, thick and soft as silk. My hands tingle at the thought, but I shove it from my mind as I prepare to see and talk to her again. I need to be on my game this time.

The dining room is ornate with red velvet cushioned chairs and blown glass hanging lights above every table that are dimmed to create a private ambiance. If an always crowded restaurant could be private, that is. I'm not out here often but remember the hostess stand is straight ahead through a row of booths and tables. My work is in the kitchen, and I don't need to know the layout of the dining room.

I bend around a corner booth and spot the hostess stand. My gaze immediately jumps to the only other body in the restaurant, sitting at a two-person table by the large front window. The high-back chair frames him in perfectly.

He doesn't have long red hair.

He doesn't have freckles lining his cheeks.

But I do see his face when I close my eyes, just like I can see Ruby's.

He steeples his fingers, the smug look on his face every bit as menacing as I remember. I clench my fists at my sides and breathe heavily through my nose.

Don't show emotion.

He's back. He's here. Now. Right now.

I don't honor his presence by saying his name. The man doesn't do anything without a plan. He's been waiting for this, to ambush me when I'm least expecting him. He possesses just enough patience to wait out his prey and enough revenge coursing through his veins to remember every indiscretion done against him. He remembers just like I do.

"Jacob," he says in a low voice. "Isn't this familiar?" He waves a hand around the restaurant, reminding me of the first time I saw Kit after all of those years. I don't need any reminding, though.

I just need to keep from punching Bobby in the face.

CHAPTER FOURTEEN

Jacob

"Sit." Bobby points at the seat across from him.

The suit he's wearing is spotless. The lines are sleek and the fabric pressed, making him look even more expensive. He's made good money. I was a small part of the whole operation but should have meant nothing to him. But he took an interest because of my connection to Kit.

I don't even have to look at it to know my answer. "I'd rather stand."

He shrugs one shoulder. "Can I get you a drink?"

The bartender is long gone by now. "We're closed," I say, hoping he'll get the hint and leave. My hands are still balled into fists at my sides. Relaxing in Bobby's presence is impossible.

The last time I saw him, he almost killed someone I love. We aren't exactly on good terms.

"Don't worry, I brought my own." He waves, and one of his guys materializes from a remote part of the restaurant and brings us a bottle of whiskey with two glasses.

He pours a finger's worth, no ice, for each of us and leaves. The bottle stays.

"Here." Bobby holds the drink out for me to take.

"I don't drink."

His expression is blank and unfeeling. "Right." He sets the cup on the table. "It's here when you're ready."

I grind my teeth together. My heart is close to exploding inside my chest based on how fast it's pumping. But if I'm going to get Bobby out of here, I need to keep my breathing steady since showing fear when cornered isn't a good idea. But I know he won't leave until he drops whatever bomb he's got.

"How's Mercedes?" he asks.

The way he says Kit's street name makes my stomach twist. "Good."

"And you?"

"Good."

His lips stretch slowly into a smile. "After a couple of years, that's all you have to say?"

"I have nothing to say to you."

"Nothing?" he asks, then crosses his legs. "I find that hard to believe."

I have plenty of things to say to him, all of which would leave a bullet in my skull.

The restaurant is empty. If Reggie hasn't gone home, yet, he will soon. There's no one else here at this hour, and I'm not about to try anything stupid. Unless he does.

He sighs. "Did you enjoy your time in jail?"

A strained laugh escapes my lips, but I don't dignify his question with an answer.

"Not much of a talker are we?" he asks, then looks at his drink. "You never really were."

I shift on my feet. He's trying to goad me into saying something, but I won't do it.

He takes a sip of the whiskey. "The first time I was in jail, I vowed to stay on the straight and narrow when I got out. I succeeded for a good couple of years, too." He swirls the liquid in his glass. "But then my mom got sick. My sister wanted to keep playing violin, and my father was gone. I needed to support my family. So, I did what I had to do."

He's trying to humanize himself, but it won't work. He's a fucking prick.

"You and I are the same in that way, Jacob. We take care of family, friends…the women we love."

I swallow hard. He saw me kissing Ruby. I didn't mean to tie her to this mess, or to me. I train my features and don't give anything away that would indicate I know who he's talking about.

He stares at the table. "I've been busy these last couple of years," he starts, changing the subject. "Business is booming, so I had to hire more employees." He draws out the last word.

He's choosing his words carefully, but it only makes me want to scream louder than I'm already doing internally. Bobby doesn't have employees. He has slaves. I shake my head slowly and clamp my mouth tightly. I won't say anything. I won't let him rattle me. Staying calm is my only option here. This is all a game to him. But to me, these are lives I'm protecting.

I continue to stare. Taking my eyes off of him wouldn't be smart. "What are you doing here?"

He points at me. "He speaks!"

I roll my eyes. I don't need this kind of shit. "I'm leaving." I turn to go.

"Stop."

I don't have to listen to him. My phone is in my pocket, and I could easily pull it out and call the cops. There are cameras everywhere in this restaurant and would act as my witness. It's not like I don't already know he wants revenge. Kit and I were the ones who got away, slipped out from under his iron grip. We didn't get away without something to show for it, though. Jail, hospitals, threats, drugs, and money. We've suffered enough at the hands of this fucker, and I don't want to get anywhere close to doing it again.

But he's here for a reason. If I leave tonight, he'll find me again. Or, he'll find Kit. I can't let that happen. Not again. She's been through enough when it comes to Bobby. And what about Ruby? He probably knows her name by now, and she knows his. Was there something between them? A history I don't know about? It wouldn't be the only thing I was in the dark on when it came to Ruby's past.

A sneer is plastered on his face when I turn around. "I'm still short thousands of dollars—thanks to your sister—but I'm willing to make a deal."

I can't help but scoff. "And what makes you think I'll make a deal with you?"

He lifts his whiskey and speaks behind the rim of the glass. "Because." He takes a drink. "You're a protector."

"Fuck off," I say, my voice hot with anger. I can't help it. The last thing I want to do is involve anyone else in Bobby's sick little game.

"Oh, but you are." He drains the rest of his drink and pours himself another. "You should know by now that most of my work is done using…collateral. Consider yourself the collateral for the damages you've caused. Apart from the money Kit owes me, the supplies you took on your little joy ride that got you caught and thrown in jail, equaled a hefty sum."

Taking the car full of drugs was reckless on my part, but it was the only way to get free. I'd already been charged once for possession and knew that by getting caught, I'd be in jail. The alternative of something happening to Kit was being Bobby's prisoner and that was worse. So, I chose jail time.

"I know you don't have that kind of money to pay me back," he says, looking around the restaurant, and then up and down at the dirty pants and sweaty t-shirt I'm wearing.

I bracket my hips with my hands. His perusal doesn't tell me anything I don't already know about my job, but at least it's honest money.

"Come work for me."

"Hell no." The words fly out of my mouth.

"You'll make good money and you can pay off your debts— yours and Kit's. Think about your family."

Does he not remember what I know? What I confessed in that letter? If he did, I don't think he'd be making this deal. He'd be trying to kill me instead. "No."

He raises both brows. "I thought they meant more to you."

I pinch the skin at my throat and shake my head. "I don't want anyone else getting hurt because of you."

His exaggerated smile causes his eyes to squint. "Then do what you have to do."

I could just tell him what I know—what I wrote. Maybe he's forgotten in his old age, I don't know. But something tells me not to. If I spook him, more people could get hurt, including Ruby this time, and I'm not willing to risk it. If he doesn't think I know, maybe something can be done. God, why does this have to be so messy? I was fine with how things were just a couple of days ago. I didn't know about Ruby or her daughter, and Bobby was minding his own business.

But I always knew it would come to this. He'd come back just like he is now and start bartering with the currency of other people's lives.

I cross my arms and clench my fists tighter. "Fuck off. I'm not working for you again."

He nods, considering my words, then tilts his head to study me.

I swallow and feel like I could choke on my own saliva.

I'm convincing myself I'm not making a huge mistake, as Bobby stands and walks out the front door. I tell myself everyone will be safe, and I'm doing this for my family. For Ruby. There was a time I jumped at a job like this. But it wasn't worth what I lost in the process. He won't stop until he gets what he wants, which means I have to figure out another way to get him off our backs.

I pick up the whiskey he poured for me and down it in one gulp.

I tell myself a lot of other things, too.

But they're all fucking lies.

CHAPTER FIFTEEN

Ruby

A knock sounds on the door causing me to startle awake.

Where am I?

I fling the covers off and rub my head, looking behind me to see if anyone else is in my bed. I'm alone. The headache is gone, but my ears are still ringing, like usual. I stare down at my mostly naked body.

What happened?

Every day starts out the same. My whole body aches, some parts more than others, and I question where I am and who I'm with. It's getting old. I check the clock on the bedside table: 10:57 a.m.

There's another knock. I grunt and cuss while standing and wrapping the sheet around my body. I attempt to smooth out my hair, but it's no use. The tangled mess will need half a bottle of conditioner and an hour with a comb to get through it.

I stand on unsteady feet and pad to the door, swinging it open and squinting at the contrast of light. The sun has been turned on full blast. "What the fu—" my words are cut off when I follow my line of sight from the man's shoes to his hair.

He's existing on the other side of the door jam, sucking all of the air out of my lungs. Despite my hardcore squint, I still notice that his face is freshly shaven and hair still wet from a shower.

"Hi," Jacob says.

I lean into the door frame and clutch the sheet tighter. "You woke me up."

His gaze darts quickly down my body, then back up to my face.

I don't hide what I'm wearing, or lack thereof. "I'm not working, yet, you know." I go to slam the door, but he stops it with his hand.

His brows relax and his mouth opens, but he pauses. "Ruby, I'm not here to sleep with you. I want to talk."

"Right. That's what they all say." A laugh bubbles up inside my chest. "I don't offer a discount for repeat customers, either."

His shoulders slump and he drops his chin to his chest. "I deserved that." His voice quiets and the red hue climbing his neck has me curious.

Why's he here?

What does he want?

Before I can ask, the drum beat in my head is back and getting louder. I lift my hand to cradle it. The sun is too damn bright and making this hangover worse.

He sighs. "Look, I didn't come here to fight, yell, or anything else."

I squeeze the door handle and glare at him, or squint. "Then, why'd you come?"

"Breakfast."

"Breakfast?"

"I came to take you to breakfast," he says, letting go of the door and tucking his hands in his front pockets. "I'll pay."

I peer down at my sheet-dress again and back at Jacob.

His gaze falls to where I'm fisting the off-white fabric at my chest, then back to my eyes. "You should probably get dressed first, though. I'll wait out here."

Before I can tell him I'm not going, he pulls the door shut.

I shake my head and mouth the word, *breakfast*, under my breath. Thinking too hard on it only makes my brain hurt more. I won't turn down free food. It doesn't mean I have to talk to him. Does that make me weak for going with him? The man who has done nothing but reject me since the first day—or night—we met. I bite my bottom lip and blink several times. My stomach growls and answers for me. It probably does, but I don't care.

Dropping the sheet, I search the floor for clean clothes to wear, but I don't have any of those. On top of that, I smell like puke and shitty decisions. I'm in the bathroom by the time I remember my water is still turned off thanks to the busted pipe, and I can't shower or even wash my face. Gritting my teeth, I stomp over to the dresser and open the top drawer, searching for my only option. Pulling out a few wet wipes, I make sure to get my face, armpits, and the stiff pieces of hair framing my face. This is so gross. I'm so gross.

My stomach gurgles again. I'm hungry and thirsty and tired. *Breakfast.*

I'm only going because of breakfast. Not Jacob. Not us.

I pull on a pair of jean shorts and a t-shirt that doesn't stink as bad as everything else, cage my hair in a high bun, and grab my purse. If being weak means taking care of myself—getting food and water to survive—then, that's exactly what I am.

A weak person might even order two breakfasts.

"ORDER WHATEVER YOU want," he says over the top of his menu.

"I will," I say, staring at the endless options.

He laughs as our waitress sidles up to the table with more cheer than jolly Saint Nick himself. "Good morning," she says in a sing-song voice. "What can I get you two lovebirds this morning?"

His gaze catches mine, a smile tugging at the corners of his mouth before looking back at the waitress. "Beth, is it?"

She nods. "Sure is."

His smile is dripping with sweetness. "Great. We'll have two coffees, two waters, and two orders of your jumbo breakfast." Snapping the menu shut, he grabs mine—that I wasn't done looking at—and hands them back to Beth. "And we'll need those coffees stat."

She winks at Jacob. "You betcha."

"And water—lots of water," I add before leaning back and slumping farther in the booth. I shoot him a dirty look. "I wanted a burger."

He shrugs. "Then order a burger, too."

I cross my arms. "I will."

Leaning in, he rests his arms on the table. "Maybe a pizza?"

I roll my eyes. "I hate pizza."

His brows lift. "That's not what I remember."

Running my tongue along the roof of my mouth, I keep my expression hard. He would stoop so low as to bring that night up. "I don't like it anymore."

He studies me. "Not even with pepperoni, pineapples, and jalapeños?"

He remembers alright. That was the pizza we ordered after…I block the memory from surfacing. Is this some kind of flex? To show me that he hasn't forgotten that night? Screw him. "That sounds gross, I would never order that." Luckily, he drops it. I shouldn't have let him bait me into talking. I refuse to make eye contact and decide to peer around the small restaurant instead.

A few old men sit around one of the center tables, their laughter rising above the other chatter. Almost every table is in use, but this place doesn't seem like five-star cuisine. The clang of kitchen pots is annoyingly loud, and though I can't see the coffee maker, I can hear it and I'm positive it's broken. My legs stick to the plastic booth that's ripped in some spots and taped in others. It's obviously cradled thousands of asses over the years. Still, something about this place causes warmth to sit high in my chest.

It reminds me of a small diner my mother used to take me to. I'd sit crossed-legged across from her, working on my homework that I didn't understand while she nursed a coffee. She'd smile over the rim and I'd smile back. To everyone else, we probably looked normal. Mother and daughter enjoying a meal together. Mother helping daughter with her homework, though she never did. Mother buying her daughter breakfast, despite that money coming from a man named Fred who dropped a picture of his family on the floor of our motel before leaving. Thanks to Fred, we got to eat that day and my mother got to buy her drugs. Everyone was happy.

Beth glides by dropping off two coffees and two waters all while humming a tune that sounds familiar. I shake my head and push thoughts of my mother away.

Jacob lifts his full mug. "Do you still sing?"

My mug pauses halfway to my mouth. "What?"

"Do you still like to sing?"

I down my water and add three sugar packets to my coffee and stir, answering his question with one of my own. "Do you still play?"

He shrugs. "Yeah, here and there. I couldn't practice in jail and don't have my own guitar. My roommate does, though, so sometimes I play his."

I gulp down more coffee, hoping it will sober me up enough to stick to what needs to be a one-sided conversation.

"So, do you still sing?"

I hate that he remembers these details about me. It would be easier if he had forgotten everything like I tried to do. "I still sing. Mostly in the shower or whenever Willow—" I stop, realizing the name that almost spilled out of my mouth. This is why I need to keep quiet. What happened to not talking to him? It's this place, reminding me of my mother and making me soft, or it's the alcohol still coursing through my bloodstream.

Cradling my coffee between two raised hands, I grip it tighter and pretend like that didn't happen. Like I didn't almost say Willow's name.

"Willow?" he asks.

My stomach turns over. Hearing Willow's name roll off Jacob's tongue makes whatever we're doing feel real. We aren't two people having consensual paid sex anymore. We are two people sitting across from each other at a family diner *talking*.

"Willow is, um. She's my…" the choppy words exiting my mouth aren't doing me any favors. "Willow is my friend."

"Cool." He nods for what feels like minutes. "Look, Ruby. I wanted to talk to you."

"Isn't that what you've been doing?" I snap.

He pauses and stares blankly at me. "Yes, but I wanted to apologize."

My heart bangs beneath my chest. I cross my arms, feeling more exposed by this statement than greeting him at the door in little more than a sheet.

"I made a mistake by leaving like I did three years ago. It was immature and stupid, and I just…reacted." He waves a vague hand. "And I'm sorry for how short I've been recently. When I picked you up from jail, I knew who you were, but I didn't know how to react, or if I should say something. But I do now." He searches my face. "I'm so sorry for never leaving a note or thanking you for one of the best nights of my life. I'm sorry for leaving the money instead of my number. I'm sorry that I treated you the opposite of how you deserve to be treated. I'm just… sorry."

My mouth and throat are dry.

One of the best nights of his life.

How I deserve to be treated.

He's sorry.

I stare blankly. Not really at him, or anything else in the restaurant. I just stare, my mind caught up in the words he said.

Beth interrupts with two large plates that she sets in front of us. "Two jumbo breakfasts for table number *love*." She wiggles her brows, and I roll my eyes.

Jacob smiles brightly. "Thanks, Beth."

"Don't mention it." She waves a hand before it finds its place on her hip. "On second thought, do mention it to my boss. He's the grumpy old fella over there," she points, her booming laughter following her as she leaves.

I widen my eyes when I look at the heaping portion of eggs, bacon, hash browns, and three stacked pancakes piled high on our plates. My appetite is stunted from the apology Jacob just served up. It felt better than how good these pancakes will taste, but I don't want it to.

He unwraps his silverware from the napkin roll. "So, will you forgive me?"

I look from my plate of food to him and sit up farther in the booth. If someone told me I'd be eating breakfast with Jacob— a.k.a. Dylan—years later, and he'd be apologizing for walking out on me the way he did, I wouldn't believe them. This is so far out of what I was expecting that I don't know how to react or what to say. What are the right words here?

Honest ones. "Maybe."

Weak and soft, that's what I am.

I unroll my fork and pierce the scrambled eggs, needing something to stab.

We sit in silence, other than the noise of our own eating. He bites into his bacon, I spear my pancakes. He drinks his coffee, I chug my third glass of water. Some of the customers filter out, but they're quickly replaced by new ones. Beth comes by once more with the check, and as promised, Jacob pays for the meal. I should say thank you but after my partial acceptance of his apology, I don't have any more nice words.

I lean back, folding my hands and resting them on my stomach. He continues to polish off his plate while I steal more glances at him, appreciating his smooth cheeks that I can see without the sun reflecting off them, and the sheer width of his biceps. Those are new. He had a nice body before, but he's different now. The hair, the muscles, the calm. It's interesting.

Clearing my head of the distraction that are his muscles, I focus on the real thing I want to know. The question I want an answer to while we're here. "Are you going to tell me why Bobby drove by?"

He stops chewing, the first time he's done that since Beth set a plate in front of him. "Has he been by again?"

I shake my head, and he nods swiftly. He pushes his plate away and wipes his hands with the napkin. Every movement he makes is slow and measured. He takes his time to answer, needing it in order to create some story I'll know is bullshit I'm sure.

"Do you know him?" he asks, twisting his coffee cup in a full circle on the table.

"I thought everyone did. He likes to mix business with pleasure. I knew about him and…Kit." Flipping uneaten food around my plate with my fork, I ask, "So, do you know him?"

"Yes." He gulps the last dregs of his coffee. "And no."

That almost sounded honest.

His forearms rest on the table again, taking up half of it. "Bobby and I have history, and I haven't seen him in awhile."

I stare him down, wondering what Jacob was wrapped up in. With Bobby, it could be anything and rarely ended well. "If it's just history, then why'd you act so shocked?"

He peers around the restaurant. "Because it is history, to me. Not to Bobby."

I nod and lower my voice to a whisper. "And what about Kit? Does she know you saw him the other night?"

The silence speaks for him, but I don't let him off that easily. Inhaling sharply, I keep my eyes trained on his face, waiting for it to tell me more than his mouth is. "Does she?"

"No." His tone is sharp. "And you can't tell her, please. Not yet."

His plea echoes in my mind. "Does Kit know…" I shift uncomfortably in my seat, "about us?"

He shakes his head and his back stiffens, sitting up straighter in the booth. "I don't like keeping secrets from Kit."

I run my tongue along my top teeth then cross my arms. "But, to be clear, you're not going to tell her about us or Bobby?"

"No."

"And you don't want me to?"

"Right," he says.

I nod, not the least bit disappointed. I don't want Kit knowing about us, either. I may not have known Jacob was Kit's brother when we slept together, but if she finds out, I can't imagine she'll be thrilled about it. I had sex with her brother, the one who's supposed to be reformed now. Bringing up the past never does any good. She can't be mad at Jacob forever, though. They're family, while Kit and I are only some version of friends. Maybe if we'd been closer, or I could hold down a friend, things would be different.

"So, we just keep these secrets forever? Is that the plan?" I press.

"Not forever. But for now, it's the best plan I've got. I'll handle Bobby, and then I'll tell her everything."

I rub my arm. Secrets are heavy. If Kit shows up at my door demanding answers, I don't know what I'd do. Not when she's done all that she has for me. But getting involved would be messy, too. "Fine. I'll keep your secrets."

He exhales and nods. "Thank you. I just want to keep everyone safe."

Safe? I drain the rest of my coffee. Bobby isn't safe. Lies aren't safe. We aren't safe together. He's trying to accomplish the impossible. It's a good thing *safe* doesn't matter to me.

I shrug. "I'm tired."

The toe-curling smile he gives me makes my stomach flutter. "Alright. Let's get out of here."

I'm in too deep with Jacob. Kissing, keeping secrets, having breakfast, kind of accepting his apology. I fell for him and his smooth words before and didn't think I'd be doing it again. But while I'm being honest, I am falling, and now we're tied together by what we know.

Why don't I feel bad then?

Maybe this isn't falling. Not this time.

Maybe this is what it would feel like to fly.

CHAPTER SIXTEEN

Jacob

Unlocking my front door, I push it open for us. "After you."

Ruby hesitantly steps inside, hands clutching tightly to the purse she always has slung over her shoulder. Her back is rigid, eyes bouncing from one thing to another once we're inside. The place isn't the picture of cleanliness. It was a last-minute decision to invite her here. I didn't think she'd agree to come back to my place, but after letting it slip that her water isn't working and something about maintenance taking a while, I opened my mouth and asked. I could have kept it shut. She could have said no. But here we are.

I shut the door and she jumps. "Sorry." I point toward the living room. "Make yourself comfortable. I'm gonna put the leftovers away."

Leaving her in the entryway, I head for the kitchen and toss the leftovers in the fridge. James is likely still at work, which I'm thankful for. It means I don't have to explain who Ruby is, or submit her to his ruthless questioning. Neither of us have brought a woman home before. James' last girlfriend was also his drug dealer, so he had to knix that relationship real quick. And I've never had a girlfriend. I prefer to keep things uncomplicated. Until now, I guess.

Our apartment is simple. We only have necessary furniture, no rugs or extra pillows that serve no purpose and make for extra cleaning. The walls are bare except for a vintage Star Wars poster in the living room that James insisted on hanging. I'm extra conscientious of the pile of dishes on the counter that I quickly gather and set in the sink. My gym bag is still on a barstool chair, so I carry it to my room then kick off my shoes. My room is better than it was last week, there's at least a path to walk through, but I pull the door shut to hide the small mess that is there.

She's sitting on the couch's armrest when I come back out. "Want anything to drink?" I slide my hands together. "We don't have a lot…water, milk, coffee. I'm sure James has some kind of frilly tea in there, too."

"Wine?" she asks while bouncing her gaze around the room. It's early for wine, but maybe this will help get her to let her guard down.

I walk into the kitchen and the two glasses I grab are dirty, so I reach for new ones, then crouch down and open the cabinet under the sink, stretching to grab the cheap wine I bought and hid. If we finish this mostly full bottle tonight, then I'll feel better about not having to hide it from James.

I know I don't deserve to see those parts of Ruby again, but I'm also hungry for them. The tension between us is still there. Like her, it burns hot at times, and then freezes in a matter of seconds. She's made a point to not touch me at all, and when I opened the door at the diner for her, she took a wide step around to avoid a potential arm graze. But she watched me as I ate, and I felt the heat of her stare in every part of my body. Then, when I apologized and she said maybe, which at least gives us a shot, I could hardly believe it. I was expecting more pushback, more explaining.

"Here." I offer her a short glass of wine filled over halfway and point to the bathroom across the apartment. "We don't have any good smelling stuff, but I've got a new bar of soap you can use and some shampoo."

"Thanks." She stands and looks at the wine glass in my hand. "I thought you didn't drink."

She remembered?

"I do today," I say quickly before moving on. "Oh, and," I open the hall closet, "a clean towel." Emphasis on the *clean*.

She takes it and clutches it to her chest, taking a long sip from her glass. "I'll be quick."

I cross my arms. "Take your time."

"I won't." She retreats to the bathroom and shuts the door.

A smile plays on my lips as the lock clicks into place. I never know what I'll get with her, but right now it's pure *ice*.

I scratch the back of my head and drain my wine only to refill it. Maybe I should have taken her to Kit's house. She's clearly not comfortable here. Does she regret coming? Likely. But the messy bun she wore on top of her head that was tilting to one side made it look like she was desperate enough for a shower, and she would have accepted the offer from anyone, including me: her ex-something.

I spend the time she's in the shower picking up random things around the apartment. I'm starting to think we're slobs. Kit scolds us for it every once in a while or brings over one of those citrus-smelling cleaners. I find it under the kitchen sink where the wine was and get to work on the counters. I'm barely done wiping down every hard surface in the living room when Ruby emerges from the bathroom.

As promised, she didn't take long and comes out with dripping wet hair. I'm wiping the coffee table, but the citrus isn't stronger than the smell of fresh soap on her skin and my shampoo, which normally smells like man but not on her. I get a waft of earthy sweetness and lick my lips. "Good shower?"

She nods and uses the towel to dry her hair. "You have good water pressure."

I'll take that as a compliment. "Thanks."

I set the cleaning spray and rag aside. "Sorry I don't have a hairdryer for you to use. It's not really part of my beauty routine and James is bald so…"

"Beauty routine?"

I don't miss the small grin pulling up the corner of her mouth. "I have a lot of hair to deal with," I say, pointing to my thick curls. "Can I fill your glass?"

She hands me the empty wine glass but doesn't say anything. I move farther into the kitchen as she hangs the towel back in the bathroom and walks through the dining room that has no table —it wouldn't get used anyway—to find a comfortable spot on the couch. My CD case sits open on the coffee table and she reaches for it, thumbing through my collection. She doesn't look like she's clambering to leave, and this might be the way to connect with her again, help her open up: music.

I hand her the full glass and set the bottle in front of us before joining her on the couch, making sure to give her plenty of room. "It's the only thing I collect."

She takes a long sip and continues to thumb through the pages. "The Beatles, Led Zeppelin, Nirvana…who are all of these bands?"

My mouth hangs open. "Are you serious? They're the classics."

"You mean old?" She glances up, a smile building on her full lips.

I take a drink and lean back, shaking my head. "No way. Classic, as in the building blocks of all other music that came afterward." I wave my hand. "Here, hand me that Nirvana CD."

Slipping the CD from the protective sleeve, she hands it over. I jump up and walk over to the CD player on our high top table along the opposite wall of the couch. This thing gets used so often enough that I have to sweet talk it into working sometimes, but it always does. Popping open the top, I push the CD in place, and shut the lid, cranking up the volume to a level that I know our neighbors won't report.

I skip to the third song, Come as You Are, and wait for it to start. My eyes don't leave Ruby as I gauge her reaction to the music that shaped me.

"Why do you like them so much?" she asks.

My eyes lock on the smooth skin of her neck that moves when she swallows.

"Well…" I clear my throat. It's a fair question, but I wasn't expecting it. I lean against the table as Kurt Cobain starts singing, and I crack my knuckles. "I guess because I moved around a lot when I was growing up. I had eleven different foster families, so my life was always changing, but music stayed the same. I could listen to the same song twenty times in a row or more," I say. "It was comforting knowing I could go back to how that song made me feel no matter what was happening." The band is older than I am, but the grunge rock musicians are my allies.

She stares, unmoving, at a spot on the floor. "Music can do that for people," she finally says. "I guess even though they're old, they aren't bad."

"I'm glad you agree." Her response makes me smile. "The first song I learned on guitar was Stairway to Heaven by Led Zeppelin. A foster dad taught me and from there, I couldn't get enough. I never learned notes, most of what I know, I learned by ear."

She nods and keeps studying the discs. "Do you have anything you can dance to?"

"Flip back a few pages," I instruct from across the room. "There, bottom right."

I shuffle toward her and grab the CD she holds out. When I turn to exchange the discs, I smile. It's a mix CD I burned, after I got out of jail when I was seventeen, full of random artists. Some were old, but most of them were new at the time. As a teen, I'd spend any money I got on my favorite albums, and then burn the rest from the internet.

The familiar funk-inspired pop song with a disco flare thumps through the speakers.

Ruby moves her shoulder to the clapping beat at the beginning. "I like this."

I bob my head and tap my heel to the ground. "Bruno Mars made some magic with this song."

She's controlling her movements, but I can tell she wants to dance the way her body moves side to side and her neck sways with ease. Her glass is empty, so I reach and pick up the wine bottle to refill it. I fill mine, too. I'm not trying to get her drunk, just to kick back. It's what I was hoping for. She's relaxing, and I catch a glimpse of the girl I spent the night with. She's so close, I can taste the memory.

"I don't remember it," she says.

"Uptown Funk? I'm surprised. It was all over the radio in 2015. I used to listen to it when I was on laundry duty in jail. It always got me moving." I move my shoulders to the beat, remembering how every pulse of the song feels in my body.

She watches me from behind the rim of her glass and I smile, adding some hips and quick glides of my feet. I can't help it. I'm feeling myself and this song. It's all muscle memory, but I throw in a few new moves I've learned since, careful not to spill what's left in my glass.

The song finishes, and Ruby stretches to clink her glass with mine as the next song plays. It's likely not what she'd consider dance music, but you can't go wrong with this one, either. Piano keys start playing the first few notes of the ballad and painting the room in a softer hue than the afternoon light filtering through the windows. I forgot how much I like this song.

I also forgot it's a love song.

Ruby smiles from her spot on the couch. "John Legend?"

I nod and smile as I finish off my wine and pour more.

She sets the binder on the coffee table and uses the open floor space as her stage. My breath catches in my throat and I cross my arms as she begins to sway. She takes up an interest in the poster. "Yours?"

I shake my head. "My roommate's."

Her arms follow her movements, and I cross mine to remind myself to stay where I'm at. The last thing I need to do is join her. The speakers are so close to my ear, Legend is practically singing the lyrics straight into my soul.

"I like this song," she says, running her finger along the TV stand. She drags the edge of the glass along her bottom lip, then throws her head back and drains it before setting it down.

My mouth runs dry the closer she gets, and I can't reply. I drink more and let the sweet flavor coat my mouth and throat. It isn't enough, though. I finish the whole glass and set it aside.

She catches me staring. "Can you dance to a slow song?"

Her gaze is pure *fire*. There's no ice now. It's all thawed.

Arms still crossed, I shrug, allowing John to do all of the talking that I can't. The words are scary-accurate, like they're revealing exactly what's going on in my heart and broadcasting all of it to Ruby and me. I didn't even know I felt this way until the song started playing.

But it's true. All of me wants all of her.

Does she feel it, too?

She laughs, spins a full circle, and bumps me in the shoulder. I stay on my feet but barely. The music is soft, but her movements are softer. Reaching her arms above her head, she twists them easily, like they're ribbons dancing above her. Body working in sync from her head, down her core to her slim hips, and following the line of her long legs. She rocks side to side on bare feet making the song come alive in ways I'll never forget.

She steps in front of me, getting closer to me at a pace that feels like she's crawling. I part my lips and flex my crossed arms. I'm afraid of the look I see in her eyes. The one that has my heart on edge and ready to free fall to whatever depths are necessary to be near her.

She reaches me, her dancing stops and if she weren't this close, I might frown. Watching her dance had all of my attention. Normally, it looks like she walks around with the weight of the world on her shoulders. When she's dancing, it looks like the world stands still. At least, mine does.

She raises her hands and places them on my forearms, tugging them out of the straight-jacket I've created for them. Her hands are on fire. It doesn't take her much effort and pretty soon she has my clammy hands cradling the sides of her hips. They tremble on her waist, but I hold her despite knowing I shouldn't. I already know what happens when she's in my arms.

I want her.

All of her.

I shouldn't want this like I do.

We sway back and forth, her fingers swirling around, creating an intricate pattern on my shoulders and back. She feels so right. Like this is where she should have been the last two years.

But she wasn't.

And I wasn't in a place I could give her anything more than a one night stand I paid for. I was in the game, making runs and doing drops. Women were a means to an end. She scared me. And if I'm honest, she still does. But things are different now. Aren't they? I wish they were. I want them to be, yet reality screams from behind me that I'm making a mistake. Things aren't different. Bobby's back, Kit's in the dark about all my secrets, and Ruby still has her job as a prostitute. How can I even be considering this? The buzz making me feel weightless doesn't care.

I inhale the smell of my soap on Ruby. It smells better on her. Everything's better when it comes to her. How has it taken me this long to remember? We were *good* together.

Until we were wrong.

I realized I'd never be able to have a woman like Ruby if I didn't want to ruin her. She knew things I didn't, and she taught me things I didn't know. In bed and about the world. She lost her mom like I lost mine: to addiction. But for that one night, we were good.

There needs to be more distance between us. But I can't seem to care about that when the ice in her has melted and the warmth of her skin is too much. To feel it is to remember. Her body on mine. My body on hers. Our mouths melding, fingers trailing over her delicate skin, her nails leaving marks along my back. It's too much. Ruby loves with as much passion as she hates.

Isn't risk the backbone that life is built on? When all of our cards are in and it seems there's more to lose than gain. It's easy to forget the gain when all that's focused on is the loss, but I've already lost so much. I want to focus on the gain just this once. What if I took a risk and leaned into whatever is happening with Ruby? What if we could be good again?

I'm dizzy with the feel of her in my arms. My chest rises and falls in sync with hers, and my taut shoulders begin to relax. Her eyes lift from my chest and land on my mouth. *Fire.* I feel it creeping into my gut. The way her freckles lead a trail between her breasts and the curve of her shoulders has me wanting to touch every one of them. They add up to all the reasons I should step away and put her out of my arms. Instead, those freckles make my fingers itch to draw her closer and kiss them like I did before. Like she asked me to.

Her endless gaze makes me wish I could read her mind. But then again, maybe I don't want to. It would tell me things about this moment that I likely wouldn't want to hear. Like this meaning more to me than it does for her. I don't want to know that.

I reach my hand to her cheek and skim the velvet of her skin with my thumb. It would be easier if one of us could be strong enough to stop this. I'm not and with Ruby leaning into my touch, I don't think she is, either. Her lashes fan the tops of her cheeks as I begin to brush short strokes along her jaw, bypassing her ear, and threading my fingers through her damp hair. My eyes are hooded, but hers are watchful. She's watching me unravel the closer she presses against me. The way my eyes drink her in, like I've never tasted her before, or how my gaze always goes back to her lips. She doesn't look away from me; it's the longest time she's stared, and I wonder what she sees. Does she see how much her touch affects me? Does she know how crazy she makes me feel? Because it's all there, I'm sure of it, and there's nothing that would make me want to break this closeness. Not after we've found it again.

I lift my other hand and trace the fullness of her lips that are already parted. I'm close enough that I can feel her breath. I wonder if she'd still taste the same: sweet and bitter, just like her.

I'm curious.

I want to know.

I *have* to know.

Swallowing, I bring my lips closer to hers. She doesn't turn away, slap me, or shove me off. Instead, she grips handfuls of my shirt. *Fire.* It spreads all over my body. I pause. I don't want to be like every other guy she's been with. The ones who take from her. I can do things differently this time. I can kiss her, please her, and stay. I won't leave this time. I'm different. I have to be.

Her breath tickles my lips, and my mouth waters with anticipation. I swallow and press a test kiss on her top lip. So soft. So sweet. *Fire.*

Her bottom lip ignites my taste buds as I angle her head so I can take it into my mouth, tugging gently. I brush my lips against hers, back and forth, sparking the first flames of the fire we're building. Her breaths are heavy as her hands drop to my hips, and she grabs more fabric in her palms. She fists and twists it as I tease her lips with mine until she raises a hand and grabs the back of my neck, crushing our lips together.

Our mouths take over, exploring one another, like we've never done this before and we've never tasted one another. My tongue teases hers but she fights back, pushing and battling like this is war. The slower I go, the faster she is. My rough squeezes meet her willing body as it melts into me. Her body fits in the creases and dips of mine and a small moan sounds from the back of her throat, forcing me to hold her tighter against me.

I feel my body temperature rising and break away from our kiss. "Are you…okay?" I ask through strained breaths. "Do you want this?"

"I want this," she says, and my mouth is on hers before she can even finish.

I should pull away.

I *should* stop this.

I can still stop this from going too far.

But as her hands touch the skin under the hem of my shirt, I know I can't.

I'm weak when it comes to her.

People make mistakes. I make mistakes. A perfect life doesn't exist, but there are perfect moments. And this right now, with Ruby in my arms and our lips working together, is a perfect moment. The mistake is worth it.

Standing straighter, I lift her by the waist until her legs are wrapped around my hips. I slide my hands under her thighs without breaking the connection of our mouths and walk her to my room. I know what happens behind closed doors, Ruby does, too. We've done them.

But this moment is too perfect to end. I don't want it to. If we're going to seize it and ignore why we shouldn't be doing this and what comes next, if Ruby is going to let me touch her, then I'm going to touch her. I'm going to experience this perfect moment in a life filled with shitty ones.

And for a few hours, I forget.

I forget about Bobby.

I forget about my roommate.

I forget about the whys and the hows.

With her legs tangled with mine, her hands memorizing every line on my body, and the door closed to the outside world, I let myself forget everyone else and remember the one that got away.

CHAPTER SEVENTEEN

Ruby

I feel around on the bed beside me with my eyes still closed. There's no warm body apart from my own, but the sheets still smell like him. Like us. I blink slowly, opening my eyes for the first time and figuring out my surroundings. My head doesn't feel like it will explode, a marked improvement from how I usually wake up, but it does throb from the full bottle of wine we drank. And, I'm alone. I peer around the room. Our clothes lay in random places on the floor, and the window lets in the evening light. We must have fallen asleep, and now, I'm completely alone just like last time.

Screw him.

I search the nightstand for a note telling me he left, and I need to be out by the time he gets back. But there isn't a note from what I can see. Only a journal, an alarm clock with numbers saying that it's hours later, and a lamp. I flip to my other side, lifting the sheet and pillow in case a piece of paper were to appear. It doesn't. I swallow. A note would be too much to ask of him.

Flinging off the sheets, I search for my clothes thrown around the room. The temperature difference between the sheets and the room causes goosebumps to rise on my arms. I ignore them and grab one of Jacob's t-shirts when I can't find my own and quickly pull it over my head. I won't let him off easy this time. I'm taking his shirt. I'm going to eat his food, and maybe take one of his precious CDs. How could he do this again?

My underwear is on the floor at the end of the bed, and I fumble to get it right side out before shoving my legs through. I'm hiking them up just as the bedroom door begins to open slowly. I rush to grab the rest of my other clothes and clutch them to my chest expecting to see the roommate. But it isn't James.

It's Jacob.

"Hi," he says with a smile, carrying two mugs and using his foot to close the door.

"Um, hi." I shake my head, trying to catch up with what happened and what didn't.

He sets one of the mugs on the nightstand and sits on the bed. "I made coffee. It's decaf."

I finally let myself breathe, inhaling the scent that fills the room, like it's crack. I don't even like crack.

He cradles his mug. "A few spoonfuls of sugar, right?"

My smile is pinched, but it's there. "Right."

I don't know what to think, or how to feel. He's good at doing that—leaving. But he was only a few steps into the kitchen. He's still here and with coffee. For those few moments, I was so mad, and now that it isn't true—he didn't leave—it's hard to calm myself down, though.

I shuffle to sit on the edge of the bed beside him and pick up the mug of coffee. It's still too hot to drink, but that doesn't stop me from inhaling the steam coming off the top.

"Were you going somewhere?" he asks.

I shoot him a questioning glance and use my mug as a shield.

He points at my clothes I have in a chokehold against my body. I loosen my grasp on them and set the clothes on the bed. "I was, uh…" I scratch my head, "going to get dressed."

"You can change in here, or the bathroom if you want." He looks at my bare legs beneath the hem of his shirt and my whole body warms. "But just to warn you, James is here."

I suck in my cheeks and stare at the ground. "Thanks, I'll get dressed and leave soon."

It's better if I go. He was supposed to have left but didn't, so now one of us needs to. What we did tonight shouldn't have happened.

"You don't have to leave. I don't work today," he adds, holding still to wait for my response.

I stare into my coffee. I need to leave. Every single one of my emotions was on display for Jacob last night. I'm sure it didn't take him long to figure out how he makes me feel. I've never acted like this with anyone, because I wasn't acting at all.

"I need to go."

His eyes fall to his coffee. "Okay. I'll drive you."

"No," I say quickly.

The mood has shifted. Awkward tension bounces between us. Last night, there was no shyness. But today, I have no clue what to say, or how to feel. It was a mistake to kiss him, and then sleep with him. I don't want him to think I have expectations, but I'd be lying. I do. I want to do this again. It was the first time I felt alive in my own skin in a long time.

I set my mug down and stand abruptly. "I have to leave." Grabbing my clothes from the bed, I say, "Busy day today." I step into my shorts.

"Are you going to work today?" he asks from his spot on the bed.

He looks from his mug to me, and I swear he's judging me. He might as well be hurling stones at me the way he asked that question.

I scoff and head for the door. "Of course I'm working today. I have to eat."

I have to buy more water until the dump of a place where I live gets the pipe fixed. Rent is due soon, and I have to start saving money.

He clenches his jaw and nods. "So, that meant nothing to you? I was just another one of your *clients*?"

Heat builds inside of me. "Are you kidding me right now? At least I'm *telling* you that I'm leaving, which is more than what you did the last time."

His cold gaze snaps to meet mine. "That was different. I didn't leave for me. I left for you."

I fling my arms wide and yell, "What does that even mean?"

He shakes his head and drops his eyes to the floor but says nothing. He doesn't try to explain or defend himself. Instead, he rubs his neck and doesn't look at me.

My face feels like it's on fire. The adrenaline floods through me, and my hands shake as I ball them into fists. Last night was different. He was nothing like any of my clients, and he never would be. Sure, it looks like I'm leaving to go sleep with someone else, but that's different. That's work, not pleasure. Can't he see that? Didn't he feel the difference? I'm sure he's slept with other prostitutes or women since me.

I breathe through my nose. "I have a daughter to take care of, and if I'm ever going to be a good enough mom, get her back, and leave L.A., I have to have money to do it." My voice cracks. "This is my job." I swallow and clear away some of the emotion wanting to come out. "Willow is my daughter. Not my friend."

I look at him and will him to understand. False hope builds inside of me. If he understood why I do what I do and for who, then maybe this could work. Maybe we could be…more.

He rubs his forehead, then drops his hand to slap his knee. "I get it. It's fine. Last night meant nothing to you." His eyes find mine, and now there's more than judgment behind them. There's hurt. "Maybe I should just pay you."

His words make my mouth fall open slowly. My body trembles, and I drop my shirt, bending fast to slip on my flip flops. I fling open his bedroom door then turn and say, "Fuck you, Jacob," before walking out and slamming his door.

My eyes are filled with angry tears before I even reach the front door. How could he say something like that after last night? After what he put me through already? He knows I have to work. So does he. But my job is sex.

He doesn't have to say it. I know what he's thinking.

I'm dirty.

He doesn't see me as a woman. He sees me as tainted, touched and fondled by other men. I huff while stomping down his apartment steps. He's like everyone else. He wants to be the only one and is threatened by me making a living this way. But he doesn't get it. I like *him*. I don't like any of those other people. They are as good as the cash they offer and nothing more.

I'm speed-walking down the sidewalk before I realize what I just admitted.

I like him.

I like Jacob.

I keep moving. How could I let this happen? He's a crusher. He crushes people, and he's doing that to me again. I can't let him do that anymore.

Tears build and course down my face, but I wipe them faster than they can fall. I hate crying. I hate that Jacob made me cry. I hate that I'm not a normal woman who can have a normal relationship with a normal man. I'm complicated.

And I'm *dirty*.

CHAPTER EIGHTEEN

Ruby

I show up early to my scheduled visit with Willow. Or, at least, I thought I was early. My sense of time feels fuzzy. I sit up straighter on the bench, but my body keeps slumping over as I wait for them to show up. It's taking them a long time. I'm so tired. I just want to sleep. I'll just close my eyes and...

"Ruby?"

I startle and turn toward the sound of my name. "Huh?"

Molly exhales. "There you are. We didn't think you were going to show today. Willow's been asking for you."

Her tone is sharp and louder than I want it to be. Pressing a finger to my mouth, I try to shush her while laying my head back down on the bench. It's heavy and hard to keep upright. "I know a Molly. She's my daughter's fake mom," I say with a smile, peering up at her.

She clutches a hand to her chest. "Ruby, are you..." she steps closer and studies my face. I try to focus on hers, but it's spinning. "Are you drunk?"

I pull myself up to sit at her question, and then decide to stand. My legs wobble, but I manage to hang onto the bench and stand to her level. "Yesss," I slur, the hiss of the "s" on my tongue feels weird.

She sighs, and I look at her through blurred vision. Her pinched brows look like two caterpillars ready to fight. "Where's Willow?" I ask.

Molly shakes her head. "I don't think it's a good idea for her to see you like this."

I scowl. "Like what? I'm fiiiine. Tired, but fine."

"No, Ruby. You're not fine."

Placing my hands on my hips, I try to glare at her, but the more I stare, the dizzier I become. Something's wrong. My balance is off, and I have to grab the bench behind me again, but it isn't where I left it.

"Careful," Molly says. She lurches forward and holds my arm.

I slither out of her grasp and waver on my feet. "I don't want *you* to touch me. Where's Willow? I'm here for Willow."

Mouth agape, she studies me. "Your eyes are bloodshot and your breath smells like alcohol. You need to sleep this off first. We'll have to reschedule."

I scoff, then bar my teeth. "You're not my mother. I'm a mother." I point a finger at my own chest and stare down at it. "I'm Willow's mother. Not you."

Exhaling, Molly rubs her forehead. "I'm sorry, Ruby. But you need to leave. Can I call you a cab?"

"No, you can't fucking call me a cab! You can call my daughter." I stomp my foot like an angry child and cross my arms. Two movements and I feel as though my body is going to fall over again.

She pulls out her phone, presses a few buttons, then places it to her ear. "Tess? Ruby showed up. Can you come back?"

"Why are you calling Tess? Hang up! I want to see Willow!"
I swipe for her phone and miss. "Willow!" I scream. "Willow, I'm
here!" Whipping around, I step forward and manage to grab the
park bench instead of falling.

Molly is whispering into her phone, and I glare at her over
my shoulder, gritting my teeth. She can't treat me like this. Like
I'm the crazy mom, and she's the perfect one. She's not even a
mom, she's a guardian. A guardian! That's it.

"Mama?"

I jerk my head forward. "Willow."

"Mama, there you are."

Leaning into the bench, I stare at Willow through my haze.
"Hiiii, baby. H-How are you?"

Willow tries to walk closer, but Molly darts around me and
grabs her shoulders.

"Ruby, Tess will be here soon to pick you up. Just sit right
here, and she'll find you." Molly slowly pulls Willow behind her.

The husband walks up. "Molly, what's going on?"

"Take Willow and go to the car," she instructs.

"You're not her mother!" I yell, then look at my daughter.
"Willow, don't go. We didn't even get to talk. I brought you a
slushie." I look at the bench I'm still holding but don't see a cup.
"I think." I turn back to Molly. "Did you take it? Did you take
Willow's slushie?"

Molly shakes her head. "No! I didn't. I wouldn't." She turns
to her husband. "Stan, please. Go."

He bends down to pick up Willow, but she starts screaming.
"Stop! I don't want to go. Mama is here now, see. She's here. We
can stay."

Molly speaks softly to Willow. "Your Mama isn't feeling well.
We'll see her next time."

Stan leaves and Willow begins to cry in his arms. Her eyes are squinted and her mouth turns down in a frown as he carries her away. I touch my cheek. I'm crying.

Turning to Molly, I spit at her feet. "You're stealing her from me. You won't get away with it. You won't!"

I start to sink to the ground, but Molly stops me. If I had more strength, I'd push her off of me and scream at her some more for taking my daughter away. But I don't fight her. Not when she wraps an arm around my shoulder, leads me back to the bench, and whispers again that *everything will be alright.*

My head is floating without a place to land and my stomach is two seconds away from revolting. "I need to see Willow. She wants to see me. I got her something."

Molly sighs loudly. "Not right now, Ruby. You aren't feeling well and you don't want Willow to see you like this, do you? Why don't you give me what you planned to give her. Where is it?"

The fight is gone. I'm tired and weak. "My purse," I whisper.

I close my eyes, and the world feels like it's being turned upside down. Spinning and spinning and spinning. It's like a ride at the fair, but I can't get off. It doesn't stop. The look on Willow's face, her tears, her hand reaching for me on repeat.

I'm not a good mom.

I'm a bad mom.

Molly tries to reach for my purse slung over my shoulder and falling to my waist, but I slap her hand away. "I'll get it."

I dig around the bottom of my purse in search of what I bought Ruby. I find it, slip it on the tip of my finger, and raise my hand in front of my face. It was in one of those twenty-five cent machines. I was on a date. Not the kind where a man takes you out, buys you food, and promises to call you. No, it was a working date. I was earning that money Jacob didn't want me to by screwing someone in the parking lot. That man bought me a drink, though.

As I was leaving, I saw the familiar twist machine. My mother used to give me a handful of quarters to play these games whenever she was on a date. Sometimes the guy she was seeing would give me a few as well. With a handful of coins, I felt rich. I could buy a sticker, candy, or try for a stuffed animal. The possibilities were endless.

When I popped off the plastic top and pulled out the mood ring, I knew I'd give it to Willow. She would like how it changes colors and her finger is the only one it could fit on. It was meant for her.

I rotate my hand, letting the sun reflect off of the circular band.

It's black.

I don't know what all the colors mean, but I'm guessing black isn't good. "Here." Tugging the ring from my own finger, I drop it in Molly's waiting hand. "Give that to Willow. From me." A surge of emotion rises up and tears fill my tired eyes as I stare at my lap. "From her mama."

Molly's hand closes over the mood ring, and she nods.

I don't see her walk away, as the tears blur my vision and make it difficult to see anything. Each one feels heavier than the last, so I droop down on the metal bench until I'm lying on my side and let them drown me. I gasp and choke on the salty tears but still, they don't relent.

Maybe this is how I'll die: a broken heart.

"Willow," I whisper, then close my eyes and wait to die.

"RUBY?" A VOICE says from above me.

I blink a few times but can't fully open my eyes. They're sore.

"Ruby, it's Tess." She lays a gentle hand on my shoulder.

"Tess?" I repeat.

"Yeah. I'm here to take you home. Let me help you up."

My head throbs as I unfold my legs and sit up slowly from the bench that represents an eternity of waiting. I'm always waiting. For Willow. For our life together to finally start. For my body to stop craving alcohol. For death. I'm tired of waiting.

"Easy now." She steadies my shoulders. "That's it, good. Here's some water."

Tess hands me a bottle, and I drink deeply. Staring at the water, I jostle it back and forth, watching the contained waves slosh around. I pretend I'm a speck inside here, trapped and drowning under every wave. I already know how it would sound. Moments of quiet, like it does in the bathtub, then loud every time my head would break the surface. Over and over I'd flip and turn at the mercy of those waves.

"Ruby?"

I shake my head and look up.

"Are you ready for me to take you home?" she asks, bending lower.

Home.

Easy for her to say. Her home is probably safe, secure, and comforting. My home isn't. I hear gunshots every night, and I don't have any water. I lock my door and act like I'm safe but I'm not. Not really. There are plenty of men that know my address.

"Do you think you can stand up? I can help you to my car."

I laugh curtly. "I've been standing on my own my whole life."

She leans closer. "I didn't mean…sorry. I just meant, can you stand on your legs? Molly said you were really wobbly."

"Molly doesn't know what she's talking about," I grind out. "I'm fine." Pitching forward, back hunched over, I stare down at the ground and swallow the fast flow of saliva filling my mouth. If I don't keep it together, I'm going to be sick.

"How'd you get here today, Ruby? Did you take a bus? Get dropped off?"

Her questions swirl around me, and I can hardly focus with my stomach contracting the way it is. I clutch it tightly, but it's no use, everything in my stomach falls out onto the cement.

She holds my hair back, but it does little to help the mess I've made.

When the convulsions finally call it quits, I sit back on the bench with a thud. "I just need to lie down," I say, already tipping over to sprawl out on the small bench.

"No, no. I'm going to walk you to my car and get you home. I can't leave you here."

"Yes, you can."

"Ruby. I will not leave you here."

I grunt. "Fine. Then don't."

Zapped of any remaining energy, I barely have the stamina to stand without the help of Tess propping me up and letting me lean into her. "That's it. One small step at a time."

The pounding in my head has only gotten louder and more rhythmic. We might as well walk to the motel, considering the thousands of miles we are already traveling to her car. I grumble in her ear. "Are we there yet?"

"Almost. Keep it moving."

"I think I'm going to be sick again."

Without any warning, I bend at the waist and retch on the sidewalk in front of us. Tess's shoes now hold the memory of this day, though I think she could've gone without the souvenir.

She clears her throat and mimics a cheerful tone as we keep walking. "Like I said. Almost there."

"I'm sorry for being such a day-suck."

She tightens her grip on my waist and exhales. "You're not a day-suck, though I barely know what that means."

"I ruined your day," I say. "I ruined Willow's. And Molly ruined mine."

"You know, if you spent as much energy liking Molly as you do hating her, I think you two would actually become good friends."

I laugh at the thought. "I don't have friends."

She sighs. "Yeah, well, maybe you could use some."

Her reply catches me off guard at the same time the sidewalk trips me up. I throw my hands forward to catch my fall, but she has a firm hold on my shoulders and doesn't let me.

I gain some balance, and we continue. "I'm not good at being anyone's friend."

"Have you tried?" Her question is more curious than snobby.

I think about the few people I've considered my friend and realize it's only a couple. Kit was one of them. Although, I'm not sure you can call it a friendship when it's only been one-sided.

I place a hand on my thundering forehead. "My head hurts."

"That's what alcohol does," she says quietly. "Ruby, the state will continue to allow for these visits if—and *only* if—you keep your end of the deal. If you want Willow to come stay with you one day, you have to get some help."

"I have help." I spit out defensively. "I have help for some things."

She tips her chin forward. "My car is right ahead."

I nod and regret the movement immediately.

She tightens her hold on me. "You know we have resources, places that you could go."

If my throat weren't so raw, I'd laugh. Instead, it just sounds like a grunt. "And how will I pay to support Willow and myself after that, huh? I'm her mother. If I don't work, how can I buy a place for us to live? How can I feed her? Or buy her clothes? I don't have time for a vacation." We wouldn't be able to get out of this city, either.

The questions I ask are tied to bombs that I just dropped in her camp. She doesn't know what it's like to struggle. To be someone like me who doesn't have a choice.

She's silent, as we take the last few steps to her car parked at the curb. Opening the door, she pauses. "I'm on your team."

I try to focus on her face, but she's moving too fast and making my head throb more. "Oh yeah? What about Willow's team? You think it's better for her to be without her mother?"

She sucks in a breath. "I'm on her team, too. But sometimes, when we aren't healthy, we need to focus on taking care of ourselves before we can take care of others. It's time to start taking care of yourself, Ruby."

The line of my mouth breaks and falls open. She leaves me to get in on my own and rounds the front of the car without another word. Gripping the door tighter to keep upright, I stare forward, tears in my eyes and leftover puke on my shirt. How did I get here? To the same place my mother had been before she left me.

I squint up at the sky, blinking back all the tears before I get into this confined space with Tess, the woman who just cut me open with her words. I know I have a problem. But life doesn't stop for problems. It keeps moving and will throw you off the ride if you don't hang on.

I drop my head and start bending down to sit but pause. Gripping the door, my heart beats faster and moves higher into my throat as I spot it, straddling the curb farther down the street. A black SUV with an arm hanging out the driver's side window and a lit cigarette balanced between two fingers. For anyone else, it wouldn't be enough to guess who's inside.

But I know.

CHAPTER NINETEEN

Jacob

"Do my arms look bigger to you?" Kit asks.

Gritting my teeth, I keep focused on finishing my last bicep curl, then set the weight down to look at her. "It doesn't work that way."

She flexes at her reflection in the mirror. "We've been coming every day for a week. They have to be bigger."

I wipe my face with a towel. "Again. It doesn't work that way." I face the mirror and flex one arm. "These took two years."

She grunts and pushes my shoulder. "I hate you. Aren't we supposed to have similar genes and all that?"

I shrug and drink my water, hoping she won't expect me to answer that one for her.

"Beau thinks my arms look bigger," she says. "And my–

I hold up a hand. "Imma stop you right there. I don't need to know what Beau thinks."

Lifting her shoulders she says, "I was going to say legs."

I shake my head. These gym hangs have been the most consistent time Kit and I have spent with each other, and I like it. I needed the distraction from the fact Ruby and I haven't talked in a week and there's nothing like sore muscles to do it. She won't answer my calls, and I'm positive she wouldn't answer her door. I was such a dick to her after that night, and I've been a dick to myself in order to make up for it. I didn't even get a chance to ask about Willow. The coffee, quiet apartment, and comfortable bed were going to help me finally ask her.

"Are you feeling okay?" she asks with her hands bracketing her hips.

The mirror beside me would show dark circles under my eyes, and the weights would say I'm tired. Even after a couple glasses of whiskey, I still haven't been able to fall asleep.

"I'm fine. Just tired." I use my sweat towel to wipe my face and cover up whatever she's looking for. "What are you doing tonight?"

Kit picks up her water bottle, and we walk to the locker rooms. "Dinner with Andrea. I haven't seen her for a while since they've been busy with the baby."

"How is Amelia? Do Allison and Peter love holding her?"

Andrea's older kids that she adopted into another family have been excited to hold their new half-sibling longer than anyone else, including Andrea.

"She's doing great." Kit smiles wide. "And you already know Allison and Peter love to hold her. She's like their baby doll."

I nod and say, "Good," before taking a sip of water. "Do you want to hit the sauna?"

She peers over at me. "I can't this time. I have to get going."

I nod and put my fist out. "I'll catch you here tomorrow then?"

She bumps it. "It's Saturday."

I stare at her without blinking. "And?"

"What about a day off?"

I lift one brow. "You want to get swole, right?"

She gives a short laugh. "Uh, not on Saturdays. I'm helping at the adopt-a-block anyway."

"Sunday?" I ask.

She smiles. "Church."

"Monday?"

"I'll be here," she says. "See you later little bro." She lifts onto her tiptoes and ruffles the hair at the top of my head, even though it's in a bun.

I squint. "I hope touching my sweaty head was worth it."

"Gross," she says, shaking her hand and holding it away from her body as she walks into the women's locker room.

I comb my hair back and walk into the men's room and stride straight to the locker for my backpack. I pull the zipper and peek inside.

The letter is still there.

It's followed me everywhere. I don't trust it anywhere other than with me. I sling the backpack over my shoulder, fill my water, and head for the sauna. I hang it on one of the outside hooks and step inside the thick, warm air.

My first mistake was thinking the letter was safe with me.

The second mistake was thinking Kit wouldn't notice.

"WHAT THE HELL is this?"

My stomach drops when I see Kit pacing in front of my car in the gym parking lot. Is she holding what I think she is?

Shit.

The letter.

I hold up a hand. "Kit—"

She cuts me off and screams louder. "What. The. Hell. Is. This?"

With the hard evidence of the letter waving between us, heat settles on my cheeks. A couple of people walk past us, and I tip my chin at them, then look at Kit. "Could we talk somewhere else?"

"No. Not until you tell me what this letter is all about. Is it true? It's dated two years ago." Her eyes are wide and moisture begins to fill them. "Are the things you wrote about in this letter true, Jacob?"

I exhale slowly, every ounce of resolve slips with my shame. Nodding, I stare at the ground.

Her voice is a whisper, so small and pleading. "Jacob."

My arms hang at my sides, lifeless and tied to bricks that are taking me to the bottom of the ocean. I can't stand looking into her eyes again and seeing the disappointment. Her disappointment in *me*.

I stare at her unmoving feet. "Did you read the whole thing?"

"Yeah," she says, but her voice cracks.

I close my eyes and let out another pained breath. How did she even get it? The letter was supposed to be safe. If I carried it around wherever I went, it wouldn't end up in the wrong hands.

"You kept this from me." Her words quake with emotion.

It's a statement that feels like a knife to my heart. It shouldn't be happening like this. I'm the one who needed to keep her safe from everything in that letter.

"Why?" she asks. "Why would you keep this from me after all the times I asked?"

My throat constricts, and I don't respond. I'm too busy seeing the damning words flash across the screen of my mind and realizing she read all of them.

I shove one hand into my shorts pocket and use the other to grip the backpack tighter over my shoulder. "I don't know."

"Bullshit," she says through a clenched jaw. "What about all the women and girls Bobby has already trafficked, because no one tried to stop him?" Her voice raises another octave. "You could have stopped this, Jacob. All you had to do was be honest."

I take a step back like I've been slapped and lower my brows. "And what about you? What about us, huh? You think I would have been believed? The drug dealer who's done time? No. Instead, I would have had to watch our backs even more than I already do."

"What does that mean?"

I shake my head. That I'm not only looking over my shoulder. I'm looking in front, behind, above, and below, because Bobby is everywhere. I never stop worrying. She looks at me like I betrayed our family.

"It means I'm always looking out for us—for you," I say.

She drops her gaze to the ground briefly. "I would have believed you," she says, pointing at her chest. "Me. Kit. Your sister. The former prostitute who still has friends on the streets who aren't safe. I would have believed you if you told me they were being trafficked."

I shake my head and swallow the emotion welling up. "And what would that have done? We wouldn't be able to stop Bobby."

"We would have figured it out. I did when looking for you!" she exclaims loudly. Throwing her arms out in front of her.

I wave a dismissive hand. "With the help of Beau's daddy who isn't even in the game anymore. How would he be any help? Bobby is too powerful."

"Marcel knows people," she says in defense then waves the letter. "We'd take this to the police. We could have figured something out instead of just hiding!"

I drop my chin to my chest then stare her down. "You don't get it."

Hands on hips she says, "Then explain it."

Wouldn't it be nice if it was as straightforward as telling the police. I scrub my hands down my face. "Bobby probably has guys on the inside too, Kit. Cops, paper pushers, you name it, he has people. We don't know who we can trust with this information. And they wouldn't believe me anyway. It's not like this letter is evidence."

"It's a testimony."

I point at myself. "*My* testimony."

She straightens, raising her hands and dropping them to her sides. "So, what about all of those girls then? We're supposed to ignore what we know so we can stay safe? There are women out there right now being traded for money like *things* and not people. How can we sit down and let it happen, Jacob? You knew where they were being held this whole time, and you did nothing. You said nothing."

I shake my head. "I knew this is how you'd react. There'd be no *we* if you hadn't read my letter. I would have taken this to my grave to protect all of us," I say, pointing between us. My pulse only continues to quicken. "I can't lose you again, Kit. Not like the first time where we were thrown into other people's homes. We already lost our parents. There's no one else. Only us." I'm close to tears, so I suck in a breath through my nose and rest my fists on my waist. "And you took that letter from me."

She bites the inside of her cheek and pins her gaze to something off in the distance.

I press, feeling anger rise up in place of my guilt. She took it. "Why'd you take this out of my backpack while I was in the sauna? How'd you know to look for it?"

"Yes, I did, but don't turn this back on me. You wrote this letter to me anyway. I can't believe you would do this. To keep information like this," her voice cracks. "And not tell *me*, at the very least."

"Kit, look—"

"Stop," she says, holding up a hand. "I don't want to hear your excuses right now." Taking a few steps forward she slaps the letter to my chest.

I grab it before it floats to the ground and watch the first tear slip from Kit's eyes.

She stares at me, emotion on full display. "I will do everything I can to find this house you mentioned and won't stop until Bobby is behind bars. I'd ask you to help, but maybe you're more of a coward than I thought."

With that, she turns and strides to her car.

I exhale and groan. "Kit, please. Don't leave. Can we talk about this?"

Holding the top of her car door she peers at me over her shoulder. "You had two years to talk. But you never opened your mouth." Bending down, she sits in the driver's seat and slams the door. It isn't long before she's peeling out of the parking lot and leaving me.

I rest my hands on top of my head and exhale long and slow. The pained look on Kit's face before she left is ingrained in my mind. I did that to her. "Shit," I say on another exhale.

Other people pass, chatting lightheartedly while my emotions are so tangled I can't make sense of how I feel. Things went from messy to impossible. Why'd I write this letter, anyway? I drop my hands and stare at it, holding it in an open palm as if it's a weapon and not a single piece of paper inside an envelope. The accusations, the names, the secrets, all written in black pen that can't be erased.

But it's not the words that could kill. It's the person behind them.

CHAPTER TWENTY

The Letter

Dear Kit,

It's weird writing you a letter you'll never read.

My roommate is gone and it's just me, sitting in our dorm room at the Journey Center. It's quiet. So quiet that I can hear my own thoughts, and they're screaming at me. I'm so damn sick of it.

Even though it's only been one year, two months, and ~~three~~ four days since I got arrested, I still remember everything. The things I admitted to and those I didn't. I've got a past, like you, and one that includes the gang leader, Bobby, also like you. I never expected to find *us* again. To love a sister I said goodbye to a long time ago, but I did. You may not understand why I've kept everything from you, but in a lot of ways, I think you do. Deep down, I think you know you'd do anything for the ones you love. You did everything you could for me, and that's what I'm doing for you.

I've been working through all my shit in therapy, and my therapist says writing is a good way to get stuff out—especially for someone like me who has kept too much locked inside for only me to know and nobody else to find out. So, that's what I'm trying to do…get it out. Except I'm not planning to show you this letter, because I love you. Remember that, okay?

It's been eating me alive these past couple of years, and now that I have family in the picture, now that you and Beau are in my life, it keeps me up at night. The information I have, the past I've been witness to, it all makes me feel ~~guilty~~ evil. But, I'm not. I just know what will happen if I open my mouth and tell somebody. It'll hurt people. It'll hurt us and now that there is an us—a family—I'd rather let it die with the old me. The one who went to prison, did drugs, and sold them. But I have to get the words out before they kill me.

So, I'm writing you a letter. I'm going to tell you everything I know, not just because I have to get it out, but because I feel I owe it to you and the past you survived. The women you've told me about and the prostitutes you worked with, I owe it to you and I owe it to them.

It's easier to think of people as a *them*. You don't know *them*, so it's easy not to care. Yet, when you give *them* a name, it changes everything. When they become a sister, a friend, or a neighbor, *them* isn't a collection of random people anymore. They're an individual, and it's personal. So, even if I could keep it all inside, I couldn't. Not when *them* is named Kit.

We've lived a ~~good~~ great life this last year. Aside from the part where I was in prison, you visited me in jail often, and I know if you could, you'd visit me here in rehab, too. Your letters keep me going while I'm in this blackout period where contact with the outside world is limited and all I have are my thoughts.

But maybe not seeing you face to face is why everything's coming up now. You're not here to ruffle my curls and for me to complain about it, even though I really don't care. I like that you do that. It reminds me of the times we had when things weren't so heavy. But they are now, and you're not here. It's just me, my memories, and this pen. A dangerous combination for someone like me who knows too much.

I hope one day I'll have the courage to admit to you what I'm going to write. That I can tell you to your face, preferably years later, and confess what I know. Maybe things will change by then. People will be caught, jailed, and killed by the time I tell you. Maybe Bobby will pay for what he's ~~done~~ doing. I hope so.

Remember, I'm doing this because I love you.

Don't forget that in the facts I'm about to tell you, okay?

Don't forget me.

Bobby is dirty. Not in the way you think, although that's enough to make anyone cringe. But there's more to him. Prostitution and drugs are just the start, but his real moneymaker is something I discovered by accident, but now I can never erase it from my thoughts. It sits in my memories, like a person holding a loaded gun to my head.

Shortly after I started working for Bobby, I learned that he has a way of doing things. There's an order of how information is passed from one person to the next. Bobby was the boss, and I was at the bottom. A soldier who was nothing more than a dispensable drug runner that took on the grunt work. I didn't know him, and he didn't know me. Very few people had a direct line to Bobby. Only a select few were privy to conversations with him. I was a nobody to him, until I became a somebody.

I'd been runnin' drugs for nearly a year when I got caught by the cops. I earned nothing more than a slap on the wrist and some community service since I was a minor. But when Bobby caught wind of it, he took an interest. He wanted to meet me.

I was shocked. It wasn't a good thing if someone like Bobby wanted to talk. I'd never spoken to him before, because I'd never had a reason to. I thought I had given him a reason by getting caught. I thought I was in trouble and wished that was the problem.

The money was good, but the hazards of the job meant that my life was always hanging by a thread. If the bosses didn't like how you handled something, you were out. They didn't answer questions; you were just done. I figured this was happening to me since I'd messed up and become a name in the police records. But why talk? Why else would Bobby want to meet?

He didn't fire me. In fact, he barely spoke to me and only confirmed my name and took my picture. I had no clue what was happening, or why he was interested. That is until I saw you at Lin's restaurant the night you met with Bobby. He favored me, because he favored you. I was just a pawn. But by the time you came into the picture, I was a pawn who had heard something he shouldn't have.

I stopped working my usual runs, but they still paid me like I was making drops. I wasn't chained up, either. It was more like I was being babysat. I was always with one of the guys that worked for Bobby. Most of the time, I was around a few. We played cards, ate together, and talked. I should say they talked; I listened. Bobby wanted me close in order to keep an eye on me, I could tell that much, but I still didn't know why. It wasn't so bad. It beat getting held up at gunpoint on the streets. It beat wondering if I'd get caught again, and it beat being alone all the time. I wasn't alone, and I guess that felt good for a while— comforting even—at least for a couple weeks.

But those guys I was with weren't always careful. They were used to talking about things with the confidence that information wouldn't get leaked. I was an outsider that was inside, not a prisoner but not an equal.

One night, we were all sitting in a private room at a restaurant, without Bobby. The drinks were flowing, and it didn't take long for them to open up. They were pulled together professionals most of the time, until they had a few drinks. Then, their tongues were as loose as the ties around their necks. I was a blurry face among the crowd that was all but forgotten after a few rounds.

Smoke filled the room, the laughter was obnoxiously loud, and stories bounced back and forth across the table. I stayed quiet, listening.

"We got another two girls," the bald one said. "Boss said it'd be lucrative. I just didn't know it would be this good."

"Not sure how to spend all your money? Need some help?" The man with a wide gut laughed loudly.

"I didn't say that." The bald man smiled broadly. "Are you transferring 'em?"

"Yeah, I'll pick 'em up and bring 'em to The Breaking House."

The Breaking House.

The name didn't sound familiar. I'd never heard anyone mention it before.

"Good. Maybe I'll get to try before buying again." The bald man's laugh was hoarse and wheezing, causing him to sputter out a cough.

Someone else said, "You know Bobby doesn't like the girls, I mean *merchandise*, tainted. Especially by your hairy ass." Everyone laughed.

Breaking House. Girls. Bobby.

"There's a reason they go there to get broken," the bald man added, boasting in his conquests.

If I weren't completely sober, I'd question whether I heard them right. Or, I would've just forgotten. But I hadn't had a lick of anything that night. I heard it all.

I listened to every conversation after that, waiting for more information to slip. The men didn't mention anything when they were sober, so I had to wait until they were drunk or high. I never asked any questions about the house. That would have put a giant target on my back, especially since I hadn't earned my place among them.

Finally, my waiting paid off.

Someone let slip what the house looked like: stucco siding, tan, nice neighborhood. They laughed until their faces turned red over the 'God Bless this Home' sign by the front door. Still, I never found out where this house was. They never said anything about the location. It could have been in a different state. But I knew just enough to be dangerous. I planned to use it as blackmail, or a last ditch effort to save myself if it came to it. But what I didn't know then was that those stories—the conversations they all had about the women—would feel like blackmail in my mind for years. I see that house when I close my eyes, and I see it when I open them.

Do you know what they do at a *Breaking House*? I didn't. Those women are shattered. Beaten, raped, held captive without basic needs, then, they're sold. It's a business exchange happening within four walls where the product is tested and created to make sure it meets the standards. There are employees and customers, buyers and sellers. It's all happening in the middle of a neighborhood. Who are these women, Kit? Could they have been you? Where did they come from?

I didn't know you were out there looking for me, or that you had history with Bobby. When all that information became clear to me, I knew I had to bury that house in the far corners of my mind. I couldn't risk letting it slip and it having the opposite effect—being killed for what I know. We were back in each other's lives again. I was in jail but still free from Bobby, and you were married. Everything was going good, so why piss off Bobby even more? I wasn't supposed to know anyway. I thought I could pretend like I never heard it.

But knowledge is heavy. Carrying all this around in my head has messed with me. I thought I could forget about it now that I'm getting help for myself. I'm not drinking or smoking anymore. I'm clean and doing good. I have a job, a family, and friends. What am I supposed to do with this information? What could I do that would change anything? I can't. But the more clear-headed I am, the more I've thought about it. Every time I see you, Kit, I think about those girls. I wonder if they will get out like you did, or if someone will come to rescue them. Did they choose that life? Were they taken? I don't know. I hate that I don't know the answer to these questions.

But at the end of the day, I don't want to lose *us*. We have a shot at a real family. I want that. After growing up with the parents we had, I didn't think I'd ever want that. You're my best friend, and I want us to stay that way more than anything.

So, no. I can't show you this letter, because I know you'll want to do something about it. In fact, I'm positive you will. You'll hate me for shoving those girls aside, like they don't matter. But hear me out. I'm not saying they don't matter. I'm just saying, *you* matter more.

You matter to me, Kit. No one has ever meant more. And for that, I'll take this to my grave. I'll bury it like it won't actually be the thing that kills me as long as I have you.

CHAPTER TWENTY-ONE

Ruby

"Ruby?"

I hear my name in the distance and groan.

"Ruby, what are you doing here?"

I blink and stare up at the looming figure above me. When I can finally make out his face, I whisper, "Jacob?"

He squats down. "What happened? How long have you been here?"

I look past him at the darkening night sky. "I–" my voice falters, "I don't know."

He exhales. "Here, let me help you up."

Reaching for my hands, he pulls me onto unsteady legs and wraps his arm around my waist so I don't fall. He unlocks his front door and pushes it open with his foot. I miss the step up and would have fallen on my face if he hadn't been holding onto me. My head is pounding again.

I get it, I get it. Too much alcohol. Blah, blah, blah.

We make it to the couch, and I plop down, keeping my eyes closed. "Water?"

"Let me get you some."

The water still isn't on at my place. Maybe that's why I ended up on his front porch.

How did I get here?

Why am I here?

He's gone and back in seconds, or at least it felt like seconds. Placing a strong hand on my back, he helps me sit and drink from the cup. I gulp deeply, refusing to stop and breathe until I've drained the glass.

I drop back on the couch and throw my arm over my eyes and groan. "My head."

He leaves again and returns with a wet washcloth and some oil. Resting the cloth over my eyes, I suck in air at how cool it is, then relax into the way it makes my head feel, like it isn't about to erupt.

He sits on the other end of the couch. "Put your feet on my lap."

"Why?" I question without looking.

"I'll show you if you put your feet up," he says.

I'm too tired to argue, so I kick off my flip flops and put my feet on his lap.

My eyes are covered by the cool cloth, but I can hear him rubbing his hands together. The slick back and forth motion is amplified by the oil he's using. He touches my foot with his warm hands and I startle, pulling it back. "What are you doing?"

"Trust me."

Easy for him to say. I don't trust people. Especially men, especially *him*. I know I shouldn't want to trust Jacob. We still haven't talked since I left his house last week. How the hell did I end up back here? I know I was drunk but still. Why would I have wanted to be here, with him, when things weren't resolved?

He slowly reaches for my foot again, and I let him pull it back into his lap. My skin prickles at his touch, but I don't pull away again. The sensation is gentle and soothing, making it hard to stay mad at him. All I want to do now is moan at the feel of his thumbs massaging the bottoms of my feet.

I exhale instead. "I said my head hurt. Not that I needed a foot massage." I can't help the edge in my tone.

I'm still upset with him, for leaving me and not leaving me. I'm irritated that he's different. The Jacob from before would have left. He wouldn't have brought me coffee and asked me to stop sleeping with other men. But he did. He did all of that.

His voice is low. "Massages can help relax your muscles and ease your headache. Sometimes my mom would get bad headaches. I'd rub her feet, and she said it helped."

I remember him sharing about his mom. She drank herself to death. I bite my tongue and try to focus on the rhythm that his hands create. His thumbs trace circular motions around my heel before he drags his thumb up the middle of my foot and down again, repeating the pattern.

It's quiet for a while, and if he weren't touching my feet, I would've thought he left.

"Why are you here, Ruby?" he finally asks.

My eyes are closed beneath the cool rag, but his voice is soft and almost makes me want to tell him. But I don't know why I'm here, so I have nothing to tell.

He continues. "You've been ignoring my texts and calls all week, and now you're here sleeping against my front door and drunk."

"Hungover," I correct, lifting the washcloth from my eyes so I can glare at him.

He isn't looking at me, though. He's watching his hands work.

I lower the washcloth. I wish I could forget last week. I remember enough of it that it makes me cringe. Maybe that's why I'm here. The pipe was still broken at my place. Without water, it felt like the walls were closing in on me, and I had to get out. Maybe it was seeing Bobby's SUV a second time while I was working the blade one night last week, or the fact that I really screwed things up with Willow, but I needed to escape. There was nowhere else to go but here.

With closed eyes and nothing to lose, I open my mouth. "I messed up."

He pauses his massage, and I wonder if I've scared him off already. But when I hear the snap of the oil bottle opening and closing, and his smooth hands work out the tension in my other foot, I relax farther into the cushions, giving them my full weight.

"Me too," he says. "I shouldn't have said what I said to you last week. It was mean and untrue. And I shouldn't have slept with you. I don't want you to think that I did that because I wanted to take advantage of you. I did that because I..." his hands knead the bottom of my foot harder, "I was weak and you deserve more. I'm really sorry."

There's that word again. The one that wants to be the salve to my wounds. "Don't be. You were right. Maybe you should have paid me."

He gives a curt laugh. "It's always hot and cold with you. One minute, the desire in your eyes is basically calling my name and the next, your heart is locked up so tight there's no way anyone could get in."

I grit my teeth, "Whatever," and pull my feet away, but he catches them in his strong grip.

"How?" he asks in a softer tone. "How do you think you messed up?"

I cross my arms over my chest and give in to his tender touch. It would be easier to be mad at him if he weren't touching me. But he is, and the gentle way he asked makes me want to say something. I feel like it's going to burst out of me if I don't.

"I saw my daughter last week and…I fucked it up." I fail to add that I showed up drunk, nearly passed out on the park bench when Molly finally found me, or that I'd worked all night the night before and couldn't remember if I ever went home. And I definitely don't mention it was the day after we slept together. I don't think he'd want to hear any of that. "I showed up like this," I say, waving a hand over my body, "but worse."

He lets out a low whistle. "What did Willow say?"

Hearing her name on Jacob's lips sends tears springing to my eyes. This is the part of my buzz where the alcohol wears off and all I have left are emotions. I don't like this part. But in order to forget for a while, I eventually have to remember, too.

I swallow the emotion in my throat. "I didn't get to see her." Not for long anyway. Only enough time for her to scream-cry my name and cement the fact I'm a horrible mom.

Making a fist, Jacob runs his knuckles up and down the sole of my foot slowly, sending a shiver up my legs, through my spine, and settling at the nape of my neck.

"Her foster parents wouldn't let me see her." Tears still linger at the backs of my eyes, turning hot at the mention of Molly and Stan.

His voice is a whisper. "I'm sorry, Ruby."

The sincerity that wraps around each word, has me shaking my head, trying to rid myself of the weight pressing against my chest. "Stop saying that. You didn't even do anything. Like I said, I fucked up. I don't even know if Tess will let me see her. She wants me to go to—" I cut myself off, realizing how close I'd come to admitting to Jacob that Tess wanted me to go to rehab.

He doesn't gloss over it, though. "Where does she want you to go?"

I rest a protective arm over my stomach. "Nowhere. Nevermind."

"Rehab?"

I stop breathing for a beat, keeping my words locked up tight behind closed lips.

"You don't have to hide yourself from me, Ruby. I've been to rehab, too, and it was the best choice I've ever made."

He draws circles around my ankle as I finally inhale the air I thought I'd lost for good. The effect of the booze clearly still has a hold of my tongue, making it loose and free with my secrets. What's even more clear is the desire I have to share it all with Jacob. I'm mad at him. But I'm finding it hard to remember why when his hands are on me.

"I've seen people go through programs, my own mother went through them, but they never helped," I scramble to explain.

His voice is as soothing as his touch. "Sometimes they do. Sounds like Willow is reason enough to try."

"She is." I squeeze my eyes tighter and whisper. "But I'm not."

It's the brutal truth. The reason I'm stuck in this loop.

The cold towel is met with my hot tears as my bottom lip begins to quiver. I'm just like my mother. Too far gone at this point. What's worth saving, anyway? Every day I fight against the voices in my head telling me I should end things. I'm tired. So fucking tired. I don't want to keep fighting. Willow is taken care of. I have no one left to worry about.

I don't know when he stopped massaging my feet and started rubbing my arm, but he did. He's closer, crowding me with his presence and sucking up all the air. He hums a tune in my ear I'm not familiar with. I focus harder. The humming fades, replacing it with his voice. He starts singing softly about the pain of a broken heart and memories that won't go away while his breath tickles the side of my cheek. I close my eyes tighter. It doesn't matter that grace comes with a heavy load, like the lyrics he's singing say. There isn't grace for someone like me. Not with what I've done, or what I'm doing. I'm hurting my own daughter. The flesh and blood I'm supposed to be better for. But I just can't be. As hard as I try, I just can't.

"We all have issues, Ruby, but it's what we do with them that matters, and going to rehab, that's doing something. You are Willow's mother and fighting for that relationship is worth it."

Pushing the washcloth to my forehead, I stare at the ceiling while tears slip down my temples and trail into my hair.

"I scared her." The small admission is all it takes for the tears to spill from the corners of my eyes in droves. "I'll probably mess up again. I don't know how to stop."

I see him nod in my peripherals, but I don't look at him. "You probably will. But you'll also make her smile again, too. And I bet that will make you smile," he says. "I want to be there when you smile."

I blink rapidly to pause the flow of tears, but they only come faster and burn hotter as they streak down my face. How can words create this much feeling? They sound like lyrics to a song, but he didn't sing them. He said them as if they were true.

He stands and grabs the guitar. When he sits on the coffee table again, quiet strums fill my ears and I release a shaky breath. The slide of his fingers against the strings scrape and creak while the melody guides his next movements. The tune is too gentle, and I silently beg him to pull and strum the strings until they break. I clench my teeth and close my eyes tightly.

He sings the song he was humming in my ear, and I listen to every word with fisted hands. I'm forcing myself not to feel, but it's impossible when music's involved. I feel too much.

I love Willow's smile. I don't want to miss her smiles. She has so many more to give. Maybe Jacob and Tess are right. Maybe rehab will help. But I've never been, and the thought of going makes my stomach knot together. Rehab is for people who have hope of getting better. They're sick and need help. But what if it's my mind that's sick? What if that can't be fixed? Rehab would be nothing more than a waste of time, because my body is only half of me. Alcohol is only part of the problem.

He finishes the song and starts from the beginning again. Every chord he plays and every word he sings untangles another knot in the pit of my stomach. But it won't last. I wish it would, but it can't, because nothing good lasts forever.

I unclench my fists but keep my eyes closed. I'm not ready to look at him.

He stops singing but continues to play. "Can I ask you something?"

My body is more relaxed now, and the tears have finally stopped. So has my breathing. "What is it?" I open my eyes and stare at the popcorn ceiling.

He stops playing, and the stillness of the apartment is deafening.

"What does Willow look like?" he asks so fast, I don't think I've heard him right.

I push the cloth off of my forehead and turn to look at him, brows pinched. "What?"

He shrugs. "Does she have red hair like you?"

I sigh loudly, lacing my hands over my stomach, and look back up at the ceiling. "No. She has blonde hair." I picture Willow, drawing out her features from memory. "And she has green eyes, like mine."

"Do you know who her father is?"

I glare at him briefly, then stare down at his guitar that lulled me into this calm state. I know he's just curious, but I don't answer questions like these often enough to have ready-made answers.

"It doesn't matter. He was just a sperm."

He leans the guitar against the coffee table he's sitting on. "But do you know who that sperm belonged to?"

Who the fuck cares? I want to say, but I hold my tongue. An improvement from earlier.

"Yes."

Silence.

"When is Willow's birthday?"

I push up to a seated position and stare him down. My head is heavy and eyes fuzzy as I sit too quickly. "Why are you asking me all these questions about Willow?" Is this his way of reminding me what I have to fight for? Why ask about her birthday then?

He runs a shaky hand over the top of his head and down the back of his neck. With his eyes trained on the ground, he asks, "You'd be honest with me right? If Willow were…you know, if she is…" he doesn't finish his thought, but he does meet my eyes.

He wants to know if Willow is his.

And the look in his eyes makes me want to tell him.

CHAPTER TWENTY-TWO

Jacob

I cradle my head in my hands, resting my elbows on the bar top when the front door opens. I'm immediately placing a finger up to my lips when James enters the kitchen.

He walks in quietly and sets a bag of groceries on the counter. "Hey, man," he says. "Why am I whispering?"

I point to the couch. "Ruby's asleep."

"Ruby?" His eyes widen as he pulls out a loaf of bread. "The girl you slept with?"

I grimace. I hate that this is how James remembers her. Not Ruby, Kit's friend, or even Ruby, the girl I like. She's *the girl I slept with.*

Nodding, I say, "She fell asleep a couple hours ago."

I don't explain that she fell asleep after I hounded her about Willow. I might as well have asked for a blood test the way her eyes bore into me.

He sifts through his bag of food, pulling out the cold items to put in the fridge. "You going to catch me up to speed on everything, or should I just guess why she's sleeping on our couch at ten o'clock at night?"

I drop my forearms to the bartop. "She fell asleep. I told you."

He shoots me a look over the fridge door. "You said she was mad at you after she left here the other morning. Did you apologize then?"

I'm regretting having said anything now. It's not like I have a long list of people I can talk to about everything. That list is two names long, and I can't talk to Kit about this. James has seen me through a lot, and I needed to tell someone about what I did— what we did.

I exhale deeply. "I don't know."

"You don't know why she's mad at you, or if you apologized?"

"Both, I guess. I thought she was mad at me, but when I got home from work, she was hungover and leaning against our door." I point toward the entryway. "She had a headache, so she laid down. I apologized, but I don't think she accepted it. I'm not even sure why she showed up here. We got to talking, and it all seemed fine until I messed it up again. Now, she's asleep and probably still mad." I sigh. "I should probably apologize again."

He shrugs a shoulder and puts a jug of milk in the fridge. "Probably."

I drop my head and stare at the counter. Her eyes were spitting fire when she said Willow's birthday through clenched teeth. *November first, twenty-thirteen.* We met after she was born.

It was stupid to think Willow could be mine. I can see that now. Ever since Kit told me that Ruby had a daughter, I lived with the possibility she was. It wasn't the truth, though. She wasn't mine. Willow was someone else's daughter.

He gives a low whistle. "You got it bad, man. You care. A lot."

James is right. I do care. How am I supposed to admit that to her, though? She threw up her walls faster and higher this time. Do I even deserve a shot? She was vulnerable and I pried. I should have just been there for her and kept my mouth shut instead of asking her about Willow.

Sitting up straight, I cross my arms and peer back toward the couch to make sure she's still asleep. I look back at James. "I have to tell you something."

He shuts the fridge quietly and goes to empty the rest of the bag. "Let's hear it."

I start bouncing my leg. "You know how I told you I had met Ruby before?"

"Before jail, right?" he asks, leaning back against the counter. The dim kitchen lights are reflecting off of his bald head and his gym clothes are rumpled.

I nod. "I didn't tell you this, but we slept together then, too."

He puts a few items in a cabinet. "Let me guess, you paid her?"

I nod again but avoid his eyes. I'm not proud of it, but that's the world we live in. "I didn't pay her this time, though. That was…" I shake my head, redirecting. "We have a connection."

I didn't mean for it to happen. In fact, I tried to make sure it wouldn't. But the way she looks at me with that thousand-mile stare seems to see straight through me, making it impossible not to feel everything at once. She saw me then, and she sees me now. And she wants to be seen, too. I don't think she knows or has been trying to communicate that without words, but she has. I feel the need as strongly as my own.

"After we were together, we talked." My voice trails off thinking about that night. If only we could've stayed in that moment. If only I could go back and write her that note I didn't leave. "I never forgot her. But you know how things were, it's not like I could start a relationship with her. She was a prostitute, and I was a drug dealer."

He leans his back against the counter and crosses his arms and ankles. "She's still a prostitute."

I cover my face with my hands. "I know, that's the problem."

"So, let me get this straight. You slept together years ago, spent the whole night talking and connecting, and then you left? No wonder she's been pissed at you."

I drop my hands and glare at him. "Not helping. And keep your voice down," I scold.

"Alright, alright." James waves his hand in the air, bringing his volume down. "Imma go out on a limb here and say you haven't told her how you feel?"

"How do I feel?"

He cocks his head to the side. "You like her, right?"

I nod.

"Does she know that?"

I shrug.

"That's not good enough, man. You gotta tell her," he says.

I grind my teeth and look down at the countertop. "I can't."

"Why?"

I shake my head but don't respond. James doesn't know about Bobby. He doesn't understand the risk I'd be taking by admitting that I care for Ruby. There's already a target on my back, but there doesn't need to be one on her's.

James and I spent enough time in rehab together at the Journey Center that I know he's just trying to help. That's why I told him about having slept with Ruby, but now I regret bringing it up, because nothing can happen. I should tell Ruby how I feel, and I almost did earlier, but I won't.

He gives me an incredulous look. "So, you're sleeping with her and she's sleeping with other dudes?"

I push off the counter and stand up abruptly. A rustle from the couch has me frozen in place as Ruby shifts. I look back at James when she settles again and I whisper, "I'm not sleeping with her. It was one time."

"Two times."

I scrub both hands down my face and march toward the pantry cabinet. "It doesn't matter. I like her, but it was a mistake to sleep with her."

I open the cabinet and reach in to grab the bottle of whiskey. It isn't here, though. It's in my room, hidden in the closet. Shutting the cabinet door, I face James.

He shifts on his feet and grips the counter behind him. "Does Kit know?"

His question guts me. Of course Kit doesn't know about the two of us. But James knows how close we are. I don't keep things from her anymore.

"No," I say.

His voice is low and measured. "You have to be honest with her and yourself. And Ruby."

I cross my arms and meet his eyes. "So, I'm supposed to tell Kit that I paid her prostitute friend for sex three years ago, ended up falling for her, and still feel that way?"

"Yes," he says emphatically. "And you need to tell someone you're struggling again."

"What?" I ask.

"Your hands. They're shaking. You've been drinking," he says to the floor.

I don't need to look at my hands to know what he's talking about, but I clench them tightly.

Ruby stirs again and we both look over, expecting her to wake up. She doesn't.

I don't turn back around and instead, let my eyes linger on the couch. I can be honest with myself. I like Ruby. A lot. But I can't act on those feelings again. Not until Bobby is dealt with. He's been quiet—too quiet. And as far as the alcohol goes, I've got that under control. But maybe I owe Kit the one thing I can be honest with her about: I can tell her about Ruby.

CHAPTER TWENTY-THREE
Then—Age 17

Then

"Come in," she said, opening the door wider for me.

I crossed through the door frame and peered around at the outdated motel decor. There were a few personal items and a coordinating color scheme of puke-green and taupe, which had probably been white at some point. The thin carpet pulled at my socks after kicking off my shoes.

"You can put your things over there," she said, pointing to the dresser across from the bed she sat down on.

I walked a few steps to the dresser and stripped off my hoodie, so I'd be more comfortable in my t-shirt, and laid it on top next to a lighter and a box of cigarettes.

"What'll it be this time?" she asked, pulling my attention back.

I cleared my throat and turned. We might have made out in my car before walking in here but being in her room is different. "Everything, I guess."

I rubbed the back of my neck, nerves kicking in. I'd never been in a situation like this before, but everyone seemed to think it was no big thing. There were plenty of strip clubs I'd been to, sure, but I still felt weird paying a woman for sex. I needed to blow off some steam, though, and remind myself that I could feel something—anything.

"It's one-hundred for everything, and I require money up front," she says, looking at her nails. She was all business.

I tried not to gape at her. Her shockingly red hair caught my attention immediately, making me think I'd enjoy this more than I originally thought. She was attractive. I was used to seeing women tweaking out or sleeping on the side of the street. Or, women on a stage where I could barely see their faces. But not her. The black satin robe tied loosely around her middle and following every one of her movements made my hands sweat. I couldn't look away. Her creamy skin and freckles brought every other feature to life, but it was her eyes that got me. Dark and light notes of green that swirled together around the black of her pupils. A whole song could be made just about her eyes.

I wanted her more than I'd wanted anything else in my whole life.

In the hours I'd known her, I'd learned she was sharp and quick-witted, relaxed while also hot-tempered. When I tried to slip my hand beneath her shirt in the backseat of the car, she slapped it away. I hadn't paid anything yet, and she wasn't about to let me cross that boundary without doing so. There was a confidence about her—a take-it-or-leave-it kind of person—but that was just the first layer. Below that, she was sad. Those green eyes told me as much.

Pulling my wallet out of my jeans, I opened it up and sifted through the cash before extending a one-hundred dollar bill between us.

She grabbed it, careful that our hands wouldn't touch, and shoved the folded bill into her robe pocket. "Knives, guns, or anything else needs to be on the dresser, too."

"I don't have any of that on me."

She stood and lowered her eyelids at me. "Good. You can sit on the bed. I'll be right back."

The woman with the endless green eyes that I was about to sleep with walked into the bathroom and shut the door. I peered around the room at nothing, until I finally walked to the bed and sat where she had been sitting. A voice sung softly from the other side of the door. Was she…singing? It was throaty and deep without rising above a whisper. I tapped my fidgeting fingers on my legs, drumming the beat to the song I didn't know, but she was singing. I couldn't make out the words, but if I were writing the lyrics, it would be about her eyes.

The digital clock on the nightstand told me it had been three minutes so far. Then four. Five. And then, the bathroom door swung open. My mouth was dry, and I could feel my heartbeat in my ears as I cataloged every part of her. She walked closer to me and stood between my knees, and my hands weren't the only thing sweating anymore. Beads of it broke out on my forehead when I inhaled her sweet scent. I wasn't new to sleeping with women, but I was new to sleeping with this one. I couldn't tell if it was because she really was that good, or if she looked at me the same way I was looking at her. Like I wanted to know more than just the landscape of her body.

I wanted to know what she was singing.

She settled her hands on top of my shoulders, running them down my arms and gripping my wrists to place my palms on her bare hips.

A shuddering breath left my parted lips, and I gulped. "Tell me something about yourself."

She laughed and combed her fingers through my hair, stepping even closer. "What do you want to know, *Dylan?*" The fake name I'd given her sounded like the strum of a guitar note coming out of her mouth.

I asked the first question that came to mind. "How old are you?"

She played with the edge of my shirt collar. "Twenty. You?"

I didn't want to tell her my real age, because maybe it would freak her out that I was only seventeen, so I lied. "Eighteen." I swallowed again. My mouth was so dry. "Do you have any family?"

Her hands stopped moving, and her whole body stiffened again. "No. Just me."

"You sing," I said.

Her lips spread into a smile. "That's not a question."

"You're right," I gulped. "It's not."

I wanted to ask about her interests or find out how she got into this line of work, but all roads led me back to the same place. My gaze dropped to my hands on her hips and followed the trail they paved down her outer thighs and back up again.

Her voice was strained and her breath hot against my lips. "Any more questions?"

I blinked slowly. "Your name," I swallowed. "What's your name?"

She paused and studied me. "Jasmine."

"Is that your real name?"

She smiled and whispered in my ear. "Yes." It sent a rush of heat down my core and between my legs.

Still bent forward, her nose traced my jawline until her lips were on mine. A piercing electric current shot through my body, the slide of her tongue against mine the only thing I could feel. But it made me feel so much. She made me feel everything all at once after years of numbness. I explored every part of her mouth, then her neck, her shoulder and collarbone. My lips never left her skin, needing to taste every flavor of her.

Her grabbing hands were everywhere—gripping and tugging, pulling and pushing. I followed her everywhere she wanted me to go. Heavy breathing was the only thing I should have heard, but when I was on top of her, inside her, I swear I heard music. It was soft and slow, then loud and all-consuming. There was a beat and stringed instruments, voices and sighs. Everything was acapella, but I'd never heard music more clearly.

It was music I could feel.

I laid next to her so close that we shared a pillow. "I've never done that before." I wasn't talking about sex. I was talking about making love.

"Me neither," she whispered in disbelief.

She felt it. Did she hear it, too?

"What's your favorite food?" I asked, tucking a strand of hair behind her ear.

Her lips turned up in a smile. "Pizza. Pepperoni with pineapple and jalapeños."

I smiled and reached for my phone hiding inside my jeans pocket that was discarded on the floor. I searched the nearest pizza shop and called them, ordering the pizza with the weird toppings for two.

She tucked her hand under her cheek still facing me. "I can't believe you just did that."

"What? Ordered us food?"

She shrugged one shoulder. "Yeah, I mean…" she shakes her head. "Never mind."

I rubbed her arm, letting my head sink deeper into the pillow. "Tell me."

All the confidence drained out of her as she rolled to her back and stared up at nothing but a water stain the size of Texas. I knew this because she had me on my back, too.

"I'm a prostitute."

I knew this, but I guess I'd forgotten. Why? Because I wasn't sharing a bed with anyone but her. She was the only one I saw and heard.

I shook my head. "You're Jasmine."

Her voice was barely above a whisper. "Yeah. I am."

I studied her downturned mouth and unblinking eyes. I didn't know her brand of pain, but I knew what mine felt like. I knew what it was like to be all alone and wanting someone to save me from that kind of torture. To save me from one more thing Life with a capital "L" could throw at me. I'd always faced it alone, because that's all I'd ever been—alone.

Jasmine looked lonely.

But with Jasmine, I wasn't alone.

Maybe with me, she wouldn't be either.

Stretching a hand out, I ran a thumb across her cheek. "I like you." It sounded ridiculous when I said it out loud, but the words would've exploded out of my chest if I tried to keep them in. I felt so much more than I had in a long time. So much that I didn't want to stop feeling. It was the new high I was chasing.

She smiled, and the corner of her eyes crinkled. "Do you say that to all the prostitutes you sleep with?"

"No." I replied so fast that she finally looked over at me. "I've never wanted to say that to anyone. But I want to say it to you." My words were honest. At least I thought they were.

She rolled over and sat up quickly, searching for her robe. Finding it, she shoved her arms through and tied it quickly. "Maybe you should go."

I propped myself up on my elbow. "Why?"

"Because."

"Because why?" I asked, not ready to leave.

"Because. I'm not capable of liking you back," she said with crossed arms and steady eye contact. But she wasn't looking at me. She stared at the bed, floor, wall, anywhere but my face. "I'm too messed up. You don't want someone like me." She laughed, but I didn't join her. "I'm a fucking prostitute! You don't like me. You just like the idea of me. I guess I gave you your money's worth, huh?"

I sat up and leapt across the bed before she turned and stormed away. Cradling her elbows, I tried to catch her gaze. If only I could see those green eyes again, maybe the music in my head would keep playing.

"Hang on. Look, I don't know what just happened," I said, pointing to the bed I was sitting on, "but that was…that was…" I stopped.

I didn't even know how to explain what that was. I'd never had that many emotions coursing through me at one time. It was confusing and weird. Explaining it to her was impossible, let alone myself. I just knew that it was different. It meant something.

"I'm messed up, too," I admitted. "What if…" I paused and sighed. "What if we can just be messed up together."

I could tell she was considering it as she bit down on her lower lip. Even though I wanted to pry it out of her mouth and kiss her like she desperately kissed me earlier, I waited. She finally smiled, and I pulled her into my arms. I removed her robe and kissed every part of her until our pizza arrived. Then, we ate. We talked and ate and made love all night that felt like music.

I waited for her to fall asleep, and then I watched her. Her chest rose and fell as each breath pushed a wavy piece of hair up and down in front of her face. She told me about her mom and I told her about mine. She talked about the motel she grew up in, and even that she wanted to leave. The life she had wasn't the life she wanted. It was then I realized we weren't both messed up. It was just me. I was the one who wouldn't get out. There were men who had guns to my head on a regular basis. But not her.

Not Jasmine.

She wanted a different life for herself and I wanted it for her. If I stayed, I would've been dragging her down with me to a depth she'd never crawl out of. I couldn't do this to her.

I slipped my clothes on and waited at the foot of the bed for her to wake up and tell me to stay. To say I'm not as jacked up as I felt. I waited for that voice in my head to tell me this was more than these handful of moments. I waited for the music to start up again. And then I waited outside the motel—alone—convincing myself that what just happened wasn't real. She deserved everything I couldn't give her. Like freedom.

That's when I realized there was no amount of waiting that could make me feel less alone. I just was.

CHAPTER TWENTY-FOUR

Ruby

"I could be there for you and Willow, you know. If you needed help, I'd be there," he had said.

"Like how you were there for me the last time," I replied.

I roll onto my back and open my eyes.

My response to Jacob the other night was harsh but honest. He'll be there for me, until he isn't. What could he do anyway? It's my life, not his. I swallowed the question creeping up my throat, until I couldn't. It wanted to come out since the moment I recognized him. Since I saw him at Kit's party. Since we slept together again. I shouldn't have asked, because there was never supposed to be anything *more* between us. He was never supposed to say things like, "If you need help, I'll be there."

But he did. So I did.

The question that actually left my mouth last night was shaped like a grenade when it finally came out.

"Why'd you leave the first time then?" I had asked him.

I turn over, and sit up, planting my feet on the ground and forcing the memory away. I peer over my shoulder and say, "You can have five minutes."

"You got another customer?" the nameless man asks.

I stare straight at the closed window curtains and nod my head.

He grunts as he rolls to the edge of the bed to stand. The man grabs his things from the dresser and walks toward the door without a second glance. I prefer it this way: no small talk.

You can find hungry, paying men just about anywhere these days. The streets, the gas station, or online. A price is set, my address given, and here we are.

I exhale when the door clicks shut, and I run both hands through my hair, digging my fingernails into my scalp at the same time.

I wish Jacob had been there for us. I wish Willow was Jacob's daughter, but her father doesn't have a name. He may not even be her real dad, because how was I really going to know? There were others around that time, too. But his face was the only one I could remember, so I'd always thought of him as her dad. He had dark hair, but he had green eyes that looked kind just like Willow's.

I didn't give Jacob a chance to respond to my question before locking myself in the bathroom until I was positive he was in his room. I said the words, but it didn't mean I wanted to know the answer. There would be too much truth attached to his explanation, and I didn't want to hear it.

I should have gone home right then and there. But it was dark, the couch was inviting, and Jacob had running water at his place. Or, maybe it's because I thought we'd talk about it or work it out after we both cooled off. I waited on the couch, but he didn't come out of his room. So, I did what any hungover woman with too much weight in her life would do: I fell asleep. I slipped out early this morning before we could talk. It was foolish to think that he'd want to. I've been nothing but a thorn in his side and he's been nothing but a pain in my ass.

I reach for the flask beside the bed and unscrew the top. My mouth waters before I even press it to my lips, inhaling the sharp burn before I taste it. It's still early in the afternoon. But by the end of the night, I won't remember half of what happens.

A cigarette is between my fingers after I set the flask on the nightstand and lay back in the bed, tucking my naked body beneath the sheets. I stare up at the ceiling and light it, watching those first few puffs of smoke take me with them. My head lolls to the side, and I stare at the pillow next to me, picturing Jacob's smiling face the first night we met. I close my eyes and feel the warm sensation in my throat spread throughout my body. If only he'd stayed, maybe life would be different. If he told me that he'd be there for Willow and me back then, I probably would've believed him. But not anymore.

Words are just words.

Another knock on the door forces me to strangle these thoughts. "Come in," I yell.

I lay back on the bed, one hand above my head and one hovering over my stomach with the cigarette in it as the next customer enters. He's tall with broad shoulders and slim hips, dressed in slacks and a button down. The working type who is probably looking for more excitement than what he gets at home. It's like a game trying to guess their stories. I never ask and I never will, but I'm always curious.

He stops at the foot of the bed, looming over me. I always meet them at the door, because I hate this feeling. Where they're higher and I'm lower. Tonight, I don't care, though. I just don't fucking care. "Empty your pockets." I point at the dresser. Even the unsuspecting men have things to hide. "I'll take the payment."

He does as I ask, bringing me the money and watching as I count it before placing it in the bedside drawer. I sit up and let the sheet fall away. His eyes roam every part of me and mine roam everywhere else.

CHAPTER TWENTY-FIVE

Jacob

I step up to Kit's front door and knock.

After multiple desperate texts and calls to her and Beau, she finally agreed to meet and talk things out. I have no idea what to expect when she opens the door. The last time I saw her she had tears running down her face and was more disappointed than I'd ever seen her.

Looking down at my feet, I close my eyes and breath in and out.

The door creaks open and her face is in view. No tears. "Hi."

I snap my head up. "Hey."

She moves aside, and I hesitantly step up and walk in. Beau is sitting on the couch, arm draped over the back as I enter and sit across from him. He nods and gives me a tight-lip smile while he stands and heads for the kitchen.

Kit settles in the spot that Beau vacated, and we both start talking at the same time.

"I–"

"I'm–"

"Sorry. You go first," I say.

She exhales. "I'm sorry."

"What?" I ask in shock. "No. I'm sorry."

Holding up a hand, she grabs a deck of cards on the side table and I smile. It's always been easier for us to talk with a handful of cards in our hands. This is how we got through those early years with our parents and after them. I think it's Kit's way of saying we'll get through this, too.

She continues while dealing. "I'm sorry that I reacted the way I did and for taking the letter. But I'm still angry that you didn't tell me about what was really going on. It hurts to know you kept it from me."

I lean forward and grab my cards, fanning them out in my hand, then I look up at her. "I know. I messed up, and I'm so sorry about that. I was just trying to protect you."

She shakes her head. "Jacob, you weren't protecting me, you were hiding."

I study my cards, hating how right she is. "Do you have any aces?"

She slides an ace of clubs across the coffee table to me and I set the match down. I've been hiding the letter from her and Bobby. But she's wrong, too. I am protecting her. I'm going to take care of the people I love. "Any fives?"

"Go fish," she says.

She ends her turn by drawing from the stack. The room is quiet other than the slip and slide of cards in our hands and on the table. "But," she exhales, "I know why you did it." Her eyes are clear. "You were scared. And if I'm honest, I was, too." She stares at the deck, debating her next words. "You've been carrying that backpack around all week, never letting it out of your sight and I thought…" she stops abruptly.

"You thought what?" I press, cinching my brows together.

Kit glances at me, then back at the suits in her hand. "I thought you were sellin' drugs again."

I say the only word in my head. "What?"

She glowers at me. "You've been carrying your backpack around like it holds a secret, and I was right, just not in the way I thought."

My head is starting to hurt. I've been clean of drugs for two years but not with alcohol. I've got a bottle of Jack in my closet right now that nobody but me knows about. I don't have to guess how disappointed she'd feel if I relapsed, because she's telling me.

Her eyes glisten with moisture as she sucks in her bottom lip. "I knew you were hiding something, but I'm sorry," she says, exhaling. "I should've known you wouldn't be selling drugs again...or using them."

The ache sitting high in my chest makes it uncomfortable to breathe. Rehab helped with the addictions, sure, but I'm not there anymore and all this lying is starting to eat away at me.

The secrets were a way of protecting everyone from the truth. From having to deal with Bobby. I tell myself it will be over soon—someday. I need to do what's right. I need to keep lying to my sister. Angry Kit isn't the version of my sister I want to see again.

But it nags at me. I should tell her everything. I need to stop lying and just come clean. Why does being honest feel so hard?

"I'd probably think the same thing."

Shame sits heavy on my shoulders, but I take it. I'd rather carry it than let Kit do it. She's been through enough when it comes to Bobby. Could I really tell her that I saw him? Talked to him? Could I tell her about the bottle of Jack? Ruby?

I clear my throat. "Do you have a king?"

She shakes her head. "You've been through rehab at the Journey Center and paid your time, but you know how common relapse is. I don't want that for you."

I shake my head and pick up a card from the deck. "Trust me, I don't either."

That's not a lie, but it's only part of the truth. What I don't say is how stressed I've been. How I'm trying to keep our lives moving forward instead of backward, and I'm only one man. A drink or two is how I'm dealing with all that stress. When it's over, I'll stop drinking.

"I should have just asked you," she says, adjusting the cards in her hand again.

"I should have just told you," I say and mean it. I could've said something about the letter so many times. I know that now. Maybe by telling her, we could have dealt with all this sooner. "I wish I could go back and do it over."

She sighs and sets her cards on the table. "There are a lot of things in the past we wish we could change, but we can't. The only thing we can do is change what we do going forward."

I drop my cards and lean back into the couch, crossing my arms. "But how? It's still dangerous and that hasn't changed just because you've read the letter." And how are we supposed to go forward with all this baggage? I could do something about it. I could tell her everything.

Kit calls out to Beau who's in the kitchen. "Do you think Marcel would help us?"

Beau walks in and sits on the back of the couch. "I don't know. It took my dad a while to get out of the game. I doubt he'd want to get mixed up again."

"What about the police then? We could tell them about the name of the place we think Bobby might be trafficking women?" Kit's words come out fast, tripping over each other.

I shrug. "We don't have an address or any evidence."

"So, we need to figure out where this Breaking House is," Kit says. "That's our evidence."

The room feels smaller as the dilemma gets bigger.

"Beau, if you could get your dad to weigh in, I'll text Ruby about the Breaking House," Kit says.

My heart plummets and I cut in before Beau says anything. "We should leave Ruby out of this. It wouldn't be safe for her."

Kit sighs. "True, but I don't have any other connections on the streets anymore. Do you?"

"No, no one." I rub the scruff lining my neck.

I try to hold onto the possibility that Kit will drop this and Bobby will, too. Maybe when I told him I wouldn't come work for him it closed that door for good. I don't want to admit to Kit that I've seen Bobby—I've talked to him—but the longer this conversation goes, the more guilty I feel. I need an antidote to all this lying. I need to tell her the truth. "Kit."

She pauses her side conversation with Beau and stares at me. "Yeah?"

I clear my throat, preparing to paint myself as an even bigger fraud in my sister's eyes. "I need to tell you something else."

"About the letter?" she asks.

I shake my head.

"It isn't about the letter," she reiterates. "So, it's something else?"

I nod, the movement painfully slow.

She sits up straighter. "Tell me."

I slide my palms back and forth and in a loud exhale, I force it out of my mouth. "It's about Ruby..." my voice shakes. "And me...and Bobby."

CHAPTER TWENTY-SIX

Ruby

Tears burn my raw cheeks. I've dried them multiple times, but they won't stay that way. They've continued falling with every sip I take from the bottle.

What happened to feeling numb?

To forgetting all the shit I have to deal with when sober?

Instead, everything surfaces. Every feeling, every struggle, every pain. It's all here.

The cheap bottle of something keeps me company on the floor as I stare at the bed that has made me and broken me. I don't have the money to take care of Willow or myself. The few dollars left in my purse and hiding under my mattress aren't enough. They are pennies compared to what I'll need to get her back and leave L.A. It's never enough. I work and work and screw and screw, and it's never enough. I'm never enough.

I cradle my head in my hands, rocking back and forth and wishing I'd never had Willow. I wish I'd never been born. It wasn't supposed to end like this—turning into my mother. But I did. I am my mother.

I'm weak like her.

I'm sad like her.

I'm broken like her.

I tip the bottle back and gulp until my throat burns, and I can't breathe. The tears staining my cheeks mix with the wet alcohol coating my lips and chin. If only love were enough to save me. I love Willow. But love isn't enough. Love is loss, and I'll do it as many times as I have to in order to give Willow a chance at a different life than what I had. I don't want this for her.

The bottle is almost empty. Back and forth I tilt it and watch the contents slosh around. I stop and rest it on my knee, and the alcohol quits dancing, too. I shake it again, harder this time, forcing the drink to move. It does. I pause again. It stops. I shake it and it moves. It has to do what I say. It doesn't have a choice and neither do I. I'm as helpless as this bottle.

Fumbling to get on my knees, I grab for the bed to pull myself up on unstable legs. The neck of the bottle is still clutched in my hand, and I refuse to let it escape as I stand and sway. It needs to pay for being so weak. I stumble backward and hit the dresser and curse loudly when it punches the middle of my back.

A groan and another cascade of tears fall from my eyes as I turn and point at the dresser. "Fuck you!" I scream. "Fuck you!" I say looking at the door that everyone walks in and out of as they please. "Fuck you!" I say to the bottle still in my hand as if it has ears and can hear me. Its silence only angers me more. Adrenaline races through every vein in my body, and I lift my arm and stare straight at the bottle. "Fuck you," I say again with no feeling this time, then thrust it at the wall, shattering it into so many pieces that it could never be put back together.

The liquid paints the wall and floor as my chest heaves. Another guttural scream rises from the depths of my pain and stabs the silence. "Fuck you," I say to no one and everyone. I don't know who I'm talking to, but the surge of heat overtaking my body keeps the coals of my anger burning hotter than the flames did.

I'd watched my mother be this person. The drunk addict who was pushed around by whoever she opened the door for. She lost it all, too. The money and her sanity. I saw it happen and swore I wouldn't be her. But here I am, staring at my reflection in the broken pieces of glass and the wet carpet absorbing what's left of me. The alcohol holds parts of me I want back. I want it out of my veins, gone from my life and my blood. I don't want to be my mother. I don't want to be Ruby. I don't want to keep doing this. I'm done with it all.

I bend down and retrieve a chunk of broken glass and fall forward on my knees. The sharp bits of glass pierce my knees, but I push that from my mind. Gray is all I see. Whoever said the world is black and white was wrong. They don't know what it feels like to live in the gray. The fringes of life where decisions are murky and misunderstood. There isn't a straightforward answer. Sometimes it's just choosing the lesser evil.

I don't want to be like my mother.

I don't want Willow to be like me.

I don't want to be me.

This is the gray.

I lift the glass in front of my face and the sharp edge catches the dim lamp light. If I ended things myself, Willow would have a family. She wouldn't become just like me. Jacob would be free of me and could live his life without always having to worry about me.

It would only take one swipe, one quick motion to end it all. Things would be better if I could go through with it this time; I would feel better. Gasping for breath between my sobs, I stare longingly at the glass. It's the only way.

I am my mother.

I shake my head, words forming through quivering lips. "Willow, I'm sorry. I'm so sorry." Squeezing my eyes shut, I rest the sharp glass against my wrist. It's cold and unforgiving. One quick move and it's all over. My tears cause my hand to shake and move the glass across my skin, pressing shallow cuts into my arm. "I'm sorry."

Gray turns to red, and I fight against the will to leave and the will to stay. *I can't do it.* But I can't stay. I have to get the alcohol out of my body. It's in my blood and I need it out, or I'll be just like her. I'll drink too much and die just like her. Shaking my head forcefully back and forth, I press the glass deeper. A little more, a little deeper.

"Willow. Willow, I'm sorry!" I slur.

Willow.

I ease up on the glass driving into my arm.

Willow.

The blood-tinged glass is in my hand.

Willow.

It drops to the floor.

Willow.

My hands are red.

Willow.

Falling to the ground, I curl up into a ball as sobs wrack my body. My cries are muffled behind my bloody hands that cover my face.

I'm just like my mother.

But I'm not her.

I'm Ruby, which somehow feels worse.

Through the tightness in my throat, I whisper, "Willow," once more.

Gray turned into red.

And red turned into black as I closed my eyes.

POUNDING SOUNDS ON the door and wakes me. My eyelids flutter open when I hear my name.

"Ruby! Open up. Ruby!" the voice yells. "I know you're in there. I need to talk to you; I have to tell you something."

I blink and look up at the ceiling. It's white. Maybe it was only red in my dream.

Where am I?

I start to roll over and wince at the sharp pain that registers everywhere on my body. My ears are ringing, but I can still make out my name.

"Ruby!"

I close my eyes and feel around on the ground with my hand. Glass. Lots of glass. I'm lying in a bed of it.

The bottle. Throwing the bottle. Glass. Blood. Damn it.

I roll to the other side slowly and the glass falls from my hair, clothes, and skin with a clink, and I feel the places where it's made its marks on my body. There are small pieces stuck in the palm of my hand, and I grit my teeth as I pull them out.

More knocking on the door causes me to startle.

I'm in my motel and someone's at the door.

"It's Jacob. Please, let me in."

My legs are shaky, but I'm able to crawl up to sit on the bed. I brush bits of glass from my knees and small, misshapen pieces leave their imprint. I rub my head again. The room is muted by the soft glow of the table lamp, but the dried blood and crushed glass tell a story.

I thought I was dreaming.

I wasn't.

He knocks again, softer this time. "Ruby, please."

I can't let him see me. Not like this. "Damn," I say under my breath, grabbing the side of my head.

The room is spinning, and I clumsily step over broken glass to make it to the bathroom. Hints of blood color my face, so I reach for a towel to clean it off, but there's still no water. I drop the towel in the sink and walk back to the bed. Every step, I feel a pinch from my cuts.

The knocking continues.

"Go away!" I yell back.

"What's wrong? Are you okay? Please, open the door."

I should've pretended not to hear him, but all the pounding is making my head hurt more. There's nothing he could say that would change anything. He'd only make everything worse. The knocking stops, so I curl up at the end of the bed and stare at the wall. I'm crying again, and I don't even know why. Everything, I guess.

It happens fast. There's silence, and then a loud bang as the door flies open and hits the wall behind it. Jacob's foot is still raised as the door swings back.

I sit up as fast as I'm able. "Did you just break my door?"

"You wouldn't open it." His chest rises and falls quickly. "Are you okay?"

I curl one leg beneath me. "I'm fine." My voice is quiet and weak though, not convincing at all.

He walks inside and checks to make sure the door still closes. It does, so he turns and the room is quiet again. I know he sees it, but I stare at my other foot grazing the floor as it swings back and forth. The dried blood that I can't wash off, the broken glass all over the floor, and my tears are on display for him to see.

"Ruby," he whispers as he steps closer. "What happened?" He searches the room and bathroom, glass crunching beneath his feet. "Are you alone?"

"It's just me," I tell him. It's always just me.

He comes closer and drops down in front of me. I don't look at him. I can't. Seeing him put the pieces together isn't anything I want to watch. He doesn't say anything as he runs his thumb along the tender spots of my forearm. I pull it back not wanting my blood to ruin him, too.

A tear slips down my cheek and before I can wipe it away, Jacob does. He cradles my cheek with his hand and I close my eyes, all the other tears following it.

His voice is a whisper. "What happened?"

I shake my head, my tongue still twisted in my mouth.

He gathers me into his arms and I don't resist. I clutch the soft cotton of his shirt, gripping it tightly in my fist at his back and refusing to let go.

"Shh-shh-shh, I'm here. I'm here," he says, over and over.

He sits on the bed and gathers me into his lap, burying his face in my hair. It's dirty and I guarantee it smells, but he doesn't pull away. He pulls me closer. I cling to him but keep my face covered. Shame. So much shame. It washes over me. I'm drowning in it.

He rocks back and forth clutching me so tightly that if I let go, I wouldn't move an inch. But I don't let go, because I need him right now. Tess was right, Jacob was right, I need help. I don't want to need him, or anyone this much, but I do.

We sit like this without a word passing between us until the light outside streams in through the cracks in the curtain and the tears dry on my face and his shirt. He lays back on the bed, pulling me with him and tucking me into his chest as he combs his fingers through my hair. It's so gentle, so tender, that my eyes well with tears again. Everything about us is wrong. I shouldn't crave his touch like I do.

He starts humming softly and I relax further into the bed, comforted by the low vibrations traveling through his chest and up his throat. It sounds like a song I know.

I sniffle. "What song are you humming?"

He pauses. "Something I've been working on."

I swallow and lift my hand to his chest to draw circles on his t-shirt. "When I was a little girl my mother used to sing me a song. It sounded similar."

He rubs my back and props his chin on the top of my head but stays quiet.

"She'd always sing it before bed." I close my eyes remembering her soft voice coupled with the way she would comb through my hair like Jacob is.

I've been thinking about my mother a lot. It's hard not to when all I see is her in me every time I look in the mirror. Even with blood staining my skin, I look like her. I hate it. But somehow I still love her. We had our good times, and those were the parts that kept me holding on.

"Some nights she would say she didn't feel well and couldn't sing. So I sang it...for both of us," I say.

"What's the name of the song?"

The lyrics are already filling my mouth. "Little Willow."

His chest vibrates as he talks in a low voice. "That's why you named your daughter Willow."

I nod and think about the first time I held Willow after she was born. I didn't need to know her father to know that I loved her. Her wispy blonde hair looked white against her creamy pink skin. Her suckling lips worked constantly in her sleep. All I could think about was that song as I held her. I sang it out loud and in my head so many times during those early days. I wanted to sing it, not because it reminded me of my mother, though it did, but because Willow made me want to sing.

"Sing it to me," he says. "Do you remember it?"

I swipe a finger beneath my eyes, stealing the tears that try to run. I nod against his chest. Reaching up, I grab the pillow above us and settle it under our heads. I finally risk looking at him. Strands of curly hair fan across the bed behind him, and his caramel eyes are light and accepting.

"Yeah, I remember it."

I swallow and clear my throat, looking down instead of into his face. I won't be able to sing it if I look at him. He rubs his hand up and down my arm, making me shiver.

I close my eyes and picture Willow. She was so fragile. I'd never held a baby until I held her. I sing about the Willow tree being tossed in the wind. I sing about the love that can't be taken away. I sing about healing. And I sing about never letting her go.

My voice quakes, but every word reminds me why I'm still here.

It's Willow. It's all for her.

CHAPTER TWENTY-SEVEN

Jacob

There are cuts on her arm deep enough to leave a permanent mark. I saw it all. The shattered bottle, the floor, the dried blood in the crook of her arm and splotched on her face. My chest tightens whenever I see the permanent decision she tried to make. I don't know what made her stop, but I'm glad it did.

She's burrowed into my side and hasn't moved since she fell asleep an hour ago. The daytime light is in full swing right outside, but with the curtain drawn, we stay paused in this moment. When I can't see the outside world, I can pretend it doesn't exist. Right now it's just us, and I'm in no rush to leave.

Her hair still has traces of alcohol soaked into it, and if her water was working, I'd wash her myself. Inch by inch, I'd wipe away every last bit of red. Unlike her, I haven't been able to sleep. She's safe, I know that now, but it doesn't bring me any comfort. Probably because safety is relative when someone has suicidal thoughts. She likely hasn't felt safe in real life and her mind for a while now. How did I not notice? Did she ever say anything? The attempt might have happened last night but the struggle didn't show up then. No, that kind of struggle is built over time.

I wish my arms could support her enough, but I'm not naive. I've been through it. The withdrawals, the constant thoughts racing through my head and telling me I just needed one more hit, one more drink. The Journey Center is the only reason I'm still here. Sure, I had the help of a jail cell to keep me clean, but it was the continued choice over the next year that proved the most difficult. It still is. Maybe I wasn't as ready to leave as I thought.

Before I kicked down Ruby's door earlier, I planned to tell her that I told Kit about us. But I also planned to ask her—beg her—to move in with Kit for a while. I didn't want to chance things with Bobby if we were going to search for his darkest secret: the house. When Ruby wakes, I'll explain things and ask her to stay with Kit. And knowing all that she's been battling, I think living with people would be good for her.

I close my eyes and kiss her forehead, letting my lips linger. If only what I feel for her were big enough to cover all of it. Kit says that's God's job and maybe it is. Maybe He is big enough to cover all of it. I wish He were for her sake. I'd do anything to take this off her shoulders.

I roll to my back and reach into my pocket for my phone. There's a text from Kit. *Did you talk to Ruby?* I exhale and stare at her message. I tap out a reply. *No, I'm a little busy.* It doesn't take her long to respond. It's past nine in the morning now, so she must be at work. *Busy doing what? You need to talk to her. Who knows how much time we have.*

I peer down at Ruby. Fearing Bobby and figuring out a plan is the last thing she needs right now. If she lets me, I'll take that on for her. If only she'd trust me, I'd show her that I wouldn't let her down this time, or any time, from here on out. I think back on the song Ruby sang earlier. Her voice is beautiful. Gritty and raw but smooth. So smooth I felt it wrapping around me like a second skin. I could tell she was nervous by the jumps in her pitch, but she thrusts so much emotion into the words she sings that I don't want her to stop. So, I asked her to sing it again when she finished. Bits and pieces of the lyrics have been bouncing around in my head since then. She sang it for Willow, but the words are for her, too. Time will heal her wounds, and I want to be there to watch it happen, if she'll let me.

My phone vibrates again. *I have the room set up for her. We can talk about a plan tonight.*

I still don't respond. I'm not sure what to do. Do I encourage Ruby to apply for the Journey Center now? Or, do I bring her to Kit's? The last thing I want to do is the wrong thing. I've never been suicidal, but I have seen people end their lives or take someone else's. I squeeze my eyes shut then stare up at the ceiling. I won't let that be Ruby.

Typing out a response, I erase it immediately. Telling her I'll call her later won't work. Kit has a way of turning into detective Carmen San Diego when things don't add up. Now that she knows what Bobby's been up to, she won't drop it. I'll have to decide whether to tell her about what Ruby attempted last night, too. Should I say something? Or, do I keep this between Ruby and me? I know she cares for Ruby. She took the news of my connection to her fairly well compared to the way she responded when finding the letter. She had more questions than anything. The how, why, and when questions came hurling at me like dodgeballs. I caught each one. What was worse was telling her that Ruby and I saw Bobby and that I talked to him.

She was hurt all over again, but I had to get out the lies and secrets I'd been holding in. Most of them, anyway. I couldn't handle them anymore. They were eating me alive.

Ruby's hands are curled beneath her chin and her breathing is steady. She's in a deep sleep and likely won't notice if I slip out for a minute. I need to gather my thoughts and figure out how to communicate them to Kit.

I peel myself off the bed and look down at her longingly. She seems more fragile today, smaller and more frail, which only makes me want to scoop her back into my arms and never let go. My feelings are growing stronger and stronger, and I want her. Every part of her. Even the parts that she didn't want. I'll take those, too.

Slipping out the door, I close it softly and lean against the stucco building. My best course of action is honesty. No more lies. But God, I've never been in this position before. This is my sister, and this is Ruby. I care about both of them. So, who do I hurt by opening my mouth?

I click on Kit's contact and listen as the phone begins to ring.

"Hey, how's it going? Are you heading to work soon?" Kit asks.

Work. I forgot. I check the time on my phone. "I have to be there in a half-hour."

"Oh." She gives me the space to add on, but I don't. The words haven't formed. "So, when are you going to see Ruby?"

I clear my throat. "I'm with Ruby."

"And…"

I drop my head. *Be honest.* "I haven't had the chance to talk to her yet. Ruby is…" my voice trails off.

"Ruby is…what?" she presses.

"Ruby is…sick," I say. My gaze finds the sky as I lean my head against the building. "She had a lot to drink last night and tried to hurt herself."

She gasps. "What?"

It doesn't feel right telling Kit what Ruby did. This isn't my place. But what choice do I have? I'm regretting opening my mouth while also knowing I can't keep this in. She didn't just get drunk. She didn't just smash a bottle on the wall. She didn't just lock herself in her room. She tried to kill herself. That warrants the truth, however hard it is to get out.

"Yeah, there are cuts on her wrist and dried blood on her skin and clothes." I exhale, the noise of the city drowning out the sound. "But she didn't go through with it, and it doesn't look like she lost that much blood." Any blood is too much, in my opinion.

"Oh my God," she says slowly as the reality sets in. "What do we do?"

Tears prick the back of my eyes. This is why I called my sister and shared this with her, because she's always there. In her mind, it's always a *we*, even when I try to mess that up by keeping things from her. She has my back, and I didn't know how much I needed to hear that until she said it.

"She needs help." I rub the back of my neck. "We haven't talked about a plan or next steps. She was hesitant to go to rehab before, but I don't know." I drop my hand. "Maybe this situation changes things. I'll ask."

Kit sighs into the phone, the weight of what we're both now carrying crystal clear. "You still like her a lot."

It isn't a question and I'm glad. I'm tired of all the questions. "Yeah, I do."

"Me too."

I blink back the tears and clear my nose. "When she wakes up, I'll talk to her about staying at your place tonight. We'll figure the rest out after that."

"Okay, and Jacob?"

"Yeah?"

"We do this together, alright? Not you more than me or me more than you. Together."

I rub my jaw. These are the same words Kit used when I sat across from her wearing orange. She's said it a couple of times since then, but the last time was when we were picking out a movie. They hold a completely different meaning now. Her words mean more now than they did then.

I repeat my usual response. "Together."

We hang up, and I shove my phone into my back pocket as I twist the knob and walk back in the room as quietly as I can. I expect to find Ruby lying on the bed still but instead, she's sitting on the edge finger-combing her curly hair.

"You're awake," I say, walking closer.

She nods. "I was cold."

The small smile on her lips is enough to warm my entire body. That one smile means so much after everything she's been through. I beam when I look at her. I can't help it. I sit beside her, pulling one leg up, and trace the smile on her lips with my thumb. "How are you feeling?"

She drops her eyes to her lap and shrugs. "Alright, I guess. My head hurts and I'm hungry."

I reach for my phone again. "I'll order us some breakfast."

She covers my hand that's searching for the nearest takeout spot. "Not yet."

Tossing my phone onto the bed, I thread my fingers through hers.

"Thank you," she whispers.

I shake my head. "Of course." She's close enough that I can see the varying green flecks of color in her eyes, and I'm glad she doesn't look away. I lower my voice. "I want to be with you, Ruby."

Water wells in her eyes, and her lips press together in a firm line.

There's a lot we need to talk about, but I forget all of it as I look at her. "Please say you feel the same."

She doesn't respond right away, but one tear falls down her cheek and I thumb it away. It gives me part of my answer, but I won't move closer until I have all of it. It's the worst time to admit all these feelings, but maybe that's exactly why I'm saying something now, because I don't want her to think for even a second that this changes what's been building between us.

I expect her to shake her head, pull back, or shove me away. To tell me she isn't ready or can't be with me. I expect the worst outcome. Instead, she nods and my pulse kicks up another notch. I lean closer, our breath mingling. There is still blood smeared across her cheek, forehead, and chin but as more of her tears fall, I use them to clean the blood off.

Her mouth tips into another smile and my eyes fall to her lips until my mouth is feeling her smile and not just seeing it. It's warm and inviting as I press closer, melding my lips to hers. She opens her mouth willingly and leans closer, setting one hand on my thigh and the other snaking up to play with my hair. I love when she does that.

I cradle the back of her head and angle her mouth giving her every feeling I've felt over the past few weeks. I don't have any doubts. It's Ruby. She's it for me, and this time, I won't run. I'll stay and be here for her however she'll let me.

Pulling her onto my lap again, I run my hands up her spine as she arches her back closer. I let my lips fall from her lips and kiss along her jaw, neck, and back to the bridge of her nose where all her freckles live. I'd kiss every single one of them if I weren't so drawn to the taste of her mouth. I kiss her like I'm desperate for her and like she is, too. I'm determined nothing will keep us apart. Not secrets, lies, or anything else could keep me from her.

I slink a hand beneath the hem of her tank top, and the heat of her skin has me moaning into her mouth. She feels so good. Ruby is a force. I've experienced her coldness, but her warmth is unmatched. It's fiery, full, and complete and is exactly how she makes me feel. I want to have all of her, right here, in this bed, but I slow our kiss, because now isn't the time. This isn't the moment. I'm not going to mess this up.

I peck her mouth a few times, then her cheek, and finally, her forehead. Her hand slides up my chest and settles on my cheek, our breath strained and ragged.

I press my forehead to hers. "Kit wants you to stay at her house tonight." The words are sudden, and maybe I should've waited a few minutes, but the luxury of time was a thing of yesterday, not today. "I do, too."

She sits straighter, staring into my eyes. Her response could go either way. I didn't outright say that I told Kit but my suggestion does. I'm waiting for her expression to shift and tell me what she's thinking like she usually does.

Sliding off of my lap and back onto the bed, she adjusts and runs a hand along her arm. The same arm she tried to end her life with.

Her voice is low when she speaks. "Okay."

"Okay?" I repeat.

She nods. "Okay."

All the feelings in my body head straight for my eyes. They fill with tears. She agreed. She'll stay with Kit. She'll be safe. That's everything I want for her.

I cradle her face in my hands. "We can talk more tonight, but I've gotta get to work. Kit said the room is ready for you and you can go there now."

"I'll take the bus," she says.

I pause, never having thought this through past step one. "The bus? Are you sure?"

She raises a brow. "Yes, I'm sure. I take the bus all the time.

I want to push back, but she's already agreeing to so much. Maybe this isn't as big a deal as I think.

I help her pack a bag and sweep up the glass, then give her some cash to buy herself breakfast on the way to Kit's. "Are you sure you're okay to get to Kit's?"

"Jacob, I can get there. Don't worry about it. You go to work, and I'll see you tonight."

Leaving her to get there on her own wasn't my plan. Maybe I should call Kit or Beau, and have one of them pick Ruby up. But, then again, they're working, too. She just went through a horrible night that could have ended with us not even having this conversation. Saying goodbye to her right now is unsettling.

She walks me to the door, and I circle my arms around her while breathing her in. She grabs my shoulders so tight, her nails likely leave indents in my skin. I kiss her cheek and say goodbye, and she kisses my mouth with tears in her eyes.

"Are you sure you'll be okay?" I ask one more time.

She stands on her toes and kisses me. "I'm good, I swear."

"Okay." I study her face. She looks good, lighter even. Better than a couple hours ago. "I'll see you later."

She smiles. "I'll see you then."

I didn't know it then, how much this goodbye would hurt.

CHAPTER TWENTY-EIGHT

Ruby

I step outside the diner, the same one Jacob and I went to more than a week ago. After being wrapped in Jacob's arms for most of the morning, I continue wanting to be close to him. So I come here, order the jumbo breakfast and coffee, then smile the whole time I eat it.

Beth, the waitress we had before, is here and she asks how my man is. I tell her he is great, because the last time I'd seen him he was great. His face was soft—relieved—as he traced my jawline and kissed me, making me dizzier than if I were buzzed. I don't know if he is *my man,* but it feels good to think of him that way.

This morning I should have woken up full of regret. I did, but I also woke up to Jacob. When I lay folded in his chest, smelling the familiar woodsy scent of him and singing, something I hadn't done in forever, a swell built behind my ribs and inside the layers of my heart. It was the same feeling that kept me from deepening the cut in my wrist last night when I thought about Willow. It stopped me from making a choice I'd regret. And today, it's leading me to Kit and Beau's house with the hope of seeing Jacob there later. What comes after that? I don't know. But I do know who will be there.

I breathe in the air my lungs are used to. It's thick and muggy, but I only inhale deeper. In downtown, everything feels hotter, even in fall, and I forget the ocean is close by. But it's there, even if I've never been. One day I'll go there. I'll stand at the water's edge and let it wash over my feet. I can almost feel it, like I feel Jacob's kisses, his touch, and his kindness.

Tonight, I promise myself. Tonight I'll see Jacob again. We'll talk more and sort everything out. All good things start with talking, right? Maybe now is our time. We've waited and tried, but maybe now we can try this—us.

I walk down the sidewalk and bend down an alleyway to cut through to the next street. There's a bus stop over there that I think will take me to Kit and Beau's house in Burbank. Jacob said that Kit was expecting me. If I had a phone I would call, but like a lot other things, it's a casualty to my need to survive. I spent the money on the bottle I broke last night.

Trash litters the ground, boxes are flattened and leaning against the brick wall, and the smell of urine is strong. Every alley is the same. I couldn't tell one from the other if I tried, but they all lead somewhere. A destination right around the next corner.

As I exit the alley to the next street, an SUV is idling near the sidewalk. Its windows are black and rolled all the way up, so I can't see anyone inside, but that's the point. The people inside don't want you to know they're in there, who they are, or what they're capable of. But I know.

I've seen this SUV before and sense the warning that comes with it. I know who's inside this one just like I did the last two times it appeared. The swell I feel inside my body fizzles out, and the blood pumping through my veins and warming my body, as I walk from point A to point B, drains from my face. Whatever I thought could happen, whatever plans I could've made with Jacob evaporate as a man exits from the back.

He's tall and bulky, twice my height and weight. We stare at one another, his eyelids low and smirk firmly in place. He knows more than I do about what the next few minutes will be like. Looking behind me, I realize how stuck I really am. There's nowhere to go. My gaze is hard, fists clenched. I don't want this to be the end. I wish it was the beginning like I thought it was a few minutes ago. Fighting or running won't do me any good. I know why he's here and who he's looking for.

He isn't here to deliver a message or a warning.

He's here for me.

And like a lamb heading to the slaughter, without a way out, I obey.

CHAPTER TWENTY-NINE

Jacob

"Where could she be?" I fist handfuls of my hair and pace Kit's living room.

"Jacob, calm down. She probably just went out for a bit," Kit says, attempting to console me. "Maybe she got lost, or maybe—"

"She's gone!" I yell, cutting her off. She left me.

I'm wearing a hole in the rug, but I don't care. This can't be happening. Ruby almost killed herself last night. The fact that she's missing isn't good. It's my fault for leaving her and not driving her back to Kit's like I knew I should have done. I should've skipped work and listened to my gut.

"Jacob." Kit's voice is fainter this time, hushed enough that I ignore her. She says my name louder, but her voice shakes. "Jacob."

I spin around abruptly. "What?"

"Do you think…" the terror in Kit's eyes raises my blood pressure.

I shake my head. I refuse to think of where or how right now. She's alive. She has to be. Finding her is the only thing I care about.

"We need to call the police," I say, surprising myself.

"You're right. We need to do something," Beau adds, leaning his tall body against the wall in the living room. "When did you say was the last time you spoke to her?"

"This morning around ten. I gave her some cash for breakfast and told her I'd see her tonight," I explain.

He crosses his arms. "It's been nine hours. We gotta go to the police."

Too many hours since my last drink.

"Dammit," I grind out, then slam my palm against the wall, but it does nothing to quell the pit in my stomach.

The last place I want to go is the police. All they're going to do is file a missing persons' report. But that won't find Ruby. Every second counts, and we've wasted too many of them.

This can't be happening.

But it is, and I did this.

I sit on the couch, hiking up my black pants that I never changed out of after work. I came straight to Kit's house, expecting to find Ruby when I didn't hear from her. James said she never came by our apartment, either, and a drive to the motel produced nothing. I pick up my phone and my thumb mindlessly scrolls without any direction. There's no one else I could call. I don't know her daughter's foster parents, or whether she has any other friends or family. I know nothing about Ruby other than the pieces she's told me. I know she likes to sing. I know she had a shitty mother. I know she likes black coffee with too much sugar. I know how she tastes and sounds. None of that will help find her, though.

I close my eyes and toss my phone on the couch. Standing, I start pacing the rug again.

"If she's alive–" Kit starts.

I cut her off. "She's alive."

Her eyes drop to the floor.

"Could someone have taken her? Do you think…" she struggles to get her thoughts out. "Do you think it was Bobby? You said he saw you and Ruby together, and then he showed up at your work. What if he…"

"No," I say harshly. "His beef is with us."

Even as I say the words, they sound wrong. There's something I'm missing, though. Bobby wanted me. I refused him. Ruby…

"Collateral," Beau says.

It's one word that tips my world. I repeat it, testing it out on my tongue. "Collateral."

"We haven't heard from Bobby, though." Kit rubs her temples. "If he took Ruby, he'd want us to know that he took her."

"Unless he wants us to seek him out," I say.

If we go searching for Bobby, we'll be on his turf, not neutral ground. As if that kind of ground really exists. This city is his playground and the people, his toys. He does what he wants, and I can't help feeling like in all this, there's something I'm missing.

Kit drops her hand, slapping her thigh. "Then, we go to the police, figure out a plan, and–"

I scoff and rake my fingers through my hair. Kit doesn't get it. She didn't see the cuts on Ruby's arm, or the blood coloring her perfect skin. Ruby is suicidal, and I left her after knowing this. How could I do that after everything she had just gone through? Did she leave because of me? I can't seem to stop making mistakes with her. It never feels like the right time. Just once, I wish it was. Just once, I wish we were both ready to say yes.

"Okay." Kit blows out a gust of air and stands. "We need to do what we can. Let's go to the station."

"I'll get the keys," Beau says, heading for the kitchen.

Shoulders slumped, I shrug, at a loss for how to turn this bad situation around. Our hands are tied. If Ruby doesn't want to be found, she won't be.

"I can't let anything happen to her. It wasn't supposed to–" I cut myself off.

My words are standing on stilts and about to topple over.

"You love her, don't you?" Kit asks.

I stare from her to the ground, shaking my head. "I don't know." My voice is barely a whisper. "I don't think I know what love is."

"Your head doesn't? Or your heart?" she asks, shifting on her feet to face me.

My sins and the reasons I shouldn't love Ruby are written all over the walls. I did this to her. Pushing her away by pushing to get closer. Maybe she wasn't ready.

She inhales through her nose, and we lock eyes. She's giving me that look. The one that makes me feel fifty shades more transparent than I feel. She can see straight through me.

I dip my head and try to hide as tears build in my eyes. "I don't know how to fix this."

Kit closes the gap between us and circles her arms around my neck. I tighten my arms, clinging to her as my tears fall. As my body shakes in Kit's arms, she whispers, "We're in this together, remember?"

I nod and whisper over her shoulder. "Together."

"Promise me again," she says. "Promise me you won't give up on Ruby. That you'll find the woman you love."

I nod my head again, my voice lost along with my heart.

She squeezes me tighter. "Say it."

Swallowing the lump in my throat, I breathe through the pain sitting high in my chest.

"I promise."

But promises can't always be kept.

CHAPTER THIRTY

Ruby

It's dark. So dark that I can barely see my hand when I raise it in front of my face. Whenever I do, I panic. My chest heaves and my cheeks flutter from my heavy breathing. I've only seen light a handful of times when I'm checked on, or food is brought in, though that isn't often. I'm completely alone.

I'm in a bedroom, and even though there's a bed, I sit on the floor with my back to the wall, staring hard at the thin strip of light taunting me through the bottom of the only door in the room. I need to get out of here. But how? The door is locked, the window too high, the men who brought me here, too strong. If there was a way out, I'd take it—I crave it—but it's the first time in the last day I'm starting to believe it isn't possible. I'm frozen to this spot on the floor, fearing the worst and expecting even more.

The hardwood chills me all the way through, and the dank, musty smell is a scent I'll remember for years. If I make it that long.

I cough a few times, expelling the dust that's swirling around the small space and trying to choke me. The man with the face tattoo of two teardrops near the corner of his eye already tried. He was close enough for me to see it well enough and to know exactly what it means: he isn't afraid to kill. Shivers steal down my spine. I'm the only one in here now, though, and while I'm not chained up to anything, my hands are zip tied behind my back. He did that, too. I've lost track of time, but the black behind the thin curtains covering the only window tells me it's night time again. Has it already been a whole day since I saw Jacob last?

Jacob.

An ache settles beneath my breastbone when I think about him, so I try not to. But his face, his long, curly hair, and those light eyes are hard to forget. He's probably wondering where I went. Is he mad? Does he think I'm dead? He probably thinks I wanted to end my life, but I don't. I've never wanted to live so badly as I do right now. It's the man who doesn't want me to. Does he work for Bobby? Is this his doing, or just my bad luck?

Muffled noises and creaks in the floor are my only indications that I'm not alone and cause me to flinch every time I hear them. He's here—or they. One or ten or more, I have no clue, because only the man with the face tattoo has walked in here since locking me in. He brought food but no water, and now my mouth is dry and my lips are cracking. My bottom lip throbs with pain, because he hit me for asking too many questions. I had to dab the blood with the sleeve of my t-shirt. *Where am I? What's happening? Can I have water?* I have a fat lip and no answers to show for it, just tight shoulders and a swirl of dread brewing in my gut. I've never been so afraid. I'm alone, and no one is coming to get me out of here. I'm a nobody, fearing for a life I barely wanted as of last night but somehow still have. What if I never see Willow again? What if I never leave this room? What if I die just like this?

I rest my head back against the wall, scrunch my knees up, and close my eyes, although it doesn't make much of a difference since the room is the same shade as the one behind my eyelids. A key sinks into the lock and the door handle jostles. Opening my eyes wide, I turn in the direction of the noise.

The door pushes open, and the dim light fills the small room, blinding me. I squint and twist my head from side to side to shield my eyes, but a dark shadowy figure is what blocks most of the light. It's the man with the permanent teardrops. No, the Grim Reaper. Maybe I'm already dead. It felt like too much of a dream, anyway.

"Ruby," a voice says, and the hair on the back of my neck rises.

I blink and focus on the dark figure. Does the Grim Reaper wear a suit?

"It's a pleasure to finally meet you."

The person talking sounds male, and his voice is hoarse and low as he talks to me, like he's greeting someone who isn't zip tied or peeing in a bowl on the other side of the room. The man sits on a stool across from me and crosses his legs. I catalog the shiny loafers on his feet and the silver cuff links at his wrists. He's not in the right place. But when I continue my journey upward, seeing the sneer on his face, I know he's exactly where he's always been and where I'm at now, too.

Hell.

I lick my sore lips and murmur. "A pleasure?"

Bobby smiles, but it doesn't reach his dark eyes. I imagine not much does. "Ruby Red."

He laces his fingers and rests them on his folded knees.

I squint at him but say nothing. Fear and rage are a weird mix inside me. I want to shrink back, but I have to stay alive.

"I'm glad you made it." He smiles while I glare. "Sorry it took me longer to get here. I've been busy. You know how it goes."

I refuse to open my mouth and jut my chin out instead, as every muscle in my body tightens.

"I'm guessing you know why you're here by now," he says.

"Because you're a lying piece of shit?" I wince at how loose my tongue is.

It's always been a problem. I need to keep quiet, but this anger at who he is and what he's done to Kit and Jacob, is hard to ignore.

He belts out a laugh while I continue to stare at his shadowed face. "That's rich coming from you," he says. "If you knew why you were here, maybe you'd have more respect." His smile turns down in a matter of seconds and the serious expression on his features sends a chill down my spine. He stands abruptly and grabs my whole chin in his palm. "You're here as debt payment."

I breathe heavily as he pulls up at an awkward angle and places a gentle kiss on my cheek. It's so at odds with the way his fingers clench mercilessly into my skin. I grit my teeth and try not to react as his face hovers in front of mine. My mouth stays closed as I breath heavily through my nose. It isn't until I make a noise of pain, he finally lets go and sits back down, adjusting his suit as I shift my lower jaw back and forth.

The leg of the stool he's sitting on is my new focal point in order to avoid his eyes. *Debt payment*. It wasn't hard to guess. I knew there was something between Bobby and Jacob that would cause Jacob to act the way he did around him.

He places a hand over his chest. "I'm willing to offer you another deal out of the kindness of my heart."

I glance at him. Fake, fake, fake. From his bald head to his unnatural smile. The words coming out of his mouth are twisted.

I have to remember that. Keeping a straight head is the only way through this.

"I'll ease up on you, give you a room with light, better food and water," he explains.

I force myself not to roll my eyes and draw my brows in closer instead.

He leans forward, elbows on his knees to study me, but I don't flinch or say anything. "But I want you to help find more recruits, more women that need a job."

I bite my cheek, but it doesn't help. The words fly out. "I thought I was just a debt payment?"

"You are. But there are a lot of debts. You have a daughter, right? Willow is it?"

Hearing her name on his lips makes my stomach turn over.

Willow.

My everything.

But Jacob.

He has a part of my heart. A bigger piece than I thought.

"Leave her out of this," I bite back.

"I will, as long as you comply."

Bobby waves at the man near the door without taking his eyes from me. The man with the face tattoo and a smug smile does his bidding and fetches a glass bottle that I know the name and taste of before I even see the label.

My mouth waters as he brings it closer and hands it to Bobby. It's been too long since my last drink. The weak limbs and sweat tell me as much.

He uncorks the top and accepts two small glasses from his guy. Pouring the dark liquid into each of the cups, I'm helpless to look away. I watch his every move and swallow repeatedly. My head is drowning. I'm hungry, but I'm also thirsty. The sound of liquid being poured and filling each glass is hard to ignore when it's so loud. I shift and angle away, lowering my gaze, and lying to myself that I'm not that thirsty. I'm not that weak.

The smashed bottle lying on the ground of my motel room pushes to the front of my mind, and I shake my head violently.

I'm crying. Throwing the bottle, picking up glass. It's hovering over my arm.

I squeeze my eyes shut and take deep, pained breaths to stop the memory. "I don't want it," I say, but even I don't believe the quiver in my voice.

He sets the glasses of alcohol on the ground, and I can't help but stare. It would taste so good. It would wet my throat, and maybe give me the courage I need to get through this. He grabs a pocket knife stashed inside his suit jacket pocket, flips it open, and moves closer to me. I press closer to the wall, expecting the knife to sink into my flesh, but he grips my shoulder, forcing me forward as he cuts my zip tie with the knife.

I take turns cradling my wrists in my hands that are sore from all the tugging I did to escape. He retrieves the cups and extends one of the glasses toward me while the alcohol dances from side to side, like a woman's skirt dancing as she twirls. My eyes are stuck on the recognizable routine. I know it well enough by now. The steps and turns, the beat and pulse. It's all familiar.

I don't take the glass, so he places it on the ground in front of me and sits back down. The chair creaks from his weight, and it's ten times louder than it was the first time. He's talking again, but his voice is like sandpaper rubbing against wood. I can't make out what he's saying. I'm trying too hard not to stare at the glass and be as weak as I feel.

The burn in my throat has already started. I swallow the bile rising higher and force my eyes to the ceiling, blinking rapidly.

Don't do it.

Don't look.

Someone laughs, but the sound is muffled. The clink of the glasses and the filling of the cup are on repeat in my head. I don't know when he left or when the door shut, but the room is dark again. I'm alone, but I'm not. I look down at the glass that hasn't left. Is it closer? It's inches from my legs tucked beneath me.

I shake my head forcefully again. No. I won't grab the glass. I can't.

Willow.

In my mind, I'm sitting with her on a park bench, her feet swinging back and forth, drinking her slushie. I'm hugging her, breathing in the strawberry scent of her shampoo as I bury my face in her hair. I'm pushing her on the swing and getting high on her laugh. I love her laugh. It's airy and high-pitched without worries to weigh it down.

"Willow," I whisper, but she doesn't hear me. She can't. I can barely hear me.

I can almost feel her blonde hair between my fingers. If she would just look at me with those big, green eyes, I'd know not to pick up the glass. I wouldn't reach for it.

Willow, please. Look at me. Tell me not to.

But she doesn't look at me.

In my thoughts and in reality, I'm on my own.

Tears begin to take away what little vision I had. I'm scared. I'm small. I don't know where I am, or what I should do. I'm ten years old again, sitting on the bathroom floor of some motel, listening to music through headphones. The volume is turned up all the way, so I can't hear my mother in the other room and I'm crying. I don't want to be alone. I want my mom. I want to count jelly beans with her. I want her to brush my hair and tell me I look pretty.

I pull my legs to my chest and rock back and forth muttering, "Mom, mom, mom," until it's the only sound I can hear. The picture of her grayish skin in my head makes me cringe. She doesn't wake. She's dead. The police come. They take her. "Mom, no. Don't go." I gasp through my tears. "Please, don't go."

I'm all alone. No one is coming to save me.

I press my palms into both of my eyes, so I can't see the glass in front of me. But I hear it. It's loud and begging. My body is weak; my mind is weaker.

I open my eyes and stare downward. My cheeks are wet, and my throat is raw. All the reasons I'm here are in that glass. I should just take it. I deserve it.

Tears and sweat mix until I can't tell which is which. I slink down and lay on my side still staring at the glass, straining to see it in the light coming through the bottom of the door. But it's there. I know it is.

I tell myself I don't want to reach for it, but I forget what that reason is.

I've lost everything already.

Nothing and no one are left.

I have no one.

I roll over onto my back and close my eyes. I'm lying in the bathtub again, remembering what it felt like to dip below the surface of the water. I take a deep breath and sink, pushing bubbles out through my closed lips. Everything is hazy underwater. Eyes and ears don't work the same. It's quiet.

I like quiet, because weaknesses can't find me here.

But I'm not underwater; it just feels like it. The alcohol is still chanting my name, *Ruby, Ruby, Ruby*, but I don't look at it. I study the ceiling. *Ruby, Ruby, Ruby.* I shake my head and tears fall, paving a trail down to my temples.

Ruby, Ruby, Ruby.

I wipe my eyes. "No!"

I turn over and push up to sit, my head throbbing from the simple movement. I grab my head, then grab the glass. Inhaling the scent makes my whole body shiver. It burns my nose, but I like it. I breathe it in again.

"Why do you have to be so cruel?" I ask the stagnant air. "Someone—anyone—please."

I rub the glass along my bottom lip.

Who cares if I drink this?

Willow has a family that will take care of her. Adopt her, even.

Jacob and Kit no longer have a debt to pay.

My mother is dead.

And me?

I close my eyes and tip the glass slowly.

I'm here. I'm here. I'm here.

I lower the glass. Jacob's voice in my memories is smooth and deep. He nuzzles my hair and tells me I'm going to be alright. That I'm loved. That *he* loves me.

I'm here. I'm here. I'm here.

"God, I need help. I know I've been bad." I never pray, but if there were ever a time to start, it's now. "I know I don't deserve your help, but I need it, please. What should I do?"

I grip the glass tighter, waiting for an answer. Waiting for anything, or anyone, to tell me to stop. My fingers strain to hold the glass, and then it's clear. I gasp through my tears, and wipe my nose and face with the back of my hand. Then, I throw the glass.

It clashes on the floor and breaks, spilling everywhere I can't see.

I close my eyes and focus on the two words that make me feel less alone: *I'm here.*

CHAPTER THIRTY-ONE

Jacob

"How much?"

"A hundred for everything," she says, her hip leaning into my car.

I let my eyes rake over her again. Her hair is dark—nothing like Ruby's—and short, hovering just above her shoulders. She's slender with perky breasts, and her eyes look past me and not at me, which is exactly what I'm doing with her.

She points to the street ahead.

I nod my agreement. "I'll meet you around the corner."

Putting my car in gear, I roll forward in that direction. My grip on the steering wheel is so tight. Am I really doing this? Is this happening? This feels so wrong, but it's the only way I know how to deal with this. How many prostitutes will it take for me to learn my lesson?

The only thing in my mind the last couple of days are questions. Questions like, where could Ruby be? Is she hurt? Is she alive? Thinking about the possibility that her green eyes are now lifeless sends a stab of pain to my heart. I rub at my chest while pulling close to the curb and putting my car in park. I inhale. I exhale. I wait. Then, I pull out my flask and take a swig that'll help me calm down.

I tap my fingers on my thigh and count the seconds in my head to keep from thinking about Ruby. I know the drill. Money was discussed, a location set, and now, the rest. I've been here enough times in the last two days to know I'm close but not close enough. Pieces are offered but never the whole, and if I'm going to find Ruby, I need the whole. I need an address.

Ruby's face flashes through my mind.

I grip the sides of my head and will the image away. I take another drink. What am I doing? Is this the only way, really? The police report was filed, but it produced nothing so far. And if Bobby is behind this like we suspected, he would have reached out. He'd want us to know if he had her. But he hasn't, so here I am, parked on the side of some random city street ready to pay for some answers.

Fingernails tap on the passenger glass and I startle, quickly putting the flask in the cupholder and pressing a button to unlock the door. Eyes wide, I lock gazes with the pretty woman I paid for as she climbs into the passenger seat and tucks her hair behind–

I freeze.

The woman doesn't wait for me to say anything or make the first move. Her hand breaches the invisible wall between the driver and passenger seats and starts rubbing my thigh. I clench my fist around the steering wheel, tighter this time, and breathe through my nose.

Her hand climbs higher, and I panic. "What's your name?" I ask, grabbing the hand stroking my leg in order to stop her progress.

"Adele. You?"

I gulp and venture a look into her deep brown eyes. "Jacob."

"Hi, Jacob." She smiles and leans closer, her cleavage pressing into my arm. "Do you have the money?"

I hand her the money, then stare forward through the windshield.

Adele's hand starts moving below mine, but I stop her again. I have to keep focused on why I'm here, on what I need. The rush skates along every nerve ending in my body, and I breathe heavily.

I roughly set her hand back to her side of the car and notice her wide, confused eyes and parted lips. Dammit, I'm scaring her. I'm such a dick. I exhale.

"I'm sorry. I'm…not here for that."

"Okay," she says, but her back is still rigid.

What would Ruby say if she saw me right now? It looks worse than what's actually going on. I'm not here to sleep with Adele, but she doesn't know that, yet.

"I shouldn't even be here," I admit. "I should just go." I cover my face with my hands and lay my head back. "I don't even know if you can help."

My voice trails off as my head falls to the side, and I look at her eyes again. They are filled with tears, and as much as I don't want to, I see Adele for who she really is. I see her as Ruby.

"Fuck. I'm so sorry. Please don't cry." I gently rub her shoulder.

She covers her face as loud gasps leave her mouth. I'm a horrible person. I don't even recognize myself. I was supposed to come here, ask some questions, and leave. Instead, I'm making a woman cry.

Still covering her face, she mumbles, "I'm sorry. I-I'm still learning. I messed up. I messed it all up."

"No. It wasn't you at all. It's just…" a gust of air leaves my mouth through pursed lips. I don't even know how to explain this. That the woman I love is a prostitute and left me. That I'm the douchebag. That I hired Adele to tell me everything she knows about Bobby, so I can find him and maybe find Ruby.

I shush her, but nothing seems to be helping.

"Please don't…don't tell," she whispers.

I knit my brows together. "Don't tell? What do you mean?"

"Him," is all she says.

Don't tell him?

"Your pimp?" I ask.

She nods again, and I bite the inside of my cheek. Reality really is a bitch as it comes crashing down on me like a tower of bricks.

Adele is Ruby.

Adele is Kit.

Adele is Andrea.

I push up the sleeves of my hoodie and grind my teeth together. What is wrong with me?

"Please…don't tell him you hated it. I-I…can't go back… there," she says through sobs.

I piece her broken speech together. Gripping her shoulder, I try to catch her eyes. "Go where, Adele?" My mind is racing. Where would her pimp take her?

Her hands fall away from her face and makeup streaks down her cheeks.

"Go where? Where would he take you?" I press.

"The house. I can't go back!" she yells louder this time.

Lowering my head, I try to catch her eyes. "What house? What do you mean?"

She shakes her head and wipes at her wet cheeks.

I'm desperate. "Please. I want to help."

She looks out the passenger window and wipes the makeup from under her eyes, doing her best to calm herself. Her voice is faint, only a whisper, but we are close enough that I can still hear her.

"He took me to the house once. Tried to sell me. I was… he…" her eyes well with tears again, and her body begins to shake.

I rub her arm. "Shh-shh-shhh. It's okay. Take your time."

She swallows and tries again, her voice cracking. "He brought me there and tried to take me back. It almost…killed me. I-I can't go back. Please."

I stare at the woman beside me. She and Ruby look nothing alike, but I can't seem to look at Adele and not see Ruby. Her tears remind me of Ruby's. Her shadowed, sleepless eyes remind me of Ruby's. And her fear like Ruby's.

Whatever she knows about the house, I have to know. Maybe it's different from the Breaking House, but maybe it's the same? Maybe Adele can help me make all of my wrongs right. Coming here might not have been the worst idea.

I close my eyes briefly. "Look, Adele. I'm here, because I love someone else. But this house…I need to know everything you know about this house." My words are frantic and scattered, but I don't care. "I want to help you. I know it's hard to trust me. But…" I pause. "I need to know. No one should experience what you experienced at that house. I want to make sure of that."

Her sobs have quieted, and her eyes bounce between me and the outside world, likely deciding whether to believe me or not. Who am I but another man trying to get what he wants? But this isn't for me. This is for her. For Ruby and Kit. Andrea. All of the women who have a name and no one to ask what it is. I'm asking.

"What's your name?"

She wipes her nose with the back of her hand and tugs at the hem of her shirt. "Adele."

I shake my head, and my eyes bore into her. "Your real name."

She studies me briefly, then fiddles with one of her rings. I'm a risk she has to decide whether to take. "Sam," she finally says.

"Sam," I whisper. "I don't know why or how we ended up in the same car tonight, but we did. And though I feel like a jerk for scaring you, I want you to know that if you tell me everything you know, I'm going to make sure you never go back to that house."

She exhales and looks into my eyes, studying parts of me that I'm not sure I know are there.

One minute ticks to two, and finally, belief blooms inside me as she says, "Okay."

CHAPTER THIRTY-TWO

Jacob

"Kit! Open up!" I yell, pounding on her front door.

No response. I try again, harder and louder this time. "Kit! Beau!"

I pace their narrow front porch like a rabid animal, clawing at my hair and redoing my bun. Calling them didn't work, so I'm here. It couldn't wait.

I stop and scowl at the unopened door. "Come on." I don't have a plan B, and I don't have time to think of one.

The lock twists on the other side of the door, and I straighten. "Kit?"

The door swings open and a rough voice answers. "Guess again."

"Beau," I say through a ragged sigh.

"What the hell man? What are you doing here so late, and why are you screamin' and knockin' like this?" he says. "We gotta work tomorrow."

I check the time on my phone: 12:08 a.m. "Sorry. I didn't check the time before coming over here. I just really need to talk to Kit. It's about the house.'"

He lowers his voice to a whisper. "The Breaking House?"

I nod but don't follow it up with any words. Instead, I peer around to make sure we're the only ones. There's no one; it's the middle of the night.

He waves me inside the house.

I start pacing the front living room, and Beau disappears down the hall. Time is ticking. It's been days, hours, minutes, seconds since I've seen Ruby. The sound of a clock moving from one second to the next is a constant noise in my head. If she's there, at the house, I know where to start looking. If she's at the house, it's Bobby's fault like we suspected. I don't want to put Sam's life in danger, but I am based on what I know. She told me everything. And it's worth the one a.m. wake-up call.

"Jacob?" Kit asks groggily, wiping sleep from her eyes. She's wearing Beau's sweatshirt and plaid pajama pants, looking every bit the hour I'm waking her up at.

"Kit. I know where the house is." I say loudly, and she flinches. Bringing my volume down, I explain. "The Breaking House."

She rubs her forehead. "What? How?"

This isn't the time to explain the *how*. She already knows that part. "It's close. Closer than we thought."

She combs through her hair. "Like how close?"

"Farther down Figueroa."

Her eyes widen. "Near the blade?"

I nod. "Close."

She sits on the couch, and Beau sinks down beside her. "I can't believe it was there the whole time. Right under our noses."

Her gaze is staring past me. This blade is known for its high concentration of prostitutes. It's a lawless land where the police only try to keep it contained rather than stop all the activity.

I slow my pacing. "What if she's there? What if—"

"Ruby?" she asks.

I nod and lace both hands on top of my head. She's there, I can feel it. If this is the same house Bobby runs, and if he took Ruby, she'll be there. "What if she's there? What if he's drawing us in?"

Kit looks down at her hands and exhales. "What if she's not with Bobby?"

"Come on, Kit," I grind out. "Even you have to admit how coincidental this all looks. How many other houses like this exist?"

As much as I don't want to believe it was Bobby, I can't ignore how things line up. I feel it in my gut.

She crosses her arms. "There could be a lot."

"There could be one," I spit back. "And this is the only one we know of."

"She might not be there," she says.

"And she might be there right now." My voice is getting louder, but I don't care. Does Kit even care? "We have to find out if this is Bobby's place."

Kit's head snaps up. "No, we don't. We need to do this the right way and that doesn't mean breaking down the doors of some human trafficking ring all on our own. We need help—backup—someone that isn't as emotionally invested. This isn't something we want to make a mistake with."

Scratching my jaw, I let out a disbelieving scoff. "You want to tell the cops."

She exhales, and Beau places a hand on her back. "We need to do this the right way."

I throw my hands up and yell, "Is there such a thing? You've got women locked up in a house like prisoners and being sold to the highest bidder."

Sam's pimp had been the highest bidder. She wasn't even from California. She was trafficked here, and now she's stuck. Andrea already has a text waiting for her about Sam. I couldn't just leave her, but there's risk involved when a woman leaves the streets, especially one who has a pimp.

One woman at a time.

I scoff. "How am I supposed to just wait around for the cops to do something? We don't have time for that. Ruby could have already been sold. Maybe we're too fucking late already!" I scream. "How can you be so calm about this, Kit? You, of all people, should know we can't wait. You've already filed the missing persons' report with the cops. We have to do something else."

Beau holds out a hand. "Hey, man. Bring it down, alright? We want to help."

I point an accusing finger at Kit. "You wanted me to do something. Well, here I am doing it, and now you're not happy about it."

She lowers her voice. "Yeah, and I also know how important it is to wait for help and be smart about this stuff. I almost lost Beau, because I wanted to get back at Bobby. We have to think this through and not just react impulsively. It won't help Ruby, and someone could get hurt."

"Fuck it! I don't care anymore!" I carve rough fingers through my hair and tear out the elastic. "We need to find her. I *have* to find her. She has a daughter." My voice cracks as I think about Willow. I cover my eyes. "We have to find her."

"Jacob," Kit says.

I let my hands drop to my sides and look over at her.

She finds my eyes and holds my gaze. "How did you figure out where this house is?"

I shrug her question off. "I have my ways."

"What ways?"

I glare at her. "Ways."

She stands and stomps toward me. "Just tell me! If we're going to figure this out, you have to be honest. No more lying, remember?"

I look past her at Beau who nods once. Does he know? He can't. There's no way.

I exhale and stare down. "I can't."

"Why?" Kit presses.

"Because it isn't as important as finding Ruby," I say, looking at my hands.

The room is silent. Beau doesn't say anything from his spot on the couch, and Kit is probably trying to piece together all the words I'm not saying with the ones that I am.

She takes a step closer. "Did you pay for this information?"

I nod but don't meet her eyes, even though she's standing right in front of me.

"Did you sleep with her?"

I jump to defend myself. "No, I swear. I just went to talk to her."

Kit lets out a long, slow breath.

I knew Kit wouldn't approve of what I wanted to do. "You hate me."

"I don't hate you. I could never. I just…" her words trail off.

I study my shoes. The room feels smaller, and Kit's short frame seems bigger. My mouth runs dry. She's going to tell me off, I can feel it.

"Jacob…"

Here we go.

"When was the last time you had a drink?" she asks.

I'm shocked by her question. It has nothing to do with going to the streets or talking to Sam. It's so far outside what I thought she'd say, I stutter and take a step back. "I…well, I–"

Her eyes well with tears. "I know you've been struggling."

"How?"

"Your eyes," she says, and I follow the tear that rolls down her cheek. "They, uh…" she looks down and up quickly, "they look just like mom's. Darker, harder, more intense, like you're trying to focus on something that's really blurry."

My nostrils flare, but I say nothing.

"Her eyes looked like yours when she had a few drinks."

My cheeks burn and I bow my head, close my eyes, and pinch the bridge of my nose to keep from cracking.

She sniffs. "You could spend the rest of your life hating yourself for your choices like mom did, or the rest of your life forgiving yourself. It's not like you can take those drinks back, but you can change how you go forward. You can apologize, admit your wrongs, and get help." Her voice pleads as she speaks the last word.

Her words are gentle, but it doesn't ease the knife lodged in my chest. "I'm not like you, Kit. I'm not like Beau. Or Jordan, or Andrea. I'm…me."

She thinks this was one, simple mistake, but maybe it's gonna be in me forever like it was for our mom. Maybe I can't get rid of it like other people can. There are tears in my eyes that make it hard to see the firm set of her jaw, but I can hear it with every passionate word she speaks.

"You aren't mom," she says.

I lean a shoulder into the wall. "How do you know?"

She expels a breath. "I was there, too, when she said all her prayers through slurred speech, stumbled more than walked, and couldn't take care of us." She steps closer. "But we were there for each other through it all. I won't let you do that to yourself, because I know you wouldn't let me, either. I'm not mad at you for slipping up. No one is other than you."

I shake my head in disbelief and inhale sharply through my nose. I don't believe that. My life is a living testament to all the mistakes I've made and keep making.

Kit crosses her arms. "You think God's mad at you?"

I roll my eyes. Of course he is. How many times do I have to mess up to prove that?

"Don't roll your eyes. Just answer me," she prods.

"Fine. You want me to say how sorry I am? How screwed up I have to be in order to have a few drinks to get through the day after I was supposed to be better—do better—after rehab and therapy?" I start pacing again, needing the movement and the space. "I'm not like you. I'm like *her*!"

I thrust an accusing finger to the heavens, the place our mother always wanted to go more than stay with us. The place she drank herself to death in order to see what it was like. I let out a disbelieving laugh. "You want me to think God isn't pissed? He should be fucking *livid*."

She shakes her head, her voice hushed. "You're wrong."

I rake my fingers through my hair again. I can't take more of this. Hating myself in my own head is better than doing it in front of them.

"You have a choice, Jacob. You can beat yourself up from now through eternity. Or, you can admit you messed up and deal with it. We all screw up, and I can't promise you won't do it again, or you won't want to do it again, but you're either going to grow through it or not." She takes another step closer and reaches for my arm. "You don't have to be like her. You aren't powerless."

"I don't want power," I spit back at her.

Kit drops her hand away. "It's what you do with that power that matters. Use that power to help Ruby. To help all the women in that house who want to leave. And then, use that power to help yourself."

I stare at Kit, then Beau. Their unwavering stares make me want to hide, but only because I know what they're saying is true.

I can be different.

I can do something.

CHAPTER THIRTY-THREE

Ruby

My legs are wobbly as I try to stand. It only makes my head spin faster, so I grab the wall to keep steady. Rubbing my temple, I swallow multiple times to keep my stomach acid from rising farther than it already has. A foul smell of body odor and urine fills the room, and I want to gag. It's only gotten worse now that I'm not alone.

They brought a girl in today, but she hasn't spoken or made any sound. I checked that she was breathing, but other than that she hasn't moved. Taking a few steps forward with my arms extended out to feel for anything in front of me, I move toward the bed. The crunch of glass beneath my sneakers forces me to move faster.

The woman groans as I approach the bed. "Are you okay?" I ask.

Another groan releases as she stretches her legs out. Her face is shadowed, and I can't see much other than the tilt of her head and strain in her neck. Hovering above her, I wince when I see how much pain this one small stretch causes her. I clear my throat, but it's still hoarse.

"I'm Ruby."

She rotates her head side to side but doesn't speak or look at me.

I touch her shoulder. "Are you hurt?"

The woman's body isn't like what I expected as I scan her. Mainly because this isn't a woman. This is a girl. She can't be more than sixteen. Her arms are tied above her to the bed frame, and her t-shirt is dirty and twisting around her torso while her skirt is hiked up. It's singed with a deep red color. I immediately cover my mouth again.

Oh my God.

I didn't know…or realize…is she…hurt? "I'm going to get closer. Maybe I can help you. What's your name?"

The girl groans once and tries to form words, but I can't understand her. "What did you say?"

"I don't know." Each word she speaks sounds like it takes more effort than the last.

"You don't know your name?" I ask, careful to keep my voice quiet.

She shakes her head slowly and winces.

There's a gash on her brow, the skin around her eye swollen and discolored. Her bottom lip juts out farther and looks to be an uncomfortable size. She's young. Sixteen might be generous.

"You don't know your name," I confirm. "Do you know how you got here?"

She shakes her head again and attempts to open her good eye, but it wouldn't do any good since it's hard to see. Daytime brought a muted brightness through the drab curtains. Enough to see what you don't want to.

I settle a hand on my stomach. I'm weak, hungry, and tired. By the looks of it, she is, too.

"When was the last time you ate?" I ask.

She tries stretching her legs again and sucks in a sharp breath.

"Your leg. Is it hurt?"

She nods, keeping her eyes closed.

I walk my gaze down her body, scanning her leg for any bones or blood. There's bruising on her pale skin from what I can see but nothing else.

I swallow, my stomach wanting to revolt again. "We have to find a way out of here."

The girl tries to speak again, but it's hard for her. The words are jumbled, making it sound like she has an accent. The only two that I can make out are, "I tried."

"You tried to leave, and they hurt you?"

She nods again.

The bruising and swelling take up the majority of her face but beneath all of that, there's just a girl. A young, hurt, tired, hungry girl.

"How old are you?"

"Don't know."

"Do you have a family?" I ask.

"Don't know."

"How long have you been here?"

Her eyes close and her swollen lip begins to tremble. I shouldn't have asked so many questions. Whoever she is, she's been through hell. Slow-rolling tears escape the corners of her eyes, trailing down purple and green skin.

"Don't know," she mouths.

She knows nothing about herself. I exhale and stare at the ceiling. "It's okay. We'll figure this out."

I look at her, then the window. "We need to get out of here."

I feel for the zip tie securing her hands to the bed. It's tight. Tighter than mine was.

"Can you lift your hands up? I'm going to try and get this off," I say.

She strains to lift her wrists higher to relieve some of the weight bearing down on the tie, but it still isn't working. My hands shake wildly as I struggle against it. I fight the urge to pull and yank, knowing it would only make it worse.

But I'm frustrated. I grunt and say through gritted teeth, "It's not working." I give up with a long sigh and grip the headboard to hold me up. "I'm going to try the window."

The window shares a wall with the end of the bed. It's like a beacon in the middle of this dark room, calling for me to test it out.

I hold onto the mattress and shuffle toward the wall. Every step feels like knives stabbing into my muscles. It's like my body has been through battle without ever lifting a finger. My veins are thirsty for alcohol, but I don't have any. I threw it, and now I'm hot and cold, sore and tired. How are we supposed to escape like this?

I reach the window and start dry heaving while I brace myself on the wall. There's nothing in my stomach, but my body doesn't get it. I gag on nothing and drop to my knees. Pressing my palms into the wood floor, I spit out the extra saliva and wipe my mouth with the back of my hand. My head continues to beat against my skull.

I don't know if I can do this. I'm not strong enough.

"Window," the girl says in a raspy voice.

I sit back on my heels and stare up. The double vision isn't helping, but I can see it, the light glowing behind the ripped drapes.

I use the footboard of the bed to help me stand, swaying before finding my balance. The window is taller than I am and would take a boost to get to it.

"I can't reach," I tell her, feeling ready to curl back up into a ball on the floor. But I can't. The girl is hurt and needs help. If this was Willow, I would do anything I could.

I look from the end of the bed to the window. Does she want me to jump? There's at least a three-feet distance, and the bed still isn't tall enough, but I have to try.

Getting out of here just became more important to me. I'll figure out what comes next on the other side. Gripping the metal bed frame tighter, I put a knee up on the bed and pull myself up.

The girl shifts, trying to move her legs, but she grunts against the pain. She needs a doctor. She needs help. I'm her only help.

The mattress bends beneath my weight.

I have to do this.

I shift until my feet are planted beneath me.

This girl needs me.

I start to stand, but my legs shake uncontrollably.

Willow needs me.

I dry heave again but close my mouth and swallow hard.

Jacob.

With my eyes focused on the window, I stand and balance. If I lean forward, I'll be able to shift the curtains and peer outside, maybe even unlock it.

"I think I can reach it," I say to her and me.

I pitch my body forward, angling until I hit the wall with my forearms, wincing at the contact from the tender spot on my wrist that almost killed me. The deepest cut is scabbed over now, but the impact may have just opened it again. I breathe heavily and grimace at the pain shooting up my arms. I shift my feet in order to make sure they are under me, even if my body is almost sideways and press my shoulder into the wall, reaching for the curtains. "Almost. There," I grunt.

The corner of the curtain is between my fingers and I tug. The room fills with more light than I thought possible and I squint. My heart beats frantically inside my chest as I bend and contort myself in order to reach the latch. I strain as far as my reach will allow. And it's just enough.

"Got it," I whisper. "It's unlocked."

There's a shallow edge running vertically where the window panes separate, and I grip it with shaking fingers and pull. I tug and yank, but it doesn't budge. "Come on."

A noise sounds on the other side of the door, and I snap my head to peer over my shoulder. Heavy footfall thumps steadily on the floor boards. I pull the curtain closed and try to push myself off of the wall. It isn't working. I'm going against gravity rather than with it when I got into this position in the first place.

Pain shoots through my limbs, highlighting every bruise and cut pressed and carved into my body. I'm being too loud, I have to get down. I shove off the wall at the same time my feet lift from the bed. The door flies open as I slide down to the floor with a thud.

"What the hell do you think you're doing?" the man yells.

He's backlit as the light from the hall fills the room and highlights every part of his body that could crush me.

He stomps closer and grabs me by the shoulders, hoisting me up until my back is to the wall and his hand is on my throat. I gasp for air and claw at his hand that's pinning me, but it doesn't work. The curl of his lip is the last thing I see before closing my eyes.

I was so close.

Close to getting help.

Closer to Willow.

Closer to believing there's a way out of this.

But there isn't one.

CHAPTER THIRTY-FOUR

Jacob

I told Kit we'd try it her way and go to the police again. I'm regretting that now.

They took down our information and sent us on our way, saying they'd handle it. Someone will go out and scope the area to determine if there's a threat. My words alone weren't good enough like I thought. They needed evidence that women were being harmed, trafficked, or both. I didn't have that. And telling them the kind of man Bobby is didn't help.

"I need to get that evidence," I tell them as we stand outside the station. "I can't just wait around."

Kit crosses her arms and stares at me. "I know."

"You know?"

She nods. "It's reckless and crazy but…I would probably feel the same way if Beau were in this situation."

"Or Kit," Beau adds, like he's been through this before and he has.

She smiles warmly at her husband, then looks back at me. "But like I said, you're not doing this alone."

With everything that Kit's been through and all that I've kept hidden, she's still here. She's got my back.

"I'll need a lookout," I say with a wry grin.

She starts walking to the parking lot and calls over her shoulder, "Let's go. I'll drive."

We're halfway to the house, riding in silence as one street turns into the next. I go back and forth between thinking this is a good idea, or one that we don't come back from. But if there's a chance I could find Ruby, I have to try.

Sam didn't know an address, but the detail she shared about the house confirms what I remember and then some. Tan stucco exterior with a red-tiled roof, black door, small front yard with a rose bush under the front window. As far as appearances go, she said it's the nicest looking one on the whole block.

I roll down my window and let in a cool breeze to relax me. This place, these streets, have me wound tight. I haven't been back since I left and for good reason, because it isn't the kind of place to end up in by accident, and we're here on purpose this time. Back in the darkest parts of the city.

The lights aren't as bright over here. Everything is cast in that late night, early morning shadow. I'm sure other areas of the city are asleep but not here. Not on Fig where working hours start when others are just climbing into bed.

Kit has a firm grip on the steering wheel as we roll through the area, and Beau's hand rests on her knee. Women walk the streets, cars idle against the curb, and other passersby stop but don't linger. Kit doesn't stop. She keeps her foot on the gas and continues on straight until we reach the cross streets where the fast food restaurant Sam described is at. We park farther down only a few blocks away.

Kit kills the engine. "You have your phone?"

I stare at her steady gaze through the rearview mirror. "Yeah."

"Good. We'll stay here until you get back," she says.

"I should go, too."

We both look at Beau and fall silent.

Her voice is shrill in the close space. "What?"

Beau shrugs. "Jacob shouldn't go in there alone. If he gets caught, it's one against however many guys they got."

"Beau," I say. "You shouldn't come, man. Stay. I'll watch my back and call if I need anything. You've got a wife."

He turns in his seat and pins me with his stare. "And my wife has a brother. You're my brother, too. I can't let you go alone." He faces Kit and cups her cheek. "This isn't like before."

She scoffs. "To hell it isn't!"

"Baby, I swear to you I'll be back and I'll bring Jacob back, too." He shoots me a look, and I smirk. "We won't be long. I'll text you if we need help, and you'll call the police."

Kit shakes her head and drops her eyes to her lap.

I rub her shoulder from the backseat. "We'll be safe, Kit."

She exhales and looks between us. "You better be."

Beau zips his jacket and kisses Kit before we both exit the car. One more look in her direction, and we're off down the street; our footfall is the only thing I can hear.

This part of the street is quieter than it is farther up Fig. By all appearances, it looks normal for a weekday night at almost two in the morning. I scan each house looking for my target. I have a pretty clear picture in my mind and tell Beau through labored breaths what to look for. He checks the houses on one side of the street, and I scan the other. Other than differing shades of tan stucco siding, all of these one-story homes look similar.

"Look for a sign out front that says: *God Bless This House*," I say.

"For real?"

I nod, remembering the man who laughed about that sign. "Can't make that up."

We keep walking, scanning each house until I spot the sign. "There."

I stop Beau with my arm and point at the house. The sign hangs to the right of the door and is lit like a beacon, thanks to the porch light.

"That's gotta be it," he whispers.

We watch the place for any activity. The front window curtains are drawn, but a dim light can be seen through the fabric. The rose bush Sam mentioned is below the window with few other plants rounding out the simple but well-maintained landscape.

"This is it," I confirm and take a deep breath. I turn to face Beau, his dark skin even darker out here. "We need to think this through. We can't just walk through the front yard. There could be cameras or security outside."

"We have to get closer. I can't see nothin' from here," he said.

I nod, my lips pressing together in a grimace. He's right, we'll have to get closer than this. Exhaling, I flip my black hood up and reach into my pocket to feel the weight of my switchblade. God, I hope I don't have to use this. I don't own a gun, but I'd be a fool to step onto a traitor's turf unprotected, even with Beau as my backup.

I start walking down the sidewalk toward the house, but Beau grabs my arm. "There's probably an alley around back. Let's check that out first."

I follow him around the block and count three houses from the corner. There isn't any movement other than ours, but I frantically check the area with wide eyes, so I don't miss anything. I step carefully, crouch low, and force my heavy breaths through my nose. My heart feels like it's in my throat with how fast it's racing, and my knees want to buckle and toss me to the ground. But keeping calm is my only choice.

The cop we spoke to at the station said he'd send someone over tonight to check it out, but a few were changing shifts and others were on different calls. Who knows how long it'll take them. Did they already come by? If they show up requesting to check out the premises and they're denied, it'll be a dead end or extra time to get a court ordered warrant. We need this evidence. No one cares like we do. This isn't urgent to the cops like it is to us, or they would be here trying to find answers like we are.

The gate to the backyard is a simple latch that I flip up. Beau holds the gate and I slide through with him on my heels until our backs are flat against the side of the detached garage.

"Do you see any cameras?" Beau asks, catching his breath like I am.

I look up and scour the roofline of the garage. "I don't see any."

But I don't trust my eyes to catch everything. The moon offers some light, but it isn't enough to spot small cameras that are meant to be hidden.

The small window near the back sliding door has light pouring out of it and highlighting the cement patio in place of grass. There's no one around. It's quiet like it should be this early in the morning, but the lights inside are on. I start to second-guess if we're at the right house. It fits the description, but I expected it wouldn't be so straight-laced and normal-looking.

"I don't see any cameras on the house, either," I say, peering back at him. "But I don't know." I shake my head. "Dammit. I can't see very well."

Darting across the patio would leave me completely exposed. Would someone be watching?

Sam's tear-streaked face comes to mind. Kit's history with Bobby. Andrea's job at the shelter. Ruby holding a piece of glass. I can't turn back even if I wanted to.

I'm here for them. All of them.

My heartbeat is erratic, and I need to get control of myself.

Beau hits my shoulder and points to the side of the house. "There's gotta be a bedroom window on the side of the house."

The patio bends around the corner of the house. Other than a garden hose curled up on the ground like a snake, I don't see anything else over there. But I have to check. "Watch my back?"

His lips press into a thin line as he nods once.

Staring at the side of the house, I straighten and check the area a few more times. I'll know soon enough if someone's staking out the backyard. I bolt across the cement in a hunched position. My eyes are trained forward, focused solely on the destination ahead. I hold my breath the whole way until I make it to the side and sink down to my heels, pressing my palm into the house and waiting for someone to call me out, shoot me, anything. I swing my head around, and Beau gives me a thumbs up.

I nod once and look up. There's a window right above my head and one closer to the front of the house. Three deep breaths, and then I'm standing. I cup my hands to peer in, but the curtain is drawn and I can't see anything.

"Shit," I whisper and crouch down again. Keep calm. Think. The curtain won't let me see into the room, but maybe the window is open.

I stand quickly and flatten my palms on the glass, pressing firmly and attempting to slide it open. The window doesn't budge. There isn't a lip to grab hold of, so I drop back down and sit on my propped heels.

There's one more window to try on this side of the house. If it's locked, I'll have to go to the other side, which means trekking across the back patio again. There's nothing to hide behind and the possibility of being seen and getting caught is higher.

Staying low, I hurry to the next window. "Please," I say quietly into the cool night air. "Please open."

The window is smaller and a lot higher than the other one. I have to stand on my toes to peer inside and can still barely see in. The curtain is mostly drawn except for one slit toward the center. My breaths fog up the glass, and I use my sleeve to try and clear it enough to see inside. But I can't see anything.

I drop down from my toes and scratch at my jaw. How am I supposed to get this evidence if I can't gain access to the house? I cradle my head in my hands. Maybe there's no one here anymore. Did the cops already show up asking questions and it spooked Bobby into moving the girls? Would Ruby even be here? If not, I'd still have to find her. The nagging thoughts make my heart skip faster, and I look back at Beau.

Pressing my palms into my eyes, I shake my head and spin around to stand on my toes again. Seeing into the room isn't working, but I press my fingertips into the glass to create tension to slide it open. I struggle to gain leverage. "Come on, please," I say through gritted teeth.

The window jostles, and I fling my eyes wide and exhale rapid breaths.

I keep pulling. My fingers scream in pain, but as it loosens in the frame, I press them harder into the glass. It's working. The window is opening. I let go and there's only an inch of space, but it's enough to hear a faint voice as it filters through the slim crack. It's soft and muted. A woman.

I hook my fingers through the one inch gap and pull with all of my strength. I don't know who is on the other side. It may not even be a woman. Doubts creep into my thoughts, and I shake my head.

Red hair.

Willow.

Tears.

Scars.

Rescue.

I drop to my heels again and angle my face up to the now two-inch gap, breathing through my nose as I whisper, "Hello?"

I'm met with silence, but no one is storming the backyard and aiming a gun at me, either. I reach for the knife in my pocket, so I'm ready in case I'm found out.

"I'm here to help. My name is Jacob and I–"

"Jacob?" the woman's voice says.

I close my eyes as emotion surges through me.

I know that voice.

CHAPTER THIRTY-FIVE

Ruby

"It's me," he replies, and my shoulders drop.

I clutch the bed frame and scramble to stand, ignoring the slice of pain that registers on my wrist from the last time I saw Jacob. Renewed energy lights a fire in me. "Someone's here to help us," I say, shaking the girl's arm to wake her. I walk over to the window and press my hands into the wall. "Jacob. It's Ruby."

"I know," he says. "Are you alright? Are you hurt?" His tone is quiet but worried.

My forehead meets the wall. "Yes. I'm okay." Now that he's here, I am. He came.

"Look, Ruby—"

"There's another girl with me. She's young."

The girl grunts from her place on the bed as she shifts.

"She's hurt. I think it's her leg. She can barely move. How are we going to get out?" I ask, the desperation rising with my adrenaline.

He pauses for a beat. "I need evidence. I need pictures or anything else that I can show the police. Can you reach the window?"

I look up and stretch my arm. "Barely."

His words are so quiet, I have to strain to hear. "I need you to grab my phone through the window and take pictures of the girl. Can you do that? Can you get the pictures?" he asks.

I stare up at the window and nod, though the room is tilting. I don't care how, but I will. "Yes."

He doesn't reply, but I see the curtain move and Jacob's phone slides through the small opening. I stand on my toes and try to reach.

My fingers graze it, but the window is still too high for me to reach, especially from my toes instead of the bed. "I can't reach."

There's a small ledge framing in the window. Jacob is here now, and I have to do this for him, for me, the girl on the bed, my daughter. It may be the only chance we have, so I grip the ledge with my fingers and pull myself up, using my feet to crawl up the wall. My entire body shakes while I grit my teeth and close my eyes. The cut in my wrist strains, and I feel a trickle of warmth running down my arm. My foot slips and I hit the ground, but I don't let it stop me. I have to do this. Adrenaline fuels me and I jump for the ledge. I stare down at my feet, which slide down the wall with every small step I take, and then at the phone. One more step, a little higher, and it's mine. Keeping my eyes on the phone, I snatch it quickly, and then land on my feet. "I got it! I got the phone!"

"Okay, take as many pictures as you can and use the flash," he whispers.

I'm trembling as I swipe to find the camera and confirm the flash is on. One snap, two, then three. I take as many pictures as I can of the girl, the room, my face, and neck. All of it looks worse as it crosses the screen.

"I think I got enough. Here." I lift up like I did before and push the phone into his hand.

"I'm going to leave you my knife," he says. "Can you try to catch it if I drop it down?"

"Yeah."

He does, but it falls to the floor and slides under the bed. I lay flat on my stomach and reach my arm under to feel for it. Once in my hand, I stand. "Got it."

He's quiet, and I worry he's left without saying goodbye. My tone is frantic. "Jacob?"

"I'm here," he says through gritted teeth. "Did Bobby do this?"

He must be looking at the photos. "No." I exhale, close my eyes, and tilt my head back. "It wasn't him. But he was here. I saw him. We talked."

"I'm going to fucking kill him," he says.

The adrenaline wanes and my shoulder slumps against the wall as I cradle my wrist. How many times had I thought the same thing? It doesn't matter, though. The only thing I care about is getting out of here alive. That getting rid of Bobby was the answer. But there are more of him.

"I'll be back, I swear. I need to show the cops this evidence, and we'll be back. I lov–" his emotion cuts him off.

I cup my mouth at the thought of him leaving. Is this the last time I'll hear his voice? Will this be the last time he hears mine? I lower my hand and tilt my head back. "I love you, too."

"I'm coming back. I'll find a way to get you out of here, okay? Swear you'll stay strong."

Fresh tears fill my eyes at the sound of the desperation in his voice. "Okay," I nod. "I will. I promise."

Quiet sobs wrack my body, and I let them. I don't know how he found this place, or what he had to risk to get here, but he did. He found me. He came for me.

I bite my fist to keep silent while I slide to the floor and cry. For once, my tears aren't because of desperation. They burn a path down my bruised face and hit my lips. The tears even taste different.

They taste like hope.

CHAPTER THIRTY-SIX

Jacob

She's alive.

I repeat this as we run all the way back to Kit's car. She turns the key in the ignition and peels away from the curb as Beau gets her up to speed, but I tune them out.

She's alive.

We navigate side streets and run red lights all while I clutch my phone.

She's alive.

We park outside of the police station, and I dart through the front doors.

She's alive.

He hands my phone to the dispatcher. "I have your evidence." Opening the camera on my phone, I find the first picture and slide it across the desk. "You need to send a team out there now. Both girls are locked in the room and are injured. One of them is underage."

The man dressed in blue swipes through the photos. His brows are drawn in concentration as he studies each photo. He grabs his radio, spouting off directions. "We'll get a team out there right away. I'm going to want copies of these to file as evidence."

I nod as the cop hands me my phone back, and I forward the photos to the email he gives me. Relief doesn't fill my chest like I thought it would. We have the evidence, a team is on their way, Ruby will be rescued. But until she's in my arms—safe—I won't believe it.

I need to be there with her. It was torture leaving her again. I would have taken her with me if I felt the girl would be safe until we got back. But Ruby refused. She told me to go, and she'd stay back, even though her voice shook. She paused multiple times trying to tell me that.

It would be best if I went home and waited for the call that Ruby was safe. They have the evidence, the guns, the sirens, so I should just leave. But instead I'm heading out to my car, telling Kit and Beau to follow me in their car, and steering the vehicle onto the freeway to catch the next exit to Fig.

Back to the house and back to where the other half of my heart is.

I'M WATCHING THE cops watch the house. What's taking them so long? Another police car pulls to the curb. More backup officers, I'm guessing. There are four of them now between the three cars. Do they need more?

Tap. Tap. Tap. Pause. Tap. Tap. Tap. Pause.

I drum the pattern into the steering wheel until my thumb hurts.

It's taking forever. Why is it taking so long?

Kit shoots me a text from their spot near the alley. *Anything?*

The cops are still in their vehicles, so I type out a quick reply. *Nothing yet.*

I push out a breath and remind myself why: hostages and armed men.

Finally, two of the cops get out of their cruisers. The other two trail them but stay close to the sidewalk. The house is still just like the rest of the neighborhood. It's almost four in the morning, but it's still just as dark outside. One of the two cops who walks up the path, knocks on the door, then backs away to stand back beside his partner.

My leg is bouncing steadily.

No one answers, so they knock again.

Nothing.

I squeeze the steering wheel, twisting my palm to conform around it.

"Open the door," I say under my breath. No one answers, though.

Whoever is in that house, watching over the girls, wouldn't just open up the door and let the cops poke around.

I open my car door and slide out, kneeling while gently shutting the door behind me, so it won't make a sound. Every noise sounds louder than it usually does, but it's too early for the city to wake up. The muted clock of night offers protection against any other distractions. No one is walking their dog or driving to work. I bend at the waist and creep around the hood of my car and round the vehicle in front of mine. The cops are still waiting for someone to answer the door. But no one does despite the lights on inside.

The blood is pumping through my heart so fast I can hear it in my ears.

The cops by the door look at each other.

The others lean against their vehicles near the curb.

Another knock.

Silence.

Then, a shot is fired from inside.

The officers dive for cover around the front of the house. They duck low, crouching behind the naked rose bushes and drawing their guns from their holsters.

The backup cops post up behind the vehicles and pull their weapons out, too, aiming directly for the house. Everyone is ready for battle, except for me.

Ruby has my knife, but that won't be enough.

Another shot.

I cover my ears.

I have to get to Ruby. She needs me.

The alleyway.

All I see is Ruby's face in my mind, and then I'm moving.

CHAPTER THIRTY-SEVEN

Ruby

The gunshot was deafening as if it went off in the house. There were low voices from the other side of the door and footsteps padding across the wood floors before the shot was fired. It's started. I'm breathing heavily as we wait. For Jacob, for help, for answers.

I drop my hands from my ears and look over at the bed as the girl begins to stir. No one has opened the door yet, friend or foe. I don't know what we'll find. Jacob hasn't been gone that long. Did he make it to the police station? Did he show them the evidence? I crawl to the door and press my cheek to the ground to see if I can see something, but there's nothing. The gap is no more than an inch tall. There's no movement and no sound. It's like silence went up with the smoke of the gun.

Scooting backward, I sit up against chnst the bed and bring my knees to my chest. This helpless feeling is back. My world is crumbling around me, and there's not a damn thing I can do about it. God, I hope that shot didn't sink into someone's body.

Seconds pass when all I can hear is the rustle of the girl shifting on the bed. Turning, I look up at her. She's breathing. For now. So I continue to rock back and forth. *Come on, Jacob.* Something's up. Where did all the noise go? A muted curse, cabinets opening and closing, a toilet flushing. None of that exists anymore. Silence ticks on but not for long.

Another gun fires, and I startle.

Breathing through my nose, I peer wildly around the room, waiting for a monster to appear from the window or door. Where will it come from? A shadow passes through the slim light under the door and the floors creak. I grip my legs tighter and keep rocking. I keep breathing.

A rock clinks against glass, and I whip my head to the window. "Jacob," I whisper and rush to stand, but my balance is off and I trip into the bed frame. "Is that you?"

There's no response, but I still wait for one. The window is still pushed open, and I stumble back. The girl moans loudly when I land on her leg. "I'm sorry, so, so, sorry. Please. We have to be quiet," I whisper, a finger in front of my lips. As I stand, the curtain pulls back and Jacob's face fills my vision. Relief floods through me. "Jacob."

"Ruby. Come on. We have to get you out of here. The cops are out front, but whoever's inside isn't going to go down easy," he says quietly, hanging onto the window ledge. His eyes are wide and wild with fear.

I look back at the bed, and then to Jacob. "I told you. I can't leave her."

"You said she can't walk." He extends a hand through the window.

I study his outstretched arm as another gunshot absorbs everything.

"Come on! We have to go now!" he says, his voice rising above a whisper.

I shake my head as tears well in my eyes. "I can't leave her."

"Ruby," he pleads.

I shake my head, clenching my fists. "I won't."

He scans the area behind him. Then, groaning he pushes the window all the way open and lifts himself up.

"You can't stay here," I say, shuffling back.

His muscles strain as his upper body hangs suspended on the other side of the window. He grits his teeth and closes his eyes as he pulls himself. It's his sheer force of will that's contorting his large frame through the small window, then sliding down the wall.

He closes the distance between us in one step and cradles my face in his palms. "I love you. I'm not leaving you here." He kisses me and whispers against my mouth. "I love you."

Tears push forward, and I smile for the first time in days, maybe even years. This feels like a real smile. The kind that is felt throughout the whole body and not just the lips. My chest expands, and I feel like I'm singing even with my mouth closed as we cling to each other and my tears mix with my smile.

My words are muffled against his shoulder. "You came back."

He circles my waist with strong hands. "I'll always come back."

"I'm scared."

His breath pushes my hair. "Me too."

The girl on the bed moans, and I whip around as she tries to move. Sweat drips from her face and her hair sticks to her temples. I step closer and press the back of my palm to her cheek then forehead. "She's burning up."

"Where is she hurt?"

"I don't know." I point at her legs and run my hands along one of them. "She makes noise like she's in pain every time she moves her legs."

"Stomach," she says through a clenched jaw. She bends her head back until her chin is pointing at the ceiling and her neck muscles strain.

"Your stomach hurts?" I ask, but she's in too much pain to respond. "I'm going to lift your shirt."

She begins roughly shaking her head while looking at Jacob.

I look over my shoulder at him. "We have to get her out of here. She needs to go to the hospital."

His lips form a straight line before saying, "We can't get her through the window, but the cops are out there. It won't be long." He pulls out his phone and uses the light to assess the girl, stopping when he sees the cuts around her wrists. "From the ties?"

The wounds are cracked and bleeding. "Yeah, I used your knife to cut the ties. They were way too tight." I cover my mouth and shake my head. All these emotions are resting on the surface and with Jacob here, it's making all of them push forward.

He rubs my back and pulls me into his side. "It's okay. It's alright. We'll get out of here and take her to the hospital. Just a little long–"

Another gunshot cuts in. And then another.

"Ruby. I–"

Two more, and I stay buried in Jacob's chest, waiting for it to end. "I love you," I say through the noise. My voice cracks. "Take care of the girl. And…if we don't…Willow."

Jacob kisses the top of my head and crushes me against him. "I will. I swear on my life."

The handle to the room jiggles and Jacob pushes me out of his arms and throws himself against the door.

"I can't get it open! Get me the key," someone yells from the other side.

Jacob presses a finger to his closed mouth and nods quickly while holding my breath.

The entire door shakes as the person on the other side rams into it. I hang onto the footboard for support and close my eyes. Jacob is still barring the door, but I can't watch.

"I know you called them," the man's voice says. "I don't know how, but you'll fucking die for this! You think Jacob will want you after this? You're a fucking slut! A whore." He rams into the door again. "You hear me! A whore!"

Bobby. Bobby is here. On the other side of the door.

I cover my mouth and tremble at his words but bite my lip to keep from yelling back at him. The room is still too dark to read every emotion on Jacob's face, but his head shakes wildly back and forth and the whites of his eyes are piercing as he holds his position at the door.

I want to scream at Bobby and tell him he was wrong.

He's wrong about Jacob.

He's wrong about me.

But with only a two-inch door between us, I bite my tongue.

We have nowhere to go.

We're stuck.

The crack of splitting wood and a loud bang forces me to fall to my knees. Jacob rushes toward me and throws his body over mine. The weight of him covers all of me. I'm safe in the most unsafe place I've ever been. I'm protected while completely vulnerable.

Voices immediately fill the house, loud and commanding.

"Hands up!"

"Put the gun down. Now!"

"I said put it down!"

A gunshot. Grunts. A loud thump on the ground.

I scream and Jacob presses his chest farther into my back.

The girl moans loudly.

The voices are yelling.

Orders are being given.

Furniture scrapes on the floor.

Curses are thrown.

Someone knocks on our door. "Police. Open the door slowly with your hands up!"

Tears skate down my face and fall to the floor. The same floor I've slept on for days. The floor that holds so many of my tears already now has more; they pour out of me as I shake.

"We need help," Jacob yells.

He starts to hum and stroke my hair.

I focus on the sound rumbling inside his chest.

"We're locked in," he adds.

He keeps humming.

The girl begins to scream and shake the entire bed.

"Now!" His voice booms. Then, he's humming in my ear.

There's yelling, more pounding against the door until it breaks. Static from a radio as voices call back and forth. More bodies—strangers, and Jacob telling me it'll be okay. Arms pulling him off of me, and my own voice raw from screaming.

It's supposed to be over.

I want it to be over.

So, why does it feel like it's just beginning?

CHAPTER THIRTY-EIGHT

Jacob

The picture of him lying in a pool of his own blood on the kitchen floor flashes through my mind.

I had to walk past him, and I know Ruby did, too. The last shot fired went straight into Bobby's heart. He died. Those lifeless eyes he had when he was alive were the same when he lay dead on the floor, staring at nothing and no one. It was over for him. He couldn't hurt anyone else now, but what it took to get here was costly.

Convincing the police I wasn't trying to hurt Ruby, or the girl, was a challenge. They didn't cuff me, but they took Ruby and the young girl out separately to tend to their injuries, then questioned me at the scene. I told the police who the dead body was, what I knew of the Breaking House, and everything else that would help them put the other men behind bars. Eventually, they let me go.

Red and blue lights rotate and the ambulance peels away from the scene toward the hospital where the girl will be taken care of. She was writhing and screaming when they brought her out, and now the sound of an emergency bounces off of the early hours of the morning. Neighbors filter out of their houses, dotting their grass and lining the yellow tape stretched across the front yard. There are more cop cars, fire trucks, and ambulances than there were an hour ago. Time speeds up again, and it no longer feels like I can hear every tick of the clock.

I hurriedly round another rig, eyes wild, searching inside for Ruby. There are two other girls with blankets wrapped around their shoulders, and they startle when they see me.

"I'm sorry," I say, holding up both hands. "Sorry."

I jog to the next one and a waterfall of red hair drapes over a wool blanket, and I'm calling out to her as I approach. "Ruby!"

She turns and throws off the blanket, running to me. "Jacob."

I wrap her in my arms again and bury my face in her hair, taking the first real breath in the last few days. My whole body relaxes at her touch. We aren't fighting for our lives or fighting each other. She's safe here, in my arms. I'm safe in hers, too. I pull back after a few minutes and study her face. The purple and blue colors on her face and neck make my body temperature rise ten degrees. I cup her face. "Who did this?"

She grabs my hands, then threads our fingers together. "It doesn't matter."

But it does, because she's trying to hide her face from me.

I bite down on my tongue to keep from saying anything else. It's over, I have to keep reminding myself. She isn't being harmed by anyone. The bruises on her face will heal. The cut on her lip will eventually be gone. All of the external reminders of tonight will fade. But it's the ones inside her that I'm worried about. The ones you can't forget when looking in the mirror.

"Ruby," Kit says, closing the distance with Beau trailing her. She pulls Ruby into a tight hug. "Are you okay?" Kit studies Ruby's face and frowns. "Don't answer that." She hugs her again.

Beau places a hand to my back, and I nod once.

Someone clears their throat from behind me and we all turn. A large man with broad shoulders and dressed in blue greets us. "I'm officer Brady. I was hoping to ask you a few questions."

Ruby looks to me, then back at the officer, nodding slowly. She's going to have to relive everything to give him the information he needs to build a case. I want to tell the guy to get lost, but I don't know if that's possible. This was a crime scene after all. Snaking my arm around her waist, I tug her into my side and give her all the support I have.

Officer Brady pulls out a pen and paper and directs his attention to Ruby. "Do you know how long you were in the house for?"

Ruby picks at her fingers and shrugs. "Maybe three or four days."

It had been four days since I kissed her at her place and said goodbye. I felt the weight of missing her every single hour.

Kit takes a sharp inhale, and Beau rests his hands on her shoulders.

Brady scratches on his notepad. "Was the other girl in your room there for just as long?"

She watches his pen. "About the same time. I was alone for maybe a day or less, and then she was there. Her hands were tied and bleeding like they'd been that way for a while, though."

Brady nods, splitting his attention between Ruby and the notepad. "And did you know Robert Cheney before you were taken to this house?" the officer asks.

Kit shoots me a look and I mouth, *Bobby*. Was he Robert in other circles, and Bobby when he was hurting women?

Ruby peers over at Kit with a tight-lip smile. "Yeah. Loosely. I knew of him since I used to work on the streets and he was representing women there, too."

She shivers, and I rub her arm. Talking about Bobby is the last thing I want to be doing right now, but the sooner we do, the sooner we can put him behind us.

"Where's Bobby?" Kit asks.

Brady opens his mouth, then closes it.

"He's dead," I say.

Kit's lips part, and her shoulders visibly relax as Beau pulls her against his chest.

It's over. Finally.

The officer wraps up his questioning. "I'm going to type out these notes. Can I reach out later today?"

We both agree and give him my number to call. Kit and Beau say they'll meet us at home and to use my key to let ourselves in.

I face Ruby and start rubbing her arms again. "You okay?"

Her eyes are red-rimmed and full of unshed tears.

I thread my hand around the nape of her neck and press my forehead to hers. "I'm here. It's alright. You're safe."

"Am I?" she asks, shaking her head. "Willow. I could have lost Willow."

"I know." I wipe the tears from her cheeks. "We'll find a way for you to see her."

She stands straighter and sniffles. "Did the girl survive? Is she okay?"

I push the hair away from her face and shake my head. "I don't know. They took her to the hospital. I'll follow up. Let me take you home."

Her brows scrunch and more tears fill her eyes.

I realize my mistake. "Kit's home. We'll stay there."

She nods and leans into me, resting her cheek on my chest.

"Thank you," she whispers into the folds of my hoodie.

I relax my jaw and rest my chin on the top of her head. "You can stay as long as you want." In Kit's house and my arms.

She shakes her head, then draws back to find my eyes. "Not that. Thank you for coming back for me."

The fact that she thinks I could have done anything but come back for her is crazy. But that's not the kind of guy Ruby's been used to. She's had to deal with the Bobby's of this world. The ones that take and take and take until there's nothing left but a shell of a woman. I was that guy. But not anymore. Not when the Ruby's of this world remind me there's more to the story.

I press a light kiss to one of her cheeks, and then the other, kissing my way around her face hoping that by some miracle I can take away the physical reminders, even if the emotional ones take longer to heal.

"You're worth everything," I whisper in her ear and grab her hand.

We navigate through the vehicles until we reach mine farther down the street. Already it's quieter. A craving for this kind of stillness hits me. I'm ready to curl around my woman and hold her without any noise or distractions. She bends and tucks herself into the passenger seat, and I shut the door only to hear my name from behind.

"Jacob." Officer Brady waves me down and walks over to the car. "I was told you were the one to tip us off to what was happening here," he says, pointing at the house.

I shove my hands into my pockets and turn my back to the car. "Yeah."

He weighs his next words before speaking. "I don't know how many women have been through here, but we rescued five tonight."

I shake my head and grit my teeth. My jaw aches from all of the clenching and unclenching I've done tonight.

"I know. Apart from the women and girls—"

I hold up a hand and narrow my eyes. "Wait. There were other young girls?"

He rests a hand on his belt and nods.

My mouth falls open, and I rub my rough jawline.

"We'll take them in for medical care and make sure we contact their families. Unfortunately, in trafficking busts like this one, finding young girls in the house is common." He pauses. "I just wanted to say thank you."

I nod once and look from my car back to Brady and extend my hand. I'm not a savior. It's people like Brady that were cuffing me and putting me in the back of a cop car once. "I should get her home. It's been a long night."

He shakes my hand. "Of course. We'll be in touch."

Brady strides over to his cruiser and starts the vehicle. The ambulances begin closing up their doors with the other girls, taking them in for the medical attention they deserve. Two other cruisers are still parked along the street, and I have no doubt they'll be here for a while longer. There's a crime scene to record and photograph.

Walking back to the driver's side, I open the door and drop into the seat beside Ruby.

I follow her gaze to the house. "Let's get out of here."

We stay quiet the entire ride back to Kit's house. Now that she's out of danger, I don't know what comes next. She's seen things and experienced even more that I can't erase from her memory. I'll wait, though. I've done it before, and I'll do it again. For her.

The sunrise is starting to peek over the horizon, and I've never been more ready for the night to end and the day to start. There's something hopeful about a new day. Whatever happens before the sun rises again seems smaller in comparison.

She grabs my hand and laces our fingers together. I squeeze once while studying the road. I won't let go. Not today, tomorrow, or any day in the future. I'll be here, by her side.

We'll get through this. Together.

CHAPTER THIRTY-NINE

Jacob

"I got a call from officer Brady."

The name alone is enough to cause Ruby to stiffen. It's only been a few days since we spoke to him at the scene, but anything referencing the house understandably puts her on edge.

She rubs her arm. "Oh yeah?"

I nod. "He said they're planning to release the girl from the hospital either today or tomorrow."

She perks up. "Really? Do they have a home for her?"

"Brady said they found her parents. They filed a missing persons' report more than a year ago."

Ruby's rigid shoulders relax, and she falls back onto the couch in Kit's living room. She's been staying here before starting a program at the Journey Center. Her idea, not mine. But I didn't argue. I think it'll be really good for her, even if we won't get to speak for a year. I know how the process goes, and I've got my own therapy to restart and focus on, too.

"Do you want to go see her?" I ask, treading carefully.

This girl has been on her mind. She talks about her nearly every day.

Ruby stares at her half-eaten bowl of oatmeal. "I don't know. Should I?"

I lean forward on my forearms. "It's up to you. I can drive you there after breakfast if you want. I don't work until later today."

She nods but continues to stare at her bowl.

"I think I should go," she finally says.

I grab her free hand. "I'll be right there with you."

She finds my gaze and smiles. It doesn't reach her eyes, but I know it's because of everything that's weighing on her. "Okay."

I PARK IN the visitor parking lot and kill the engine. I shift to face her. "Are you sure you want to do this?"

She stares blankly out the front window, then meets my eyes. "I need to. We both went through this and that ties us together in some weird way." Her eyes fall to her lap. "She's so young."

I stroke the back of her hand with my thumb and listen.

"She reminds me of me." Her voice is low and strained.

I want to scoop her into my lap and hold her, because I want to protect her from everything. But if she feels she needs to do this, I trust her, and will support her regardless.

I lean over and kiss her cheek. "I'm going to buy you the biggest slushie when you're finished."

She laughs and makes my heart sing with that one sound. "Promise?"

"Promise," I say definitively. "That'll be our first stop."

She nods, then takes a deep breath. "I'm ready."

A tap on the passenger window startles Ruby. "Kit?"

I open my door and round the hood just as Ruby gets out to embrace Kit.

"What are you doing here?" Ruby asks. "I thought you were at work."

Kit nods in my direction. "Jacob thought you could use some extra support."

Ruby looks at me. It's enough to make me fall in love with her all over again. There's gratitude and love and everything in between. All of it flashing across her features in a split second before she turns back to Kit. She pulls her in for another hug.

I invited Kit, because she knows what it's like to live in fear of a man. But she also knows what it's like to create a life afterward. I'm a small part of that rebuild and if anyone can show Ruby it's possible, it's Kit. Ruby doesn't have to do this alone. She has people. We are those people.

Turning on her heel, Ruby wraps her arms around my neck and buries her face in my shoulder. "Thank you."

I rub her back and trail my hand down her arm to grasp her hand. "I'll see you in a bit."

She smiles and a little bit of warmth reaches those deep green eyes. Kit loops her arm through Ruby's, and the two walk across the parking lot. The red of Ruby's hair catches the light and dances like fire licking the air. It's as bold as she is. As confident as she's becoming. It's a glimpse of every part of her that I love on the inside but on the outside.

CHAPTER FORTY

Ruby

Elevators, stairs, hallways, doors, and then finally, we're checking in at the nurses' station and facing the open door of a near stranger. I don't know why I want to do this. But there's something tugging at me that I have to.

Kit squeezes my arm. "Do you want me to come in with you?"

I shake my head and pivot on my heel to face her. "I need to do this…alone"

She nods and hugs me. "I won't be far."

She leaves, and I turn back to the open door. All I have to do is walk in, and then the words will come, right? I can do this. Whatever I find in this room, I can handle it. It's just emotions. Just feelings. Just memories I'll have to relive. Kit said this was part of the healing process—facing the past in order to live in the future.

But this is hard. This is a recent past. *Last week* kind of recent.

My heart is racing, hands sweating. Is it supposed to feel like this? Like I'm walking back into that house with bound wrists and a hand gripping my arm?

I peer down at my wrists. No ties.

They aren't real.

What if I'm not ready to face everything that happened? What if this girl isn't ready to face me? I do a full circle, looking for which direction Kit walked off in. I need to find her. I don't think I can do this, yet.

"Hi, you must be Ruby."

I whip around to the door and stare blankly. Brady must have mentioned I was coming. I didn't expect to be known.

"I'm Esther, Hannah's mom," she says.

I don't respond right away. I'm stunned. *Hannah.* That's the girl's name. And this…this is her mom. I look her up and down. She's wearing jeans, a sweater, and sneakers. She looks so normal. Not like a mother who would lock their daughter in a bathroom. Not like my mother.

"Uh, h-hi," I start, then shake my head. "Yeah. I'm Ruby."

She clasps her hands in front of her. "I'm so glad you came. Hannah hasn't said much. A few one-word answers here and there but nothing more. It's…" her voice catches, and she covers her mouth with her hand. "It's so unlike her." Her eyes find the ground. "It *was* so unlike her. She was taken when she was only fifteen, now she's sixteen, but…a totally different person."

Sixteen.

I nod slowly and wipe my hands on my jeans. I didn't know the Hannah before the house, but after spending days with her in that room, I know there's more to what happened. She heard and saw things I didn't.

She dabs her cheeks with a tissue she pulled from her pocket. "Sorry. This is all just…a lot. We want to help her, but her father and I don't know how."

I swallow the lump in my throat. I've never known a mom like this. One that wants to help her daughter through everything she's been through. Not one that puts her through it, like mine did. Hannah has everything she needs and she's right in front of me. I don't know what I could say or do that would help any more than the love of her parents already is.

"It's okay." I look through the open door and back at Esther, her eyes pleading. "Keep being there for her," I say. "Don't stop, even if it seems like nothing is happening. She'll feel it."

More tears overflow from Esther's eyes, but she nods and mouths the words, *thank you.*

I smile then hesitantly step into the room. The shades are wide open, letting a stream of sunshine through the windows. It's deceiving, really. I've been outside and know how crisp the fall air feels today. The bed is empty, and Hannah is seated in one of the chairs by the window, staring. Most people don't appreciate the light of the sun until all they've seen is darkness. Then, the sun is pure magic in how it lights the whole earth. It's the biggest and brightest star there is, so I guess God should get some props for creating it.

Not wanting to startle her, I tap a knuckle on the wall. "Hey."

She looks over at me with a blank expression that tips into a pinched smile before looking back out the window.

Her warm brown eyes compliment her chestnut hair, and there's a rosy tint to her cheeks that can be seen over the fading bruises. Her back is hunched and the huge hospital gown seems to swallow her tiny body. But she's a beautiful girl. The kind that looks innocent and homely here in a hospital room or tied to a bed.

I approach slowly, my destination the chair across from hers. She continues to stare out the window as I sit, and I follow her gaze. Maybe there's something out there that I'm not seeing. But the more I look, the more I think it's just the fact that an outside exists.

I cross my legs and look between her and the window. "I hear you'll be going home with your parents today."

She glances at me briefly and nods.

I close my eyes. She should have been living with her family this whole time, going to school, hanging out with friends, and writing her crush's name in her diary. Instead, she saw the ugliest parts of humanity.

Opening my eyes, I swallow. I never had any of that either. "Your mom seems nice."

She picks at a nail, gaze locked on the world outside.

I keep trying. "Your eye is almost completely healed."

She stills, and I bite the inside of my cheek. I shouldn't have said that. What is wrong with me? I don't have the words she needs. I don't know what to say. It's not like we shared a good experience. We shared a nightmare.

A nightmare.

The bracelet I spin around my wrist hides the marks left from the ties. "I've had nightmares about…the house." I steal a glance at her before looking out the window again. "At first I thought I could handle it. They'd go away, right? But they haven't. They've gotten stronger, more violent, more terrifying."

She shifts in her chair and crosses her socked feet.

I lean back in my seat. "I'm going to get help. I need someone to talk to about everything that happened. I don't want to, but if I don't…" my thumbs chase each other in my lap, and I sigh. "If I don't, then they won't stop."

She fiddles with her gown, shifting uncomfortably.

"Your family is here to help you get through this. But…" I stare at her face. "I am, too."

Her lips press firmly together and turn down in a frown as her eyes fill with tears. She's trying to stop them with the sheer force of her own will, but the emotions are too powerful. They want out.

She blinks rapidly and stares at the ceiling, trying to stop them. But they won't listen. She gasps and covers her mouth. Her eyes shut and tears pour out of her one after the other.

I'm hesitant to reach out and comfort her. Touch isn't something that feels good when it's felt so bad. Instead, I lean closer and lower my voice.

"You should have never experienced this. I'm so sorry you did." My own tears press against the backs of my eyes. "If you ever need someone to talk to, I'm here."

It's the same thing that Jacob's been saying to me all along—Kit, too. I think the only reason I can say those words at this moment is because I've heard them. I know what they sound like coming from someone else's mouth.

She palms her cheeks to clear the tears, but more rush forward and fall down her face. She presses a hand to her stomach. "My baby."

My baby?

It all starts to come together. She was pregnant. This baby would have been a problem in Bobby's world. A problem that needed to be solved. My head spins and a flash of anger fills my chest, causing me to sit up straight.

Her shoulders shake, and she's gripping the fabric at her stomach, twisting it in her bony hand until her fingers turn white.

I was twenty-one when I had Willow. Not a child, but not an adult, either. She's the only good that came from everything. Holding her for the first time felt like I was holding hope. Like there was more to life than what I'd seen. She made me want to be better. I still do, even though I've failed her. I want to be better for her.

I extend my hand toward her, palm facing up. Her eyes are still spilling tears as she looks at me but grabs my hand with all her strength. The same strength that got her through hell. And the same strength that will get her through this. There's a bridge between us now, and it isn't just our shared experience that has built it. It's our shared pain and the hope for healing.

I don't know what the journey looks like for her.

I don't know what it looks like for me.

But, I want to know.

CHAPTER FORTY-ONE

Three Months Later

Ruby

The room is dark. Why is it so dark? Why can't I see?

The floor is cold, but the room is colder.

I'm alone.

A hand caresses my face, but I jerk back and hit the wall. The hand doesn't care, though. It follows me. It laughs deeply and takes over the silence. That laugh. This hand.

Panic tightens around my throat.

The laughing gets louder.

"Stop!" I scream and scramble to my feet, but they're bound. I can't move them, like I can't move my hands.

The laughing is louder, filling my ears to the point I can't think. I forget my name. Who am I? How did I get here? Who is this?

"Please," I beg.

More laughter.

I wake with a jolt and sit up straight in bed, panting, then flip on the light. Air. I need more air. My forehead is damp with sweat, and I wipe at it like I try to wipe away the memories.

"It was just a dream," I tell myself in a hushed tone.

I breathe through my nose and try to stay calm, but the echo of laughter is on replay in my head. Kicking off my covers, I sit up and pull my knees into my chest.

"Ruby?"

I manage to croak out, "Yeah."

Andrea is already walking into the room.

"Bad dream," I whisper.

She sits on the end of my bed. "Another one, huh?"

I nod. It doesn't matter the months that separate me from that house, the nightmares make it feel like it just happened.

The light casts the small shared room in a soft glow, and the sight of it puts me at ease. I'm not in the house. There's a dresser, clothes hanging in the closet, my roommate, and Andrea. It's nothing like the Breaking House. I'm at the Journey Center, a rehab center nestled in the heart of L.A., exactly where I've been for the last two months.

"Is it the same dream or different this time?" Andrea asks, curling one leg up on the bed.

My fingers are ice, and I press them to my face. "The same one. He uh…" my mouth is so dry, so I swallow and clear my throat. "He was laughing this time, though."

Her brows knit together. "Why do you think he was doing that?"

She doesn't have to say his name. She knows exactly who my dream was about—who they're always about: Bobby. There have been plenty of nights she sat on the end of my bed while I fell back asleep, because his image was burned in my brain. Him laughing; him pouring alcohol down my throat; him holding a knife to my neck.

I start picking at my cuticles and lower my voice. "I don't know."

She extends her hand for me to grab. I squeeze all of the support out of her gesture.

"You might want to write it down in your journal." She nods at the notebook sitting on my nightstand. I've had it since day one. A gift from Kit when I started the recovery program here. "You see your therapist tomorrow, right? Might be a good time to talk to her," she says.

My breathing has finally hit normal and come down from frantic. "Yeah, I'll see her tomorrow." I meet Andrea's eyes. "Thanks."

She smiles. "Of course. Do you want me to stay?"

I pause for a second to consider but shake my head.

She pats my folded knee and stands.

"Do you think they'll ever stop?" I ask in a small voice.

She turns to face me and smiles. "I do. The only things waking me up in the middle of the night anymore are Amelia, and the nightshift here."

I smile. "Don't take this the wrong way or anything, but do you ever wish you had a different job? You know, not one that reminds you every day what you went through?"

I don't know if I'd want to watch people detox like Andrea has to. In the trafficking house, I went days without alcohol. But I'd also gone long stretches without food or water, too. The process had already begun, but after I was rescued and started eating and drinking water again, my body begged for a drink. Just one, I'd say. Then two or three later, I'd hate myself. It didn't matter that I didn't want it, because my body did. I had to go cold turkey just to be here, and in a couple months, I can't even count the number of times I've thought about it. Too many times.

She steps closer, keeping her voice down. "That's exactly why I wanted this job—to remind me of everything I've been through."

I lift one brow. "Why?"

She crosses her arms and shifts on her feet. "It probably seems crazy to say it that way, but when I see the women who come through these doors, it's humbling. I remember what it felt like to be them—to be you—and honestly, it gives me all the hope in the world. Addiction isn't the end. It can be a beginning, too. It's a beautiful process, really. We aren't broken because of our traumas, we are forgiven because of them."

I nod slowly then look at my hands. "If you say so."

"One day, Ruby," she says, then quietly backs toward the door. "You'll know it. Call if you need anything."

Closing the door softly, I lay down and hug my pillow. Everyone keeps saying that it'll get easier. The cravings, the new habits, the nightmares. Hell, I told Hannah it would get better, too. Now I'm not so sure, though. I'm tired of counting the days. Thirty days sober, thirty-nine, forty. I'm ready to start my life again.

I close my eyes. *Willow needs me to count the days*. I'll keep counting and marking off my calendar until I get to wrap her in my arms. Jacob, too. I have people counting on me. It's why I wake up every morning, get dressed, do my chores, eat, and pray. I have people that I want to have the healthiest version of me.

Instead of clicking off the light and falling back asleep, I sit up and grab my journal and pen, and flip through it to a blank page. One day, I'll give all these letters to her. She'll know what I went through, and that I thought about her every day and every second it was hard. In the meantime, I put pen to paper and scrawl at the top of the page like all the others: Dear Willow.

LIGHT FILTERS INTO the room, and I'm bathed in warmth. I stretch my arms above my head and feel the heat of the sun on my skin. A quick scan of the room tells me my roommate is already up and dressed, so I hurry to do the same.

Every day is the same here. I wake up with intention and not a headache.

After writing the last words in my letter to Willow last night —All my love, Mama—I went to bed wanting to call her. To hear her little voice on the other end of the phone ask me if I've had the new slushie flavor at 7-Eleven, or if I could be any animal, which would I choose. The first time we spoke on the phone before I came to the Journey Center, she asked if she could come to my house.

I stuttered, unsure how I should answer that. "I, uh, well. I don't know. Maybe. Someday." When I have a home.

"Do you have a dog?"

I laughed. "No. I've never owned a dog before."

"Never?" she asked.

"Never. But I've always wanted one."

"Me too. Molly and Stan have a cat. It's fine," she said.

I coughed out a laugh. "Cats are sweet, too."

She blew out a breath. "I guess."

"Maybe one day we'll get a dog then," I said.

I smile just thinking about it as I tie my sneakers. She reminds me of that dog we're gonna get one day every time we talk. And it's the promise of the dog I don't own yet that reminds me our story isn't over, yet.

I head out of the room and walk to the small office on this floor. There are so many long hallways and doors in this renovated hospital building turned rehab center that I'm still figuring it out. For now, I know the route to the cafeteria, the thrift store I work at, and the chapel where we meet daily. It helps that all of my time over the next year will be spent on this campus, and I'll have plenty of time to learn it.

I knock on the door and peek inside to spy Janet, the women's floor supervisor, at her desk. "Hey."

She pauses what she's doing on her computer and staples her chair around. "Hey, Ruby. How are you?"

I tuck my hands in my back pockets and smile. "I'm good."

She smiles back. "What can I do for you?"

I hook a thumb behind me. "I was going to do some chores, and then I was hoping to call Willow."

"No problem. Let me know when you're finished and you can use my desk phone," she says with a wide smile that causes her eyes to crinkle at the sides.

I thank her and head to the storage closet to get the broom and mop to start my chores. It takes me the next hour to finish them, and then I'm back in the office, dialing Molly's number. Calling her to speak with Willow was approved since Willow is still so young. But other than my daughter, I can't speak to anyone outside these walls, so my entire focus can be on the program.

Molly picks up. "Hello?"

"Hi, it's Ruby."

"Hi! Let me get Willow for you."

"Thanks, Molly."

Things haven't gone back to the way they were before I showed up drunk to the park. Then again, I'm pretty sure things were worse before. I didn't like Molly and Stan, and even though I still worry that Willow likes them more than me, I've accepted them for who they are: foster parents. I'm grateful for them, even if I struggle with how to feel.

"Hi, Mama!" Willow exclaims.

"Hey, baby!" I lean back in the chair, my smile wide. "How are you? What are you up to?"

"I'm playing stuffies."

"Oh yeah, do your stuffies have names?" I ask.

She goes on to tell me each and every one of her stuffed animals' names as well as their favorite foods and activities, which sound a lot like hers. I can't keep the smile off my face the entire time. It makes everything feel worth it. The pain, the growing, the long days, and even longer nights. And the moment I get to hug her will bring it all together.

"I want a gold dog with long hair," she says out of nowhere.

I twirl a lock of my hair. "Okay. What should we name it?"

She's quiet for a few seconds. "Olaf."

I scrunch my nose. "Olaf?" I laugh. "Where'd you hear that?"

"He's in my favorite movie. He's a snowman, but he's funny. I think our dog will be funny."

I hold the phone tighter and rest my head on the back of the chair. "I like that name. Olaf it is."

I check the time on the wall clock. Almost time for work. "I have to go soon."

"Okay," she groans. "Mama, before you go, can you sing me my song?"

I sit higher in the chair and dip my chin to my chest. "Yeah, I can do that."

My voice isn't as rusty these days. I sing all the time. In the shower, during church, walking to and from the cafeteria. There's always a song on my mind but never as often as Willow's song— our song, Little Willow.

The weeks after I was rescued from the house, I stayed at Kit's and every night before Jacob went home, he would sing me this song while I fell asleep. Just like my mom did. For all the struggles my mother faced, she gave me something with that song.

She gave me a prayer.

I didn't know it, but those words were an anchor in the middle of my storms. It still is. And now, it's Willow's, too.

I close my eyes, letting the words form on my tongue and work the magic they're so good at doing. Like every other time I've sung our song, I finish and Willow claps.

"I love you, baby," I say with tears clouding my vision.

"I love you, too, Mama."

CHAPTER FORTY-TWO

Ten Months Later

Ruby

I smile while sitting on my bed, journal propped on my lap while I twirl my hair. There isn't a single word written between the lines. They all still live in my head.

Graduation was tonight. I completed my program.

Three-hundred and sixty-five days down and a lifetime of recovery to go. I'll keep counting days, marking them off on my calendar and celebrating when I hit milestones, because every one of them is a miracle I want to remember.

Soon, I'll move out of this room and back in with Kit and Beau. I have plans to keep working at the thrift store here on campus and continue therapy. There's so much good ahead.

I doodle along the top of the page and hum softly. I've missed Jacob's voice. I want to listen to him sing and play guitar while I just stare. Tonight was the first time I'd seen him in an entire year. His hair was the same, tied back in his usual bun. His light eyes that saw only me were the same. His hands as they wrapped around me were the same. But his kiss felt new.

Everyone else was around, watching us as we hugged, and he gave me a chaste kiss to my lips that has left a vibrating hum in my veins since that moment. I cried and didn't stop crying until he hugged me goodbye and said he'd pick me up tomorrow. I miss him. Like Willow, I've written him letters. Ones that will make him cry and others that will make him blush.

Time hasn't been our friend. We'd be good together, I think, but every chance we've had hasn't been the right one.

I hope now is the right time. *Tomorrow.*

A rhythmic knock on the door pulls me from my thoughts. "Come in."

Kit appears with a wide smile. "Hey. Are you busy?"

I shake my head and set my journal beside me on the bed. "I was just journaling, and then probably going to go to bed."

"Are you up for a little fun?" she asks with a smirk.

"I'll grab my hoodie."

WE DRIVE OUTSIDE the city toward the coast. Los Angeles can feel like its own island. But the farther we drive, the more I realize there's more. The air is different out here. Heavy moisture hangs low, and it's cooler than in the city. Kit hasn't told me where we're going, but I haven't asked, either. It'll be well past curfew by the time we get back, but she said Andrea is fine with it. We pass the time talking and swapping stories. She tells me about the time she broke a heel while walking the blade and had to go barefoot. I tell her about the time I put my wig on the wrong way. There's laughter now where there wasn't before.

"Almost there," she says as we roll down a street with palm trees lining the way.

The white caps of the waves as they rise and fall are still visible, even with the darkening sky. It's calming in the way it makes music. Crashing and thundering as it echoes off of the earth. It's confident in its strength while also boasting of it every time a wave rolls over the sand, higher and higher each time.

"I've never been to the ocean before," I admit.

"What?" Kit's voice is at least five octaves higher than mine.

I keep staring at the water. "I mean, I've seen the ocean but never stopped at the beach."

My mother never brought me as a kid. We didn't have a car, and bus fare to visit the ocean wasn't a priority. The few foster families I stayed with lived inland, and by the time I left and was on my own, I focused on work.

"That's criminal," Kit says with a disbelieving laugh. "It's time to change that."

I look back at the road as she pulls into a parking spot that's a sidewalk's distance from the sand. "Wait. Really? This is what we're doing? It's dark."

She smiles wide and reaches for a couple of blankets in the backseat. "Come on," she says, opening her door and heading for the sand.

I quickly follow her lead, but she stops me with a hand on my arm, pointing at my shoes. "It's better if you take them off."

We slip off our sandals and trek through the sand. It's softer than I imagined it would be as my feet sink with every step, making it difficult to walk. I look down, bypassing sticks, jumping over wet and dry seaweed, and eventually, screeching when cold water touches my skin.

Kit laughs and pulls me back. "Can you swim?"

I shrug. "I don't know…is it hard?"

I think about the bathtub. How I'd sink below the water and wish I'd never surface. It didn't require swimming, only sinking. Ending my own life feels like a smaller part of me today than it did back when I started the program. It's still there on those hard days, but the same people who are there for the good ones are there for the bad. I have support and ways to cope that work better than alcohol.

She shakes her head. "But you better stick close to me."

The air is saltier here. I can almost taste it on my tongue, and my skin is sticky to the touch. Being at the beach makes me wonder what else I'm missing out on. I haven't been to the mountains, either. Are they just as amazing as the waves?

Kit walks at a clipped pace, but I hardly notice. I'm focused on looking out as far as I can to the point where the water and sky meet. It doesn't exist as far as I can tell. But it does, and I think that's what it's like to have faith. Knowing something's there even if you can't see it. One day, I want to see it. I want to go to the places that my eyes can't see.

The waves crash loudly, absorbing any other sound around us. A large fire that comes into view with a group of people surrounding it. Kit heads straight for them and soon multiple sets of eyes are on us, some familiar, others not.

"Ruby, I want you to meet some of the most amazing women I know." She waves her hand around the circle. "Andrea, Janet, Olive, and Dina."

"Hi, Ruby," the group says at different times and volumes.

I lift my hand in a shy wave since everyone is staring at me. Then, Kit trudges through the sand to the other side of the fire, pulling me with her, and we sit in beach chairs between Andrea and Janet.

"Hey, I'm Olive," one of the women with straight black hair says, pointing to the woman beside her. "And this is Dina."

Dina adjusts her glasses and waves with a smile.

I nod and smile back warmly. "Hi."

Kit drapes a blanket around my shoulders, then snuggles one around hers. Her tanned face glows in the light of the fire, and she reminds me so much of Jacob. I feel my stomach drop and press a hand to it. Every time I think about what it will be like to see him again tomorrow, my entire body responds. I'm ready for every one of our tomorrows.

She looks at me, her hand drawing an invisible circle around the group. "We've been getting together for more than a year, meeting on the beach, someone's house, or wherever else we can find."

Low chuckles break up the quiet. "Like the roof of the Journey Center?" Dina asks.

"It has the best view, that's for sure," Andrea adds.

Janet croaks out a laugh. "Until you got us caught by security for laughing so loud, Olive."

Dina covers one-half of her mouth and speaks to me. "Olive does have a really loud laugh—"

Olive cuts Dina off by pinching her leg.

Dina screeches and rubs her knee. "Feeling spicy are we?"

Kit laughs and turns back to me. "We wanted to create a safe space for each other. We've had therapists, coaches, mentors, and teachers, but friends are important too."

Andrea leans forward. "Everyone in this circle has a past, a lot of them similar to yours. And we wanted support." Her voice quiets. "We wanted to know we weren't alone."

Kit nods. "There's no judgment here. Only listening ears, plenty of hugs, honesty, and love. We don't all have the same story, but we have the same desire to keep growing. To keep living."

"We're here for you," Janet says with a smile. "For now and later."

There's a weird thing that happens when you go without something for so long that it makes it feel normal. Until, it's in your life and you realize what once felt normal just isn't anymore. That's how I feel looking at these women. I've never had *friends* before. Acquaintances, sure, but friends, never. I didn't think I needed them.

Well, I need them. I don't know how I survived so long without them.

The conversation flows easily for the next couple of hours. I learned that Olive's laugh really is unmatched in volume. Dina is blind without her glasses, thanks to drugs. Andrea went back to visit her mother's graves last month, which is something she'd never done. I learned that Janet has never been on a real date—one that she wasn't paid to go on that only included sex—and Kit and Beau are going to start the process of adoption.

I learned other things, too.

I'm not the only one who's been abandoned.

I'm not the only one who's had a messed up family.

I'm not the only one who's struggled with addiction.

And I'm not the only one trying to heal.

CHAPTER FORTY-THREE

Jacob

"I have another stop I want to make."

There's no turning back now.

I head down a side street, prepared to take the next right, and then a left before we're there.

Ruby's hard stare burns a question mark into my cheek. "Where? I thought it was only going to be me and you today?"

I picked her up from the Journey Center bright and early. I didn't want to waste another minute before being able to see her. Kit had to beg me to give her space after graduation last night. And even that came with a bribe. She owes me groceries and a car wash. Seeing her walk across the stage made me eager to hold her. I never wanted to kiss her so badly. So, when she walked out the door with sleepy eyes and sluggish feet, I picked her up and kissed her like I meant it.

A smile tugs at the corner of my mouth. "You'll see."

She peers out the window, looking for more answers.

"Will I cry?" Ruby asks, stirring her slushie that I brought her.

I glance over as she raises the straw to her mouth. With windblown hair and rosy cheeks, she steals my breath. Her, like this, alive and looking lighter than I've ever seen her.

"Yeah. You'll cry," I say, looking between her and the road.

She bites her straw and stares straight ahead.

One more turn, and then she'll know. She's been here before. Regularly, in fact.

I pull up to the curb, throw my car in park, and cut the engine. Hopping out, I jog to open her door. I offer her my hand, and the tears have already started their path down her cheeks.

She cups her mouth and her eyes well with tears. "She's here?"

I reach behind her and grab the slushie out of the cupholder —the slushie I got but didn't drink—and hand it to her. "She's here."

As much as I wanted to keep Ruby all to myself today, it wouldn't be fair. Not when Willow has been waiting for this moment, too.

She grabs my hand, and I help her out only to wrap an arm around her shoulder. "Are these happy tears?" I ask.

She nods. "How did you do this?"

"I made some calls," I say with a shrug.

Janet played a large part in reaching out to Molly, and then Tess to plan this. They were more than willing to help organize the surprise. All we had to do was show up.

She slowly shakes her head, then looks out at the park. Molly, Stan, and Tess wave at us from a park bench near the playground.

"Ready?" I whisper into her hair. "I'll be here when you get back."

She nods and starts walking in their direction, eyes locked on her destination.

I lean my back against the passenger door and stare at the ground with a drawn out sigh. We pulled it off, and I know seeing them together, even from afar, will only cement that.

"Jacob?"

I snap my head up to find Ruby walking back, so I push off the car. "Yeah?"

She holds out her hand in invitation.

I don't hesitate. I walk toward her and lace my fingers with hers.

"Come meet my daughter."

I swallow multiple times, emotion trying to best me, then let Ruby lead us to the waiting group. We're met with smiles, hugs, hellos, and how are yous. That is until Willow comes bounding over, wisps of blonde hair flowing behind her, smiling as big as Ruby.

"Mama!" she shouts. "You're here!"

Ruby kneels and opens her arms. "I am. I'm here."

Willow jumps into her arms and hugs her neck. "You brought my slushie!"

Ruby stares up at me, and then back at Willow. "Yeah, baby. We brought your slushie. I can't see my favorite girl without one."

"Did you bring the puppy?" Willow asks.

Ruby laughs so hard she loses her balance and falls back. "I don't have a puppy…yet."

Willow crosses her arms. "When?"

"Soon, baby. Real soon," Ruby assures her.

I help Ruby to her feet, and she introduces us. It takes Willow no time at all to tell me all of her doll's names. I can't stop smiling at how she possesses the skill to bounce while talking. I'm not around many kids, but she's mesmerizing. The constant movement, laughter, and interrupted stories all add to her charm. Ruby oohs and ahhs at different times and I look on, seeing another layer of her in Willow that has me thanking God I'm here.

"You can be it," Willow says, pointing at me.

I look to Ruby for an explanation and happen to catch the wink she gives Willow. She then meets my eyes and when they connect, I'm positive every feeling and thought I've had in the last five minutes is written on my face.

But Ruby only shoves my shoulder and says, "Tag, you're it," and takes off running while holding Willow's hand.

I rock back on my heels and close my gaping mouth. Molly, Tess, and Stan snicker as I try to figure out what just happened. Smiling, I cup my hands and call to them. "You've got a ten-second head start!"

I start counting under my breath.

One Mississippi. Two Mississippi. Three Mississippi…

Is this what it's like to have a family?

Four Mississippi. Five Mississippi. Six Mississippi…

If it is, I think I want one.

Seven Mississippi. Eight Mississippi. Nine Mississippi…

I want family dinners. I want bedtime stories. I want slow mornings in bed. I want tag. I want holidays. I want movie nights. I want red hair splayed across my chest and blonde hair in every family photo.

I inhale through my nose. There's so much wanting that lives inside me. It's been growing. And now, it's like an explosion beneath my rib cage. I rub my chest, trying to ease all of the want coursing through me. But it doesn't help. This isn't the kind of ache that goes away. It's here for good, I think, because that's exactly how long I'll love Ruby: forever.

I start jogging to the playground where Ruby and Willow are, pumping my arms and finally calling out, "Ten!" I wiggle my arms through the bars on the structure, trying to reach them, but I can't. They both squeal and run to the other side. My smile gets bigger with every near touch. They keep slipping out of my reach, and it only fires me up more. "I'm going to catch you!" I yell to their backs.

Ruby wiggles her foot off the side of the steps, and I leap but miss. Again.

"Hurry! Down the slide," Willow whispers loudly to Ruby, gripping her hand tightly.

I pretend not to hear them and run to the opposite side of the play structure. It isn't until they are both flying down the spiral slide, Willow sitting on Ruby's lap, that I reroute and meet them at the bottom.

"Gotcha!" I say, lifting their feet off the ground in a big bear hug and tickling their sides. They both squirm, and I set them down.

We're all panting hard and stumbling around the bed of wood chips on unsteady feet. Ruby reaches up and brushes the hair from my face. I don't even remember when my hair tie came out. Somewhere between running toward everything I want and finally stretching my arms to grab them.

I catch Ruby's hand in mine and smile at her. Emotion swells on the inside of my chest, and it's spreading. It's taking over my body and making its home here. I'm not complaining. It's new and different from the love I have for Kit. For Beau or James, or anyone else.

This love was fought for. It was buried treasure I had to find.

I press Ruby's hand to my cheek and close my eyes.

A small hand pushes my stomach, and I grunt.

"You're it!" Willow screams before taking off again.

She's laughing so hard and tripping over her fast moving feet. She manages to stay upright as she dashes up the steps and runs across the floating bridge.

"No head starts this time," I call to her.

Pressing a kiss to Ruby's cheek, I chase after Willow.

I never thought I'd see Ruby again after we first met, or that I would fall in love with her. Meeting Willow isn't something I expected to happen, either. But that's just it. There are parts about loving someone that I didn't understand until I was in it. The unexplainable joys. The unplanned turns. The good, hard, ugly, confusing, beautiful parts.

But somehow, love finds a way.

CHAPTER FORTY-FOUR

Jacob

I'm so nervous. My stomach drops every time I think about the next hour. Am I ready? Is it too soon? Will I mess up?

I pace the living room, rehearsing everything under my breath until the doorbell finally rings. Half-tripping to answer the door, I manage to open it quickly.

Ruby's full lips greet me with a smile, and her green eyes are bright without any makeup on them. "Hi."

I exhale a sharp breath. "Hi."

She's effortless in cotton shorts and a t-shirt, her hair spilling down her back and over her shoulders makes my heart race faster.

I can do this.

I step aside for her to come inside my apartment, and when the door closes, I slide my arms around her waist and crush her against me. "It's good to see you."

I've been waiting for this moment all week. With our work schedules and individual therapy groups, it's difficult to find a day we're both free. But today is that day.

And now is the time.

"I missed you," she murmurs against my neck.

Goosebumps rise all over my body at the feel of her breath on my skin. It's been a while since Ruby and I have been together physically. We've kissed and hugged, but the feel of her body against mine might as well be foreign at this point. We need to change that.

"I missed you, too." I stand taller. "Are you hungry?"

She shakes her head. "I had lunch with Kit at the Journey Center."

"Thirsty?"

She smiles. "I'm good, I swear. I know where all of that is anyway and can get it myself."

Jabbing a finger into my rib cage, I twist away as she passes me and heads for the living room. I like that she's comfortable here.

It's been a long week. I picked up more shifts at the restaurant, because I have plans. There are things I want now and making them happen has taken time. The weeks and months Ruby spent at the Center, I spent scraping together every dollar I could. I've been surviving off of whatever leftovers Kit and Beau have in their fridge in order to make things happen.

But Ruby is worth it.

I sit beside her on the couch, propping my feet up on the coffee table. James is gone tonight, and I confirmed repeatedly that he better not show up. I don't want any interruptions. No sister, friends, brother-in-law. I made sure to lock the door, because I'm close to finding an excuse to not do what I'm about to do.

She rests her head on my shoulder.

My heart thumps faster. "I've been writing," I say, clearing my throat. "Can I play you a song?"

Her eyes find mine. They're soft and inviting, like a warm blanket on a cold day. "Let's hear it."

I stand and walk over to my guitar stand. Every step makes my pulse thrum with anticipation. Picking it up, I sit on the coffee table across from her and strum the first note. I've practiced this hundreds of times. The words, the notes, the meaning behind all of it. James was sick of hearing it, but I didn't care. I kept at it, practicing until every chord and every word felt right.

Ruby nestles deeper into the couch and puts her feet on the table next to my legs. She nudges me, and I smile without looking into her eyes. If I do, I won't be able to focus. I'll get distracted by the love there.

I lit a candle before she got here. The smell of cinnamon and vanilla fills my senses, and I focus on that while my hands instinctively play the chords, sliding up and down the neck of the guitar. I pick at the strings and bob my head to the beat I'm creating and the rhythm of love I'm sharing.

She taps her feet as the music builds, her legs picking up the beat. The words are on the tip of my tongue, ready to free fall along with my heart. I didn't know it would feel like this. That love would feel like I'm flying. And when I'm not soaring, I'm diving deep, the waves crashing over me. I'm helpless and buried, a complete goner.

My voice is low and gravelly as the story begins to take shape. The struggle, the regret, and the wanting all come into focus as I let my heart lead. From the moment we met, the space in between, and now—all of my time—is hers.

> *I want you to stand*
> *Right here by my side*
> *To place your hand in mine*

I steal glances at her, careful not to linger for long or else my nerves will quiet me. She leans forward and laces her fingers, resting them under her chin as I ease into the song. I bounce my leg as the string picking turns into strumming and melds into a full crescendo of sound that fills my whole world. I hear nothing else. Only the promises.

I want you to be mine

For then, for now, forever

My strumming slows. I'm no longer living in the words but in the reality of them. I look up and meet Ruby's tear-filled eyes. She wipes at a falling tear, and then another.

I pluck softly, more weightless than I thought possible.

"Marry me." My voice is nothing more than a faint whisper, but it sounds loud. The loudest kind of sound when the rest of your life hangs in the balance, waiting for what comes next.

More tears appear in her eyes and spill over. "Yes," she says, and then her lips are on mine, her fingers threading in my hair.

I drop my pick and cradle her face in my hands, kissing her soundly, sealing everything I just sang.

The tears hiding out behind my eyes push forward and fall. I run my thumb along her cheek. It's so smooth and delicate. Opposite of mine and so perfect. The scars are still there, but the cuts have turned to faded memories. I swear I'll spend the rest of my life paying special attention to those scars. Especially the scars.

"I love you, Ruby. I love Willow. I love *us*."

She holds my wrists, her watery gaze connecting with mine. "I love you, too." Her eyes fall to her lap and another tear drops. "We're…a lot. It isn't just me. It's Willow. And Molly and Stan. Tess." Her voice gets louder as she waves a hand through the air. "It's my problems and issues. This isn't going to be easy. I'm… complicated."

I relax my brows. "Ruby, look at me." My gaze is strong and unwavering. "I want *you*. I want to walk through the mess with *you*, because there will always be a mess."

Fresh tears are in her eyes when she lifts her head. Her voice is barely above a whisper. "Promise?"

I set my guitar on the couch and pull her onto my lap, smoothing my hand over the back of her hair. "I promise." My voice shakes with each word.

I want so badly for her to believe and trust me. But it isn't one moment that will do this. It's every moment going forward. All the minutes between now and forever.

I shift my weight and reach into my pocket, extracting the ring I bought weeks ago. It's simple. Nothing big or extravagant, just a gold band that never ends.

I slip it onto her left ring finger and trace the continuous circle with my thumb. "Forever," I say. "That's the name of the song."

Her mouth curves upward. "Forever."

EPILOGUE
One Year Later

Ruby

His back is facing me as he flips something on the stovetop with a spatula. Wet curly hair swivels around his shoulders as he moves barefoot around the kitchen. Some days, I lean against the door frame and watch him. This man with the smooth voice that makes my toes curl and sings his girls to sleep every night is ours.

The music is turned down low, but I can feel the beat in my chest from across the room.

He moonwalks backward, turns on his heel to spy me watching, and throws me a saucy grin. Olaf, our one-year-old golden retriever, comes sprinting out of the bedroom from behind me, tangling himself in Jacob's legs.

"Hey, buddy." He scratches the dog's ears, and they flop from side to side.

I don't hide my amusement as I walk toward them. "You had time for shower sex and pancakes?"

He smiles and turns back to the stove to flip a pancake on the plate. "I always have time for both."

I come up behind him and wrap my arms around his waist, resting my chin on his shoulder while he pours more batter in the pan. "Pancakes on a special day."

Olaf barks, and we both turn to shush him. "Jealous are we?" I ask the dog. Apart from Willow, Jacob is his favorite. I just feed and walk him every day.

He wags his tail, then trots to the living room to chew on his favorite bone when he sees I have no intention of letting go of his favorite person.

Jacob spins around and grabs my hands. "A special day means dancing."

"Willow is still asleep," I say. "And I don't want Olaf to bark again. You know how he gets when we dance."

He peers up at the clock, and then at the dog. "Willow will be up soon, and Olaf is chill. Come on, please?" He peppers my face and neck with kisses.

I already know what I'll say. With my lips to his ear, I whisper, "I'll dance."

The words aren't even out of my mouth before he's grabbing my hand and spinning me in a full circle. My hair is damp as it floats around me, and I swivel my hips in sync with his.

Olaf is too busy chewing his bone to care about the dancing for once.

Jacob does a full circle, rotating his feet in and out as he follows me around the kitchen. Back and forth we trail one another, leading the other in a rhythm that we take turns repeating. We aren't strangers to kitchen dancing. It happens at least once a day. With music playing in the background anytime we're home, it's not hard to get swept up.

I sit on the beat and raise my hands above my head, snapping my fingers to the bass coming through the speaker. His large t-shirt nearly swallows me and the pajama pants I stole from him are tied as tight as they would go, both billowing with every move I make.

The trumpets in the song meld with the hip-hop roots, and I love it. Feeling him this close lights me on fire. We got married six months ago and haven't spent a night apart. Maybe we're still in the honeymoon phase of our love, but life has never tasted so sweet.

He reaches for my hand and spins me until my back meets his chest, and he scoots us toward the stove so he can flip the pancakes. I laugh when he refuses to let me go. His chin settles on my shoulder, and every nerve ending in my body comes alive at his touch. I feel everything. The fresh scent of mint rolls off of his skin and hair from the shampoo I rubbed into his scalp earlier and the earthy, spiced scent of his aftershave on his neck makes my skin flush.

I turn to face him and put my other hand on his chest just above his heart. His beautiful, kind, loving heart. The one that somehow accepts me, even when I don't accept myself. The heart that fights for me, even though I'm tapped of strength. And the heart that made room for two instead of one.

His lips are so close to mine that I can feel his breath on my face as he sings me the rest of the song. I can hardly find my own breath pattern with him singing about wanting to love me, trust me, and never let me go. All of it skipping my ears and sinking straight into my heart.

His thumb traces my bottom lip with slow movements that make my head spin. Every touch, every word, means something with him. Words that had no meaning before I met him. They were empty and dull. But now they're full and sharp.

He presses his lips to mine, moving my head with only the strength of his mouth. I wrap my hands around his neck and play with the long hair falling down his back. Tugging gently, I angle his mouth and sink deeper into him.

"Ew."

We both fling our heads in the direction of the small but demanding voice.

Olaf barks a few times, then sidles up to Willow as she rubs her tired eyes. "Do I smell pancakes?"

Jacob squeezes my waist and lets go, rushing to grab the pancakes he forgot about while kissing me. They're burnt to a crisp, but he holds up the plate with the other hot cakes. "Your favorite."

"Did you get the good syrup?" she asks, plopping down in a seat at the table. Olaf sits
dutifully at her feet ready to eat his breakfast of fallen pancakes and lap up drips of syrup.

He gives me a side eye then says to her, "Only pure maple syrup for our girl."

"Good. I don't like that fake shit."

Our mouths drop open when we hear Willow curse, then immediately look at one another and point.

"You!" he says.

"No way! That's your cuss word," I say with a breathy laugh.

Willow props her head up with her hand. "A kid in preschool told me, okay?" she sighs. "He said it's another word for poop. Fake syrup tastes like poop."

We both start laughing so hard and don't stop until our sides ache and tears stream down our cheeks.

"Is someone gonna get me my pancakes?" Willow yells. "We have to go soon!"

I sober up first. "I got it."

"Wait." Willow holds up one small hand. "I think I want dad to cut them. He makes the pieces bigger."

I shoot a smile at Jacob. "Dad?"

He wipes happy tears from his cheeks. "I got you, baby girl."

Jacob

"DO I LOOK alright?" I tug at the neckline of my button up shirt nervously. It's tight and stifling. I'm already sweating beneath this suit jacket, and we haven't even left.

Ruby walks out of the bathroom, and I forget how uncomfortable I am. She's stunning. The broad smile on her pink lips and thick curly hair she spent an hour on warrant my gaping mouth. I would understand if I'm drooling. The outfit she chose is a forest green form-fitting dress with a curved neckline and long sleeves. It flares out just above her knees and highlights all of the parts of her I love. I eat her up with my eyes, and then my mouth, placing a few kisses on the soft skin of her neck.

She straightens my tie and smooths her hands over my lapels. "You look great," she says, kissing the corner of my mouth. "Nervous, but great."

I exhale and play with the top button on my jacket. "I don't want to mess this up."

She crosses her arms and smiles. "You won't."

God, her smile is so pretty. It eases some of the tension in my shoulders.

I turn back to the full-length mirror, and she wraps her arms around my torso, peering around me. "You're going to do great. Everyone we love will be there."

Before I can say anything else, a big voice and small body bounds into the room. "I'm ready!" Willow announces. Olaf is on her heels but isn't able to stop as fast and slides on the slick floors, bumping into my leg. I pet long strokes down his back and tell myself I'll need another pass with the lint roller.

The glimpse I catch in the mirror of Willow isn't enough. I spin quickly to take in the beautiful pink dress with ruffles, lace, and sparkles everywhere that she picked out. Ruby gave her free reign to choose whatever dress she wanted. This was the first one she spotted and the only one she considered. It's perfect. Willow is beaming. The light blush on her cheeks only highlights her joy.

"You're beautiful, Willow. Good call on the dress," Ruby says.

She fluffs the layers. "You look pretty, too, Mama."

Ruby does a full spin in her heels and curtsies. "Thank you."

I kneel down, and Willow does another full spin in front of me while Olaf tries to lick my face. I nudge him away so he doesn't get more hair on my suit. "I think you found the best dress in the whole store."

"Mhm," she hums and tips her hips side to side like a bell. "The whole world actually."

I wink up at Ruby. The smile on Willow's face is contagious. "I'm looking forward to today."

She steps closer and smooths my hair back. It's longer now, held back by an elastic and butterfly clip that Willow gave me. Her hand finds it right away and she tilts my head. "You're wearing it!"

I laugh. "Of course. You gave it to me to wear. So, I'm wearing it."

We were at the last park visit before Willow came to live with us four months ago, and she told me if I have long hair that I'll need a clip to wear. I accepted the clip with purple butterflies painted on it and wore it the entire day. Its permanent home is next to a picture on the dresser of the three of us. But today, I wanted every reminder of Willow with me.

She studies me through a squint and nods her approval. "It looks good."

"Thank you," I say, kissing her cheek and standing back up. "Are you ready?"

She does another twirl with Olaf. "Ready!" Her short heels click on the floor as she walks out of the room, a hand on her hip, and Olaf trailing her. "Come on, guys!" She waves for us to follow.

"Go find Auntie Kit and Uncle Beau. We'll be right there," Ruby says. She sucks in a breath beside me and releases it slowly, reaching for my hand.

I kiss her cheek. "Are *you* ready?"

She folds into my chest, and I settle my hands on her hips as her arms circle my neck. Her nose trails along my freshly shaved jawline, and she inhales deeply before kissing me softly. I forget where I am and what's happening when she kisses me like this.

She pulls back. "I'm more than ready. This might just turn out to be the best day of my life."

I lift an eyebrow. "Even more than our wedding day?"

She nods and kisses me again, running slow fingers along the nape of my neck.

I cradle her face in my hands. "Our wedding day was special. You in that white, beaded dress walking barefoot down the beach was…" I kiss my fingers, like a chef who made a perfect dish would. "It was perfect. You were a dream," I say. "You still are."

She laughs and hooks a thumb toward the closet. "Maybe I should wear that dress."

I lock my arms around her tighter and shake my head. "No time. This dress is perfect, too."

She smiles, and I kiss her cheek. "What about the day we bought this condo, and you and Willow moved in? Is today better than that day?"

Her nose scrunches, and she nods. "I think so."

This condo wasn't cheap. It took months to save up the down payment. I worked extra hours at the restaurant whenever I could, including as a server, which earned me extra tips. Surprising Ruby with our own place to call home was priceless.

She screamed, cried, and leapt into my arms. Then, she kissed me until we were close to giving Willow a sibling.

I kiss her forehead. "Okay, okay. I got a good one. What about the day you graduated from your program?"

Her hands run along my shoulders, picking off stray pieces of dog hair.

It took months and a few close calls before she held that certificate in her hands. She hasn't had a sip of alcohol for over a year and neither have I. It was a hard win, which made it all the more sweet. I framed that piece of paper and hung it in our bedroom. Every time I see it, I remember the pride in the set of her shoulders and the glow radiating off of when they gave it to her.

She bites her lip in thought. "Today will be better."

I kiss her bottom lip that was trapped between her teeth, giving it extra attention as my lips press lightly to hers.

I smile against her mouth.

"What?" she asks.

"I got it," I say with excitement. "Willow's fourth birthday party. The bounce house; the clown who made those balloon animals that looked more like penises than animals; her cake that you made and used three bottles of sprinkles on."

She throws her head back and laughs. "Oh, I remember. It was only two bottles and for my first cake, I think it turned out pretty good."

I laugh with her. "It was great. The best cake in the world."

"Don't even joke. You had three pieces!" She slaps my arm, and I grab her hand. "Today is still going to be the best day of my life. But I'm not sure Willow will agree. That party was epic."

She presses her forehead to mine, and I rub my hands along the soft fabric covering her arms. "I think you're right. Today is the day we're going to celebrate every year until we die," I say in a hushed tone. "We'll write books about it. Tell random strangers in the grocery store how it happened. Our grandkids will know every detail of today by heart. And every night for the rest of our lives, after I make love to you, I'm going to thank you for making this day a reality for me. For choosing us."

Her voice cracks and her eyes fill with tears. I catch the first one that falls, like I do every time she cries, then kiss each of her hands. "I love you, Ruby. I love Willow," I say. "Let's go have the best day of our lives."

She grips my hand tighter and nods.

I'm nervous as hell, because I've never done this before. But there are no doubts living inside me. None. I'm confident in this decision.

"Are you coming?"

We look at the doorway, and Willow has both hands on her hips, tapping a foot on the floor as Olaf's tail beats rhythmically on the door.

"Hey, we just got here." Kit peeks around the door frame. "Sorry, I tried to keep her busy, but she's excited."

Beau steps around Kit and shoves his hands in his pockets. "We all are."

I laugh and lace my fingers with Ruby's. "Let's go then!" I shout, and Willow pumps her fist in the air.

Beau and Kit clap their hands and dance their way down the hallway, spinning Willow like a ballerina.

Today is the most important day on the calendar. We've all been looking forward to it since the moment I said, "I do," and Ruby is right: it'll be the best day of the rest of our lives.

It's the day I legally adopt Willow and make her my daughter. Forever.

WHEN I SAID my vows to Ruby with the waves dancing behind us, I told her I'd take care of her and Willow. I'd lay down my life again and again. To be there in all times and all seasons. When temptations knock on our door and the sun doesn't feel bright enough. I promised to love like my life depended on it.

I meant every word then.

And I feel every word now.

"Please rise for Judge Brown," the bailiff instructs.

I stand up from my place beside Ruby and grab her hand. Willow is on the other side of me, and she slips her hand in mine. The tears are close today. I can taste them in the back of my mouth and feel the pressure behind my eyes. Kit and Beau sit in the row behind us along with James, Molly, Stan, and Tess. Everyone's here as witnesses, friends, but mostly family.

When I thought that Willow was my biological daughter, I would've supported Ruby, but knowing that once those papers are signed, she's my daughter by choice; it only intensifies my commitment.

Judge Brown takes his seat at the podium, shuffles a few papers, and then locks eyes with me. "You're here to adopt Willow Red I understand?"

The quiver in my voice is obvious. "Yes, your honor."

He nods, looking between Ruby and me before locking eyes with Willow. She's been sitting for twenty minutes already, and for a four-year-old, that's too long. Her feet rhythmically tap the ground, causing her body to twist and jostle my hand.

Judge Brown smiles. "You must be Willow."

Willow nods with an exaggerated flare.

He looks at Ruby, and then at me again. "Big day for your family."

"The biggest," I reply.

Ruby squeezes my hand twice, and I let out a slow breath. The next few minutes are a series of papers, signatures, and questions for our lawyer. We have everything we need and the process goes smoothly.

Before the ink dries, Willow is in my arms. I lift her off her feet and spin her in a full circle. Setting her back down, I sink to her level. "You're officially a Lopez now."

"Willow Lopez," she says with a smile.

I nod, and the tears that I've kept at bay all day spill out of my eyes. "That's right."

Her brows crease, and she touches a tear running down my cheek. "Are you happy?"

I wipe my cheeks with my palm. "So happy." I look up at Ruby as she places her hand on my shoulder, then back at my little girl. "The happiest I've ever felt in my whole life."

"It's picture time!" Tess says from behind us.

Molly and Stan high-five Willow, eyes brimming with fresh tears I've seen running down their faces before. Today is bittersweet for them, like the day Willow left their home and came to ours. They didn't see Willow as a sojourner passing through their lives; they loved her as if she were theirs, and for that, I'll always be grateful to them. Even they have a place in our family.

I stand up straight, but I can't stop crying. There are so many tears, and I don't know where they all came from, or how they fit inside my eyes. I pinch the bridge of my nose while they pour out.

Kit pulls me into a side hug. "Tears look good on you, brother."

Good. Because I think I just signed up for a lifetime of them.

IT'S LATE BY the time we pull into the garage. The sun set hours ago, but we were too busy laughing over a fancy dinner where we held our pinkies out every time we drank our water. We played on the beach with Olaf who ran in and out of the waves, spraying us all with salt water as he shook out his fur. And we took more pictures than will fit on our walls.

Ruby peers into the backseat. "She's asleep."

I turn around to find Willow slumped sideways in her carseat. Her hair is sticking up in every direction and she's barefoot.

I look at Ruby, and we both smile. "I'll carry her in."

Willow doesn't stir as I unstrap her from her seat and sling her into my arms, or when I change her pajamas and brush caked sand off her feet. She's limp in my arms, safe and loved.

I start to sway and hum before laying her down. The tears are back as I replay every part of today in my mind. It really was the best day of my life. Today, we became a legal family and though our days won't change much, our lives will.

Today became forever.

Paul McCartney's words fill my mouth and the velvety hums morph into words. I remember the first time Ruby sang me this song. She was desperate and had lost everything. But now, every night I sing it to Willow, I think about the journey it took to get here.

Nothing will shake this love.

Nothing can take it away.

Because that's the thing about love. It seeks us out. Through the darkest of moments. The hardest of seasons. The most jacked up situations that seem hopeless. Our pasts that seem impossible to overcome. Our present moments that feel heavy. Our futures that we try to kill off.

Love is searching for us, so we hang on.

It'll find a way through.

The End.

JACOB & RUBY'S PLAYLIST

01. **All of Me** Chapter 16
John Legend

02. **Uptown Funk** Chapter 16
Bruno Mars

03. **A Place Only You Can Go** Chapter 21
NEEDTOBREATHE

04. **Little Willow** Chapter 26
Paul McCartney

05. **Still (feat. DaniLeigh)** Epilogue
Lecrae

06. **I'll Find You (feat. Tori Kelly)**
Lecrae

07. **Blue**
Madison Beer

Afterword & Acknowledgements
(Contains Spoilers)

As a writer, this book changed me. Being the voice of Ruby and Jacob was hard at times. I don't always think like they do. But it challenged me in ways that will affect every other book I write.

As a reader, I found myself getting caught up in the story. These characters have become friends, and now with this third book, the conclusion of the Love Series, I'm saying goodbye to some pretty fantastic people. I'm so proud of them and the journeys they have taken, and to see them at the end of it all, accepting and giving love, is everything. There was heartbreak along the way, like every person's life has, but there's also so much hope. So. Much.

With each of the female main characters in this series, Ruby's life is modeled after real women working the streets. It's also a representation of those I know who have chosen to find help in the areas they need it most. I'm proud of Ruby and the women like her seeking to better their mental health, living situation, family life, and relationships. In many ways, I found myself relating to her internal struggles, even if the external ones were different.

For Love Finds a Way, I knew I wanted to highlight human trafficking in some form. I've come to learn just how common it is in the states, and even more so how close it really is. In many instances, our own backyards. Cities, especially port cities, hold greater risk and access for the selling and buying of women. The Breaking House was based on multiple articles and personal accounts that describe the places in which women and girls have been held when being trafficked. They are places where women are bought, sold, and broken. Sex workers, like Ruby, are often targeted as well.

I wanted this story to also reflect the process of what it looks like to be rescued from a place like this. During my research, I read more of Jordan Turpin's story and how she saved her siblings from being continually harmed at the hands of their parents—another form of exploitation that is both staggering and heartbreaking. They were rescued because of Jordan's bravery to escape and find help. She was seventeen. A young girl who was desperate enough to change the story for her and her siblings. It was a staggering act of heroism, and I knew then that I wanted Jacob and Ruby to embody this in their own rights.

Jacob taught me that healing isn't linear. Sometimes, we fall back on the sword we just pulled from our sides. But through his loving perseverance, he found a way through the darkness, just like Ruby. I also wanted Jacob's character to reflect what it looks like to be a man who is about empowering women. He's a compilation of the men I've known in my life who would go to great lengths to support the women around them. My hope is that you have men like this in your life, too. One's that encourage you to turn up the volume of your voice, support you even when the colors fade and the world looks more bleak, and cherish you in all times and seasons. I believe there are some good ones out there.

As highlighted in the first two books, the Journey Center is a real place, though I have changed the name. This organization has been a light to downtown L.A. for years, offering acceptance and hope in the form of meeting basic needs. Families who need housing, individuals coming off drugs, women who are exploited, foster care youth, veterans, and other humans looking for help have benefited greatly because of the resources at this Center. I am so honored to have had the opportunity to work with them over the course of this series. Chances are, there is a similar institution in your city that could use your support however you're able to give it.

Lastly, there are so many elements to writing a book, but one of my favorites is getting to work with other writers to help hone the story into the finished product you have in your hands. Ruby and Jacob's book wouldn't be the same without some incredible people.

I've written a few books now, and each has been read by my friend, Marie, some of them being terrible early drafts. You've been with me since the beginning, girl, and have truly witnessed the evolution of my writing and storytelling. I'm so glad you've stuck around and even more grateful for your friendship.

Haley, we started this journey together, and I am so looking forward to the many books we have in our futures. You have also been faithful to read my early drafts to the completed ones, and your feedback has been instrumental, and your excitement is an encouragement to keep going. Keep writing. I'm looking forward to being in the same room again soon!

To all of my other early readers for this book—Jill, Erica, Rene', and Hannah—thank you for loving these characters through the hard times and into growth. And all of my other indie author friends that would take multiple pages to name. Thank you for being the best coworkers in a career that is largely done solo. I adore each one of you.

To my editor, Krys—Consider me a fangirl of your work. Having your eyes on my books has given them the polish they need to shine. You have become a new friend in the process, and I am incredibly grateful for you. I swear I'll get better with commas! Someday…

My husband, Samuel—Thank you for talking out scenes with me and being willing to read each of my books. There are pieces of you in this one, too. Readers have you to thank for the scene with Adele/Sam.

My kids, the Fab Four—Thank you for making me set my alarm at four a.m. to get writing in since you are all early risers that require breakfast ASAP. Your pride in these books is the best kind of encouragement. Thank you for telling your teachers, friends, and random strangers that your mom writes books and they should buy one!

Mom and Dad—You are always supportive from start to finish. I appreciate you so much for asking me what I'm writing and getting just as excited about that book as the one I told you about the week before.

To my new and longtime readers, thank you for all the love and support! For reading, reviewing, messaging me with your excitement over a book. It's this enthusiasm that keeps me going when I'm in the middle of writing a book and about ready to burn it.

If you are interested in seeing my inspiration for some of the characters, scenes, outfits, etc. discussed in this book, you can find me on Pinterest @authorchristinahill.

I also love connecting with readers on Instagram and TikTok: @authorchristinahill. If you loved the book, please consider writing a review on Amazon and Goodreads. This is such a tangible way to help indie authors and for the message of this book to reach more beating hearts.

With all of my love,
Christina

About the Author

Christina is a lover of love and has been writing stories in her head for years. She is living her own story on an island in the stunning Pacific Northwest with her husband and four children. Christina loves to connect with readers on social media.

For more information or to sign up for my newsletter, visit www.authorchristinahill.com.

9 798985 719949